The Innovation Approach

David Roach's *The Innovation Approach: Overcoming the Limitations of Design Thinking and the Lean Startup* addresses a critical challenge in product innovation: perfecting the front end of the innovation process. Roach introduces a robust approach that guides innovation towards creating robust product concepts that are desirable, feasible, and viable. His model presents a novel, well-constructed iterative process, each cycle comprising four core activities: secondary research, benchmarking, primary research, and ideation. Each cycle in his model is meticulously detailed, combining the strengths of Design Thinking and Lean Startup methodologies while skillfully avoiding their common pitfalls. Clear, insightful, and engaging, this book is not only an enjoyable read but also an indispensable resource for managers in product and service innovation. A must-read for those seeking to drive successful innovation in their organizations.

—*Robert G. Cooper*, **Professor Emeritus at McMaster University, Canada, and ISBM Distinguished Research Fellow at Pennsylvania State University, USA**

The Innovation Approach: Overcoming the Limitations of Design Thinking and the Lean Startup

BY

DAVID C. ROACH

Dalhousie University, Canada

United Kingdom – North America – Japan – India – Malaysia – China

Emerald Publishing Limited
Emerald Publishing, Floor 5, Northspring, 21-23 Wellington Street, Leeds LS1 4DL.

First edition 2025

Reprints and permissions service
Contact: www.copyright.com

British Library Cataloguing in Publication Data
A catalogue record for this book is available from the British Library

ISBN: 978-1-83797-800-7 (Print)
ISBN: 978-1-83797-799-4 (Online)
ISBN: 978-1-83797-801-4 (Epub)

INVESTOR IN PEOPLE

This book is dedicated to "mon frère" Professor Dr. med Michael Klaus Schmidt, an innovator and passionate clinician whose generosity of spirit I will forever miss.

Contents

List of Figures and Tables   *xv*

About the Author   *xvii*

Preface   *xix*

Acknowledgments   *xxiii*

Section I: Introduction

Chapter 1   Systems of Innovation   *3*
Introduction   *3*
Innovation Approaches   *3*
   Product Development Management Association   *4*
   Stage Gate ™ System   *5*
   Integrated Product Development   *6*
   Lean Product Development and Innovation   *6*
   Agile Product Innovation   *7*
   The MIT Model – Product Design and Development   *8*
   Design Thinking   *9*
   Lean Startup   *9*
Other Innovation Systems, Tools and Techniques   *10*
Lead User Research   *10*
   Quality Function Deployment   *11*
   Basadur Applied Innovation – Simplex System   *12*
   TRIZ   *12*
Common Themes and Approaches   *13*
   Internal and External Communication   *13*
   Cross-functional and Multidisciplinary   *14*
   Information Driven, Agile and Effective   *14*
   Requirements and Attributes   *15*
   Problem Focused not Solution Focused   *16*

Creativity Enhanced, not Driven   *16*
Relative Value   *17*
Boundaries   *17*
Check-in, Check-out   *18*
Innovation Invariably Collides with the Business Model   *18*
There is a Project Management Component   *19*
Uncertainty Management   *20*
Conclusion   *20*

Chapter 2   Limitations of Design Thinking and the Lean Startup   *23*
Design Thinking as a System   *23*
Introduction: A Brief History   *23*
Modern Incarnation   *24*
What is DT?   *24*
Strengths of the System   *26*
Weaknesses in Practice   *27*
The LS as a Methodology   *29*
A Brief History   *29*
What is the LS?   *30*
Strengths of the System   *32*
Weaknesses of the System   *33*
Implications   *35*
Conclusions and Recommendations   *38*

Chapter 3   A Complimentary Model of Innovation Management   *39*
Introduction   *39*
What Is Innovation?   *40*
From an Economics Lens   *40*
From a Creativity Lens   *41*
From a Strategic Management Perspective   *41*
From an Entrepreneurial Standpoint   *42*
Innovation Defined   *43*
Innovation and the Business Model   *45*
The Innovation Approach   *47*
Problem Statement   *50*
In Practice – Problem Statement   *52*
The Innovation Helix   *53*
Conclusion   *54*

Section II: Core Steps and Capabilities

Chapter 4 Secondary Research *57*
Introduction *57*
What Is Secondary Research and Why Is It Important? *57*
Perspectives of Secondary Research *58*
Market Research Perspective *59*
Entrepreneurship Perspective *60*
Technology Management Perspective *60*
    DT Perspective *61*
    LS Perspective *62*
What Secondary Research Information Is Important
    for Innovation Management *63*
Guiding Models *63*
    The KANO Model *63*
    The User-centered Model *65*
Secondary Research in Action *66*
Case Example – IDEO Deep Dive (Secondary Research) *67*
Informing the Next Steps *69*
Conclusion *70*

Chapter 5 Benchmarking *73*
Introduction *73*
Consumers' Relationship to Products *74*
Category Features and Benefits *75*
Systematic Evaluation *76*
In Practice: Summary Table Example *77*
Benchmark Orientation Matrix *79*
Benchmarking Example *80*
Case Example: Benchmark Orientation
    Matrix – Golf Putter *81*
Evaluation and Analysis *83*
Analogs and Complementors *84*
Conclusion *84*

Chapter 6 Primary Research *87*
Introduction *87*
Approach to Primary Research *87*
Types of Primary Research *88*

Primary Research Best Practices   *91*
Developing, Executing and Analyzing Interviews   *91*
Discussion Guide   *93*
In Practice – Probe and Learn (Part 1)   *94*
Conducting the Interview   *95*
In Practice – Probe and Learn (Part 2)   *96*
Observation Within Interviews   *97*
Case Study – Observation   *98*
Artifacts as Focal Points   *99*
Interpreting Results   *100*
   Customer Journey Mapping   *100*
   Cognitive Mapping   *101*
Case Study – Handheld GPS   *102*
Conclusion   *104*

Chapter 7   Concept Development   *107*
Introduction   *107*
Tools and Techniques   *108*
Brainstorming   *108*
Lateral Thinking and Diverging   *110*
Case Study – IDEO Deep Dive   *113*
Converging   *115*
Quantitative Approach   *116*
Qualitative Approach   *117*
Concept Selection   *118*
Case Study – Wakeup Light   *118*
Conclusion   *119*

Chapter 8   Concept Evaluation and the MVP   *121*
Introduction   *121*
Evaluation Models   *122*
   Stage Gate™ Approach   *122*
   Lean Startup   *123*
   Design Thinking   *123*
Evaluation Approach   *124*
Viability   *125*
Desirability   *125*
Feasibility   *126*
Prototyping and the MVP   *127*
Prototyping Approach   *128*
In Practice – Prototyping and the MVP   *129*
Conclusion   *130*

Section III: Advanced Tools and Techniques

Chapter 9   Adoption Theory in Practice *133*
Introduction *133*
What Is Adoption? *134*
Case Example – Google Glass *138*
How and When to Mobilize Adoption *140*
Case Example – memsorb™ *141*
In Practice – Adoption *145*
Conclusion *146*

Chapter 10   Learning from Lead Users *149*
Introduction *149*
Who Are Lead Users? *150*
Lead User Misconceptions *152*
Lead User Research *153*
Case Example – Lead User in Market *156*
Downside of LUR *157*
Case Example – Lead User Attributes *158*
How and When to Use Lead Users *160*
Example – Lead User Analog *162*
Conclusion *163*
In Practice – Lead User Research *164*

Chapter 11   Sustainability *167*
Introduction *167*
Eco-development *168*
   Eco-development and Consumer Behavior *169*
   Eco-behavior *169*
   The Elusive Green Consumer *169*
Eco-development and LCA *171*
   What Is LCA? *171*
   What Are the Limitations of LCA? *172*
Case Example – Nappies *172*
Eco-development and Innovation Management *174*
   It's a Material Problem *174*
Cradle to Cradle (C2C) *175*
   How Does It Work? *176*
Case Example – Mirra™ Chair *177*
How Is It Used in the Innovation Approach? *179*
What About the Other Aspects of Sustainability? *180*
   Case Example – ETEE™ *181*
Conclusion *182*

Section IV: System Level Capabilities

Chapter 12   Team Selection, Structure and Governance   *187*
Introduction   *187*
Why a Team Approach?   *188*
Team Selection Approaches   *189*
Profiling Tools and Techniques   *190*
   Myers-Briggs   *191*
   IDEO Ten Faces of Innovation   *191*
   Basadur Problem-Solving Index   *192*
Other   *193*
Structure, Leadership and Management Support   *194*
   Project Structure   *194*
   Leadership   *196*
   Management Support   *196*
   Other   *197*
Conclusion   *197*

Chapter 13   Project Management Essentials   *199*
Introduction   *199*
What Is PM?   *200*
   Knowledge   *200*
   Skills   *202*
Tools and Techniques   *204*
   What Is Necessary to Manage the FEI?   *204*
Uncertainty   *205*
   Team Resource Management   *206*
   PM Software   *208*
Other Project-Related Issues   *209*
   Self-management   *210*
In Practice   *212*
Conclusion   *214*

Chapter 14   Heuristic Business Modeling   *215*
What Is a Business Model?   *215*
   Introduction: A Brief History   *215*
   Modern Incarnation   *216*
   Business Model versus the Business Plan   *217*
Heuristic Approach to Business Modeling   *219*
   Fixed Cost Model   *220*

Case Example – Golf putter (fixed costs)   *223*
  Revenue Model   *225*
Case Example – Golf putter (Revenue model)   *226*
  Variable Cost Model   *228*
Case Example – Golf putter (Variable cost model)   *228*
Case Example – Golf putter (Variable channel – i.e., selling costs)   *231*
Heuristic Business Modeling and Hypothesis Development   *233*
Conclusion   *236*

Postface   *237*

References   *239*

Suggested Readings   *245*

Index   *247*

List of Figures and Tables

Figures

Fig. 1.   QFD House of Quality.   11
Fig. 2.   Adapted from IDEOs Design Thinking Framework.   25
Fig. 3.   The Business Model.   46
Fig. 4.   Cycle of Innovation.   48
Fig. 5.   The Innovation Helix.   49
Fig. 6.   KANO Model.   65
Fig. 7.   User-centered Model.   66
Fig. 8.   Titleist Scotty. Cameron Newport 2 Plus.   77
Fig. 9.   Cognitive Map for Handheld GPS.   103
Fig. 10.   Wakeup Light Concepts.   119
Fig. 11.   Types of Prototypes.   128
Fig. 12.   Google Glass.   138
Fig. 13.   memsorb™   144
Fig. 14.   Handheld GPS.   157
Fig. 15.   3D Interlocking Sphere.   160
Fig. 16.   Pelican™ case.   163
Fig. 17.   Cradle to Cradle (C2C) Approach.   177
Fig. 18.   Mirra™ Chair.   178
Fig. 19.   Compostable Pod.   182
Fig. 20.   Product/Process Synergy.   195
Fig. 21.   Project Management Trade-offs.   201
Fig. 22.   Business Model Inverted-T.   220

Tables

Table 1.   Innovation System Gap Analysis.   37
Table 2.   Product Summary Table.   76
Table 3.   Benchmark Orientation Matrix Structure.   79
Table 4.   Benchmarking Orientation Matrix.   82
Table 5.   Fixed Cost Model.   225
Table 6.   Pricing Model.   226
Table 7.   Variable Cost Model.   229
Table 8.   Revised Variable Cost Model.   230
Table 9.   Revised Variable Cost Model.   232

About the Author

Dr. David C. Roach received his BEng degree in 1983, MBA degree in 1992 and PhD degree in 2011. He is an Associate Professor with the Faculty of Management at Dalhousie University, Halifax, NS, Canada, where he teaches graduate courses in entrepreneurship, innovation and the commercialization of biomedical technologies. He lectures internationally in the areas of innovation, entrepreneurship, product development and marketing technology products. He has been instrumental in many early-stage companies ranging from aerospace to biotechnology and brings a hands-on approach to the innovation process. He sits on the Board of Directors and acts in an advisory capacity for several small- and medium-sized enterprises (SMEs) in Canada. He is Co-founder, President and CEO of DMF Medical Incorporated, a MedTech company focused on making anesthesia safer. He has authored and co-authored several publications in the areas of innovation, entrepreneurship and product management. His academic research interests include product management practices of SMEs and early-stage ventures. In his spare time, he is an avid ice hockey player and a passionate scale modeller of First World War aircraft. He can be contacted at: david.roach@dal.ca.

Preface

You are a progressive group. You believe that innovation is crucial to your organization's long-term vision. You keep up to date with emerging trends both in the marketplace and the modes of organization. You tend not to be at the bleeding edge but consider yourself a fast follower. You're not seduced by fads but employ techniques that stand the test of time. The intuitive appeal of Design Thinking makes sense to you and seems to be a great fit for your organization. Its empathetic, team-based approach and collaborative work style are exactly what your organization espouses. However, after the initial excitement and perhaps some early wins, it doesn't seem to be delivering the benefits that you thought. Perhaps it's because your organization has lost its entrepreneurial drive, but after dabbling with methods like the Lean Startup, it seems to have only confounded the problem. You continue to search for answers…

If this reminds you of your journey…this book is for you…

THIS BOOK IS NOT A CRITIQUE OF EITHER DESIGN THINKING OR THE LEAN STARTUP, BUT A WAKE-UP CALL TO THE GENERALLY POOR IMPLEMENTATION OF THESE FRAMEWORKS

This book has been in various forms of development for close to four decades. Over my career, I have always been relatively successful at innovation, but my early career was characterized by ad hoc "hit and miss" approaches, based more on entrepreneurial intuition than a consistent methodology. What always fascinated me was whether there was a modest approach with broad enough application to improve the outcomes of the innovation process? Today, when I interact with executives or my graduate students, I liken the innovation process to America's pastime – baseball. Baseball is one of the few sports where a 70% failure rate makes a player a superstar. A player who can put the ball "in play" 30% of the time (a.k.a. a "0.300 hitter") is rare in a game where *all players* have developed the "skills," but few have mastered the *consistency* required to reach this pinnacle. Surely, innovation management must have a similar process …

At the time, one of my former bosses challenged me by stating that although I may have shown some ability to create successful innovations, it likely wasn't repeatable and certainly could not be "systematized." As with most things in life, I took this as a challenge and have spent the past decades researching, applying and modifying best practices. My journey has taken me to top institutions such as Harvard, MIT, Babson, Kellogg, University of Chicago, to name a few ... to learn from the best of the best. After applying many of these "broad-brush" approaches, I eventually reached a point where a deeper dive into the academic field was necessary – receiving a PhD in the area of product management. Throughout this process I continued to apply this knowledge, resulting in several breakthrough innovations in aerospace, medical devices and consumer products. It also resulted in many failures, but my hit rate approached that of a 0.300 hitter. What became clear is that there are fundamental principles and building blocks that form the basis for successful innovation management approaches.

It also became clear that there is an unbreakable relationship between innovation and entrepreneurship. These two somewhat complementary constructs are conjoined and can either work synergistically or be at cross purposes. From an academic perspective, firms or individuals have what we refer to in strategic management studies as "capabilities." These capabilities differ between innovation and entrepreneurship but have often been incorrectly lumped together. Innovation is the process of *creating value for a target audience*, while entrepreneurship is about *recognizing, crafting and exploiting* commercial (or social) opportunities. These are two disparate types of capabilities which when managed synergistically often lead to success, while when in conflict almost inevitably lead to failure. My research and the overwhelming anecdotal evidence suggest that individual actors often mistake their capabilities in either of these spheres leading to poor outcomes. The capability required to research, conceptualize and execute innovations differs radically from the capability to recognize (i.e., uncover) opportunities and craft them into something commercially or socially viable. Successful innovators surround themselves with entrepreneurial talent, while successful entrepreneurs surround themselves with innovation talent. But more about this in Chapter 1.

Although initially thrilled by the advent of novel methodologies such as Design Thinking and the Lean Startup, I quickly became disillusioned by their implementation. Although the lines between innovation and entrepreneurship have always been blurred, these methods quickly reached an unmanageable level of populism driven by a surge of internet-based promotion. Both methods have many merits. However, neither adequately addresses the innovation–entrepreneurship interface, specifically from a "capabilities" perspective. Moreover, in practice, they suffer from what I refer to as the "boardgame" principle, where individuals follow a planned route somewhat analogous to the boardgame *Snakes and Ladders*. In *Snakes and Ladders*, players move their token on a board in a quasi-linear fashion, where ladders are used to fast forward through the process, while snakes result in sliding back. Conceptually, Design Thinking advocates for a nonlinear approach where assumptions should be challenged or revisited throughout the process. On the other hand, the Lean Startup promotes "pivots" when new information comes to light. In practice, however, individual actors once locked into a path rarely revisit key facts and assumptions, while pivoting is often the outcome of poor management of the innovation process, once the team has effectively reached a dead end. Compounding this situation are the many "how to" books and websites written on these subjects. Each in their own way provides lengthy checklists, questions to be answered and case examples (note: mostly from behemoths such as Apple, Google, Tesla, etc.) which are mostly unsuitable for typical organizations. In practice, individuals and/or teams become overwhelmed by these choice options and retract to simplified heuristics, in effect cherry-picking areas of comfort. In keeping with my analogy, they fast forward through steps only to inevitably slide back. This is neither *effective* nor *efficient*. For instance, a favorite comfort area is the brainstorming process, which is creative, fun and highly visible to management and/or investors. This approach mostly ignores decades of well-established best practices and is *inconsistent* with the successful management of the innovation process.

This book chronicles my journey through the merits and obstacles of innovation management. It is not about criticizing or altering best practices developed and tested over time. As a matter of fact, this book is complimentary to these methods and practices. For instance, there is no benefit in reiterating the approach and/or benefits of brainstorming or customer discovery. These steps are well documented and generally well understood. Instead, I hope to build upon these many solid foundations from both a practitioner and academic perspective. As a result, I will endeavor where possible to link recent tools and techniques back to their origins to convey an understanding of the lineage of these concepts. Once core principles are fully understood, it is much easier for individuals to apply them in the correct manner, context and measure. I will also go beyond the narrow confines of core concepts into advanced tools and techniques, as well as system-level capabilities that support a robust innovation management system.

This book is divided into four broad categories. The first section revisits *systems of innovation* and how they relate to new methodologies such as Design Thinking and the Lean Startup. This knowledge is used to propose a *complimentary* model of innovation management. Building upon this model, *core steps and capabilities* are discussed under the presumption that successful management of these steps increases the overall *effectiveness* of the process. When steps are more effective, they also become more *efficient* in the long run. Core steps include background research (secondary and benchmarking) followed by primary research. Once these steps are completed, ideation activities can then be undertaken to generate meaningful concepts. I will argue that these core activities are sequential in nature and build upon each other. They represent the core of an *innovation cycle*, which provides the basis for the next iterative cycle, where the innovation problem is redefined and enriched. This is the transition to the next phase where *advanced tools and techniques* are engaged. These techniques or *themes* involve the application of adoption theory, lead user research and design for sustainability. Each of these themes involves a repetition of the *innovation cycle*, albeit with a refined focus. This allows fledgling concepts to be amplified, improved and stress-tested. The book concludes with a discussion of *system-level capabilities* which include team selection and governance, project management essentials and business model innovation. Together these form the innovation approach.

The book is structured to blend theory with practical application of techniques. To accomplish this CASE STUDIES and IN PRACTICE sections are highlighted throughout. Case studies emphasize examples of innovation management at work. The in practice sections feature the application of techniques described within the chapters. Throughout, key concepts are highlighted to reinforce *effective* steps within the innovation approach.

For managers, my hope is that "the approach" can breathe new life into their innovation practices by allowing them to increase the effectiveness of their innovation activities. For founders, practitioners and consultants, the approach may lead them to fine-tuning their processes, resulting in better outcomes for their organizations or clients. For my academic colleagues, my hope is that the opinions throughout this manuscript may become the kernel for new avenues of research inquiry that are so badly needed at the innovation–entrepreneurship interface.

In closing, innovation and entrepreneurship have always had a strong and synergistic relationship. Innovations that are not adopted commercially or socially remain inventions. Every entrepreneurial endeavor requires some form of innovation. As a result, many tools, techniques, and systems have been developed to reconcile these somewhat disparate approaches. Design Thinking has emerged as the de facto standard for innovation management, while the Lean Startup methodology has become the prevailing approach for entrepreneurial pursuits. While both systems have significant strengths, they suffer in practice from philosophical gaps. In practice, Design Thinking has become subservient to the brainstorming process, while the Lean Startup suffers from the notion that "pivoting" is the solution to all that ails the business model. Based on almost four decades of practice and research, this book begins with the philosophy that *a poor concept can rarely be converted into a success*, while *the most robust concepts often suffer from an unachievable business model*. Rather than a critique of these popular methodologies, this book serves as a *compliment to these approaches* focusing on the front end of innovation where most of the critical innovation and entrepreneurial decisions take place.

My hope is that this book will be somewhat controversial, but embraced by most …

Acknowledgments

First and foremost, I would like to thank my "number one," Katy Schurman. A former student and now indispensable colleague, she has painstakingly reviewed every aspect of this manuscript. She not only contributed her superior organizational skills but also provided many insightful comments and suggestions. I'd also like to extend a special thanks to Dr. Nancy Kilcup who has always graciously accepted the role of "number two." She, along with Katy, have allowed me the privilege of writing this book by taking care of all the other things happening in my hectic world. I will look forward to supporting them in all their future endeavors.

As always, I'd like to thank Professor Emeritus, Jack Duffy, for all his insights throughout the years. Although he did not have time to review much of this work, a lot of what I learned from Jack is embedded in this book. His wit and boundless anecdotes always seem to get directly to the heart of the matter!

To my friend and colleague Jenny Baechler who provided a welcome sounding board for some of the concepts in this book – thank you for your support and tolerating me throughout the years. To my part-time partner in crime Professor Glen Hogan, a very talented industrial designer and teacher. Glen has a unique talent for getting directly to the core of issues and our chats over the years have reinforced a lot of my thinking.

There are many others too numerous to mention that have all played a role in my journey. These range from my academic colleagues to the many business associates I have had the pleasure to learn from. A few notable mentions include Dr. Robert Cooper, whom I met in the mid-1990s whose approach charted the direction of a lot of my practice and his Austrian colleague Dr. Angelika Dreher whom I met over the course of writing this book. Her understanding of the relationship between Design Thinking and the Stage Gate™ system mirrored my practical experience in countries such as Germany. I'll look forward to keeping in touch with her.

Finally, my family. My wife, who has always been there no matter what crazy directions I decided to pursue. It is now my turn to support her as she embarks on her own adventure in creative writing, where her poetry will certainly shine. To my children, who when asked, generally know what their pappa has been up to. They've always been an inspiration to me and have become adults that we genuinely enjoy spending time with.

Finally, my dear friend, colleague and business partner Professor Dr. med Michael Klaus Schmidt. I wish I could have handed him the first copy of this book.

Section I

Introduction

Chapter 1

Systems of Innovation

Several approaches to innovation management have been developed over the decades. This chapter provides an overview of these approaches, distinguishing between systems, methods, processes and techniques. Approaches such as Lean, Agile and Stage Gate™ are reviewed and their relationship to both Design Thinking and Lean Startup are explored. These approaches are then examined for a common set of best practices. The chapter concludes with a set of criteria which form the basis of effective innovation management approaches for the front end of innovation.

Introduction

Innovation management is a broad topic, ranging from approaches to research and development (R&D) to economics and government policy. Since this book is about the innovation approach, it is focused on the development of innovation capabilities for the management of the process. These capabilities form the foundation for the fundamental premise of this book, namely that *a poor concept can rarely be converted into a success*. As a result, the focus will be on what is often considered the front end of innovation (FEI) where *ideas are transformed into robust concepts*. These activities range from the initial vision or inspiration for the project to the development and evaluation of concepts. Once concepts are considered desirable, feasible and viable (usually resulting in an Alpha-level prototype) they are then ready for the more rigorous back end of innovation (BEI) process, where detailed design, testing and launch activities dominate.

This chapter will focus on various innovation approaches to establish best practices. These will then be compared to current popular approaches such as Design Thinking (DT) and the Lean Startup (LS).

Innovation Approaches

Several approaches to innovation management have been developed over the years. Most involve approaches to R&D or new product development. These often involve confirming customer requirements, establishing economic viability or determining product–market fit. As a result, the field is littered with

The Innovation Approach:
Overcoming the Limitations of Design Thinking and the Lean Startup, 3–21
Copyright © 2025 by David C. Roach
Published under exclusive licence by Emerald Publishing Limited
doi:10.1108/978-1-83797-799-420241001

intersecting strategic approaches, including methodologies, systems, processes and techniques. Thus, it is crucial for both practitioners and academics to clearly distinguish between these often-interchangeable terms.

Systems refer to a set of interconnected or interdependent elements that work together to achieve a common goal. They involve the integration of various components and processes, whose interactions create a functional whole. *Systems thinking* involves understanding how these mechanisms interact, knowing that all interactions synergistically impact outcomes. The best description I have heard to describe systems thinking is to picture a windchime at rest. When you touch the windchime at any point, all parts are affected, which determines the outcome (i.e., creation of sounds through chiming). This demonstrates systems are only as strong as their components and the synergy between their interaction.

Methods describe organized approaches within a system to accomplish specific tasks or solve problems. They provide a structured approach to achieve outcomes, normally through step-by-step procedures, guidelines or protocols. They provide a framework to ensure consistency and efficiency in achieving desired results.

Processes are sequences of interrelated activities or steps that transform inputs into outputs. They are often used to define how work is done within an organization, system or method. Processes provide a structured way to manage resources and tasks, providing consistency and repeatability. These are the mainstay of organizational efficiency and quality assurance systems.

Tools or techniques are instruments or resources that aid in performing tasks. They facilitate the application of processes and can be tangible, intangible or conceptual in nature. For instance, open-ended, probe and learn interviewing techniques (somewhat intangible) form the basis for customer listening methodology. Conversely, a well-designed questionnaire (tangible) would follow a process to elicit customer feedback. Both can be used within an innovation management system to provide input into customer requirements. As a result, tools and techniques can take the form of templates, guidelines or software programs.

Last is *philosophy*. Many of the approaches rely on a "vision" or an overriding aspirational set of principles. This vision sets in motion all of the above.

In summary, a *system* is a broad framework of interconnected components, *methods* are orderly approaches to accomplish tasks, *processes* are sequences of activities that transform inputs into outputs and *techniques* are resources that aid in implementing processes effectively. Understanding the distinctions between these terms is essential for effectively applying these somewhat convoluted concepts in practice.

These simple definitions will aid in understanding the vast body of work related to innovation management in the next sections.

Product Development Management Association

The most comprehensive resource for innovation management is the Product Development Management Association (PDMA). The PDMA is considered the ultimate source of best practices in managing new product development and comprehensively covers most of the systems, methods and processes considered state-of-the-art. They stress three key areas, specifically (i) portfolio, (ii) process and (iii) product life cycle management as part of an overall innovation management strategy. Supporting this strategic framework is the role of teams (and their leadership), various innovation management techniques and market research used for decision-making. Together they form what they refer to at their Body of Knowledge (BOK) (PMBOK Guide, 2021).

From an innovation management perspective, portfolio management is a *project selection* activity. It is a necessary step in most organizations to align corporate strategy with innovation objectives of the firm. Its fundamental purpose is to manage and spread risk across the range of innovation projects. These innovation undertakings have been categorized as incremental, derivatives, hybrids, platforms and lastly, R&D projects (Wheelwright & Clark, 1992). Product life cycle management on the other hand refers to the management of in-market products which require periodic maintenance to keep them positioned within the market. These activities range from incremental product improvements, to adjustments in features and pricing. This leaves the systems on how to move from project selection (i.e., portfolio) to market-ready innovations.

Stage Gate™ System

Foundational to the PDMA BOK is the most well-known product innovation management approach – Dr. Robert Cooper's Stage Gate™ system. This system emanated from his PhD research in the late 1970s, driven by his fascination with the significant differences between company success rates in new product development. Traditional methods at the time involved a stepwise approach most often performed by narrowly focused departments. In this epoch, R&D would hand off their design to engineering, who would hand it off to manufacturing, who would eventually hand it off to the marketing department to launch the product. The process was functionally disciplinary, linear and time-consuming. His research uncovered best practices (and by association limitations) of this approach. He recommended a management structure to not only "do the right projects but do the projects right." Key to his recommendations was the importance of upfront homework, a truly cross-functional team approach, unique differentiated products and strong market orientation throughout the process. As a result he developed an idea-to-launch management system that he trademarked as the Stage Gate™ system. It covers both the FEI and BEI through to post launch review. In effect it provided a macro-level structure designed to systematize the business innovation management process. More recently he has refined his system to align with agile techniques where he incorporates sprints, scrums and interim gates which he refers to as "upgates" (Cooper & Fürst, 2023).

By the turn of this century, this method became the de facto standard for managing the innovation process within both large- and medium-size firms. However, it had limited adoption in small and micro enterprises mostly due to the significant management overhead imposed on these organizations. It did not provide enough "how to" knowledge (i.e., techniques), only providing guidelines on what should be considered at each stage between gates. Also hindering these smaller firms was the general lack of management experience, which left technique selection to nascent management teams.

As a result, the Stage Gate™ system was not widely adopted or was poorly executed by most small enterprises and virtually unknown in the startup and early-stage community. Where it was occasionally applied in early-stage companies, it was mostly forced upon founders by their financial partners who mistakenly applied "big business" management systems to the innovation process. This proved to be time-consuming, bureaucratic and generally inefficient and as a result quickly fell out of favor in the startup community, paving the way for approaches such as the Lean Startup (LS).

The Stage Gate™ methodology is a blend of *solution-driven* and *problem-driven* innovation.

Integrated Product Development

Integrated product development (IPD) evolved from concurrent engineering, where design is integrated throughout the product life cycle from conceptualization to end-of-life. Based on a holistic approach, this system forces innovation processes to align with the product life cycle, to design in (or out) aspects of the product's value proposition. It relies on the premise that careful consideration at the early stages of development (i.e., the FEI) will result in a more thoughtful life cycle impact. This notion is strongly supported by many practitioners and academics who posit that up to 80% of product life cycle impacts are embedded once the innovation concept is locked in (Ulrich & Eppinger, 2012). This approach fundamentally relies on stacking the FEI to establish richer early product definition, one of the key tenants of the Stage Gate™ system.

Thus, IPD forces the design team to simultaneously consider such things as functionality, production, maintenance, quality and disposal. It differs from conventional methods by advocating that these areas should be contemplated concurrently, simultaneously impacting the quality of the product and productivity of the process. Like the Stage Gate™ system, it builds upon orderly decision points to move from one part of the process to another. It accomplishes this by relying on many of the same techniques including, voice of the customer (VoC), strategic alignment (e.g., portfolio selection), cross-functional teams and basic project management techniques.

This system tends to be *solution-centric* rather than problem-centric.

Lean Product Development and Innovation

Often referred to as Lean Product Innovation (or Lean for short), this innovation *methodology* has its roots in the lean production approach pioneered by the Toyota Motor Company (Kennedy, 2003). At its core, the Lean system is about waste elimination. Its success within automotive manufacturing spurred interest in expanding its principles outside of this area. As companies such as Toyota began to push the limits of waste reduction within their production systems, it became clear that the logical next frontier was to eliminate waste at the source (i.e., the design of the product itself). Not only could it streamline the design process by improving quality, cost and timeliness, much like IPD it would also impact the entire product life cycle. This was one of the driving forces behind Eric Ries' LS philosophy (Ries, 2011).

This methodology by its nature is best deployed by large organizations for complex but generally incremental products. Incremental innovation projects rely on tried and tested technologies reconfigured to the application at hand. In the automotive industry, most of the novelty of a new product involves minor adjustments to component architecture. For instance, the styling of the vehicle may undergo cosmetic changes, but the remainder of the vehicle remains unchanged. As a result, there is little uncertainty in retooling a production line to make different parts. One of the key outputs from this system is its proactive risk management approach. Lean innovation understands that it is based on incremental innovation, not advanced or radical innovation. As a result, one of the highlights is that it proactively reduces risk by *parallel processing activities.* Keeping the project requirements "flexible" as long as possible allows for the more uncertain aspects of the project to be fully road-tested (no pun intended). When the technology is "ready for prime time" (i.e., effective, robust and scalable), it replaces the incumbent technology on the product roadmap.

As with all best practices in innovation management, it relies on significant upfront information gathering. Also like both the Stage Gate™ system and IPD, its success is based upon a truly cross-functional team that is empowered by senior management to act in the best interest of the product, rather than their functional specialty. Much of the thinking supporting the LS is based on this Lean philosophy.

This methodology tends to be *solution-centric* rather than problem-centric.

Agile Product Innovation

Agile Product Innovation (or Agile for short) is a *methodology* that evolved from the software industry in the mid to late 1990s where quick iterative bursts of development are followed by rapid tests. The objective is to get to an optimum solution quicker, better and cheaper. The premise being that short, focused development cycles are preferred over longer more comprehensive development cycles. Often used terminology includes such things as sprints and scrums. Scrums refer to nonlinear, fixed-length iterations akin to a rugby scrum, where the players huddle, determine the next play, then execute a short burst play, only to re-huddle and do it again.[1] Similarly, sprints refer to the period of work involved between evaluation processes, akin to the stage portion of the Stage Gate™ system. Foundational to the entire methodology are quick and dirty iterations leading to artifacts that can be assessed. Daily builds result in artifacts often referred to as focused prototypes (Ulrich & Eppinger, 2012).

---

[1]Although the term has been bandied around for decades, the concept was first introduced to describe the nonlinear team approach as espoused by Robert Cooper's Stage Gate™ system.

In the software industry today, daily build and test iterations are the norm. Unlike tangible products, software is continuously and infinitely changeable. However, some of this rational has spilled into tangible product development methodologies over the years. For instance, the Stage Gate™ system was modified to include aspects of agile through their Agile Stage Gate™ approach (Cooper & Fürst, 2023). Thus, Agile should be considered a *methodology* rather than a system, since its fundamental principles are integrated throughout other innovation *systems*.

In practice however it has delivered mixed results. Trying to apply software project management philosophy does not necessarily deliver the gains but can often deliver losses. Tangible or hardware products are time-consuming, expensive and not forgiving to rework. When software-based Agile is superimposed on hardware projects it often comes with unrealistic scope, timelines and costs. The Silicon Valley approach, based on agile thinking and advocated by the LS community, often suffers from this approach.

This methodology tends to be *solution-centric* rather than problem-centric.

The MIT Model – Product Design and Development

In 1995, Karl Ulrich and Steven Eppinger published their seminal book – Product Design and Development sometimes referred to as the MIT model (Ulrich & Eppinger, 2012). Their focus was on physical products, however, they emphasize that their broad approach is adaptable to all innovation projects. Although their book takes a very linear approach, they go to great lengths to emphasize that innovation is not a linear process. They also emphasize the importance of cross-disciplinary capabilities of the team, which range from business, engineering to operational functions. Their approach is based on the core functions of marketing, design and manufacturing.

They frame the development process as a set of physical steps analogous to baking a cake or assembling an automobile. Like a cake, not only are the proper ingredients required, but the appropriate sequence of activities is necessary to produce an acceptable result. Like baking, the wrong sequence of activities can produce unwanted interactions even though the ingredients are appropriate. Like bakers, no organization or team follows the same recipe or process. This they contend highlights that innovation management is part science and part art.

Ulrich and Eppinger (2012) spend an entire chapter, discussing how to build requirement definitions through first identifying customer needs; specifically, their experience in their use environments. They stress that the team should identify customer needs *without* knowing how they will eventually address those needs. They emphasize that the process of gathering needs from raw customer data and subjectively interpreting these needs is key to establishing early requirements. To accomplish this, they don't differentiate between secondary and primary research activities, suggesting multiple approaches ranging from interviews, focus groups, observation to surveys. They state that greater than 90% of customer needs should be revealed after 25 hours of data collection. As a practical guide, they suggest that fewer than 10 interviews are probably inadequate, while 50 is too many.

Following Griffin and Hauser's (1993) approach, they further suggest that interviews be based on interview guides versus a series of questionnaire items. Finally, they propose guidelines for the difficult task of interpreting raw data. They later go into detail about the BEI where they discuss later stages in the design process (e.g., the role of industrial design, design for manufacturing).

This system is mostly *problem-centric* rather than solution-centric.

Design Thinking

As discussed earlier, a *system* is a broad framework of interconnected components, which is only as strong as (i) its components and (ii) the synergy of their interaction. DT can thus be thought of as a *system* that purports to use *methods* to accomplish its goals. The methods however tend to be applied in an ad hoc fashion, and their related processes are somewhat ambiguous. This may be the reason that no definite study has concluded that this system outperforms others. In many quarters it is taken on the status of innovation mindset or *philosophy* rather than a structured approach.

Although there is a myriad of definitions, at its core DT is a human-centered, innovation-focused problem-solving approach that engages various *methods, processes* and *tools* for creative purposes (Daymond & Knight, 2023). It relies on an iterative approach to problem definition through need-finding, information gathering/analysis and creativity/ideation. As a *system* it relies on a lose combination of *methods, processes* and *techniques* to achieve its ends. This has led several critics to describe DT as a disparate set of tools and techniques often poorly executed and/or applied (Carlgren et al., 2016). This has created general confusion about its merits as a management approach, some going as far as proclaiming that the confusion has reached a crisis point (Dorst, 2011). However, these approaches have found support in a willing community looking for alternatives to traditional analytical methods, which have often failed to produce successful results. A more detailed discussion of DT is provided in the following chapter.

For the purposes of this book, DT is considered a *system* based on a set of principles designed to reduce (or manage) *uncertainty* in the innovation management process. It is *problem-centric* rather than solution-centric.

Lean Startup

The LS *philosophy* developed by Eric Ries is now considered the de facto approach to entrepreneurship. It is widely touted as a methodology rooted in the doctrine of lean manufacturing and agile development, although its supporting processes and techniques can be considered somewhat weak. It seeks to minimize waste and maximize learning through iterative cycles of experimentation and validation.

LS fundamentally involves three mechanisms that include business model development, customer validation and agile development, supported by what is referred to as minimum viable product (MVP) testing. In essence, it combines innovation management tools (i.e., customer learning and agile development) with aspects of entrepreneurship (i.e., business modeling). Since neither set of mechanisms cover the entire spectrum of entrepreneurship nor innovation, it is frequently criticized for lacking rigor.

The primarily outcome of LS is business model development based on iterative hypothesis testing, where "MVPs" are used to establish a viable (then scalable) business model. The system also relies on established *methods* such as the business model canvas, which looks at various aspects of the business model and their relationships. This build–measure–learn feedback loop terminates once development and testing of the MVP results in a valid/scalable business model.

Although strength and weaknesses of the method will be discussed in finer detail in the next chapter, LS has nevertheless reached "enlightenment" status among its proponents. It does however have some drawbacks. The emphasis on speed also leads to an insufficient understanding of the problem or problem space. It also confounds the innovation and entrepreneurship approaches, often leading to superficial coverage of both areas. In many cases the product or service innovations that emerge have significant adoption issues. If the innovation does not deliver on its value proposition, the business model may not be executable. The strength of the innovation is foundational to establishing a viable business model.

Since it comes from an entrepreneurial perspective, it tends to be *solution-focused* rather than *problem-focused*. Thus, for the purposes of this book, LS is considered a *system* born of the philosophy that agile and lean principles are the driving force to entrepreneurial success.

Other Innovation Systems, Tools and Techniques

Lead User Research

Dr. von Hippel defines lead users as individuals or groups who exhibit strong needs ahead of the mainstream market. These users serve as a foresight laboratory for marketing research due to their atypical needs. Lead users typically face extreme needs that current products or services fail to address, compelling them to create their own solutions.

In contrast to traditional market research whose focus is on the mainstream market, the lead user method gathers insights from the edges of the target market as well as analog markets and markets facing similar challenges in a more pronounced manner. Lead users can be categorized into three distinct types: those within the *market*, those in *analogous* markets and those focused on key *attributes*.

Lead users in the market occupy fringe segments often overlooked by conventional research. As an example, 3M Corporation looking to develop cost-effective surgical bandages engaged with surgeons in third-world markets. In analogous markets they engaged veterinary surgeons developing infection control techniques for pets. For key attributes they worked with Hollywood makeup artists whose expertise was skin adhesion (von Hippel et al., 1999).

While lead users are rare and challenging to find, they are distinct from early adopters, DIY enthusiasts or extreme customers. Confusion often arises due to misunderstandings of lead user criteria and distinctions from other user types, such as lead use experts or inventors. Successfully identifying lead users requires exploratory research skills akin to investigative reporting, rather than relying on traditional market research techniques.

Initially conceived for market research, lead user research has evolved into a system offering valuable insights into the FEI. Despite its decline in usage, it remains a fruitful technique for uncovering latent (unspoken) delight needs and enhancing innovation management processes.

For the purposes of this book, Lead User Research is considered a *methodology*. Chapter 10 will cover this methodology in greater detail.

Quality Function Deployment

Quality Function Deployment (QFD) is a systematic approach to product and process development. It originated in Japan in the 1960s as part of the quality assurance movement. Its aim is to align customer needs with the design, development and quality processes.

At its core, QFD is a structured planning tool that facilitates communication between different functional areas of an organization, ensuring a holistic and customer-centric approach. The process typically begins with the identification of customer requirements. These "whats" are the essential attributes and features that customers desire in a product or service. These requirements are then converted into engineering characteristics, or "hows," represented by technical specifications. QFD utilizes a matrix called the House of Quality, shown in Fig. 1, to visualize the relationships between customer requirements and engineering characteristics. This matrix serves as a communication tool, providing a structured framework for cross-functional teams.

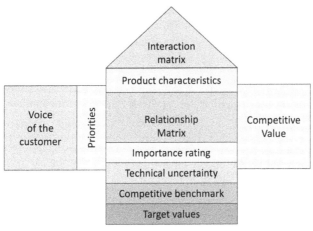

Fig. 1.   QFD House of Quality.

One of the key principles of QFD is the prioritization of customer requirements based on their importance and impact. Weighted factors, such as customer preferences and competitive benchmarks, are assigned to each requirement to guide the development team. As a result, it goes beyond the initial product design phase and extends into the entire product life cycle.

QFD reached its peak in the late 1980s where it was championed by technical factions of organizations to quantify all aspects of design, development, manufacturing and quality. It was perceived to link fuzzy marketing requirements to hard product specifications. Its fundamental flaw was believing that the voice-of-the-customer (VoC) could be systematically quantified. This and its complexity made the system unmanageable, and it is now rarely used although some of its underlying principles are still beneficial.

For the purposes of this book, QFD is considered as *methodology* supported by a set of *techniques*.

Basadur Applied Innovation – Simplex System

The Basadur Innovation methodology, developed by Dr. Min Basadur, is a structured approach to innovative thinking and problem-solving, aimed at guiding individuals and teams through the stages of problem identification, idea generation, evaluation and implementation. It emphasizes the importance of involving all team members in an unbiased and open-minded manner.

At the core of the Basadur method are four problem-solving styles: Generators, Conceptualizers, Optimizers and Implementers. Each style contributes differently to the innovation process, from generating ideas to executing solutions. Dr. Basadur developed a profiling tool based on cognitive psychology to identify individuals' problem-solving approaches, aiding teams in understanding each member's role suitability.

His process begins with problem formulation, stressing the need for a comprehensive understanding of the problem space before moving to idea generation. This involves viewing problems from multiple perspectives to gain clarity and insight. It then employs classic brainstorming techniques, often led by Generators, to produce diverse ideas. Ideas are generally evaluated by Conceptualizers.

It diverges from DT in its emphasis on rigorously *defining problems before ideation*. While both adopt user-centric, iterative approaches, Basadur's focus on problem definition and tailored problem-solving techniques distinguishes it. DT typically starts with an empathetic exploration, with the problem evolving throughout the process.

The Basadur methodology is outcome-oriented, prioritizing actionable ideas and solutions. It provides a structured framework for multidisciplinary collaboration, facilitating the transition from creative concepts to practical implementation.

For the purposes of this book, it is considered as *methodology* supported by a set of *techniques*.

TRIZ

TRIZ is a Russian innovation system that roughly translates to the "Theory of Inventive Problem-Solving." It is based on extensive analysis of thousands of patents to identify recurring patterns and principles underlying successful inventions. At its core, it deems that inventive problem-solving follows specific patterns that can be identified, codified and applied universally. It comprises several key principles, including the use of contradictions, ideality and inventive principles. The methodology encourages practitioners to recognize contradictions within a problem, such as conflicting requirements or limitations. This sets the stage to systematically explore inventive solutions that resolve these contradictions. Although it still relies on the ideation activities of the team, it effectively *concentrates the creative space* by focusing it on the most likely solution areas. In practical terms, TRIZ provides a toolkit of problem-solving techniques across 40 inventive principles referenced to a contradiction matrix.

Over the years, I have used TRIZ on some projects and have found it to be very useful when the solution space requires the resolution of fundamental contradictions. For instance, size and weight of an object are related. If weight reduction is the innovation objective, it will likely impact size. Being able to narrow the field of possibilities by exploring the likely solution space can be a very effective approach. It creates boundaries around the ideation process increasing its *effectiveness.*

For the purposes of this book, it is considered a set of *techniques.*

Common Themes and Approaches

As discussed, each approach relies on a loose combination of methods, processes and techniques to achieve its desired results. Invariably, there are significant overlaps in each approach, using slightly different arrangements to achieve their end points. Depending on the desired outcome, more weight is given to some aspects of the approach versus others. For instance, some highlight speed, others flexibility, while others propose rigid guidelines and checkmarks. Nevertheless, from an innovation management perspective, it stands to reason that these aggregate systems, when critically examined, should provide insights into best practices.

Next, an examination of common themes and approaches is discussed.

Internal and External Communication

Every modern innovation management system relies on strong internal and external communications. During the FEI, internal communication is based on the ability to effectively communicate often incomplete thoughts, partially explicated concepts and multifaceted constructs. Standard verbal or written communication is often inadequate to translate these nuances. As a result, virtually every innovation management system encourages the creation of tactile objects or artifacts as a focal point for internal communication. This approach has been widely used by designers dating back to the 1960s. Artifacts can be rough three-dimensional models of an idea, explanatory sketches, or even audible or olfactive representations. They can be used to communicate a team member's idea, represent learning garnered from field research or characterization of a customer's experience. Together they create a team-centric language for mutual understanding.

Once concepts are clearly communicated, they can then be used to extract deeper knowledge and understanding with a wider audience. For instance, in medical applications the term "sterilization" can have radically different associations whether you are communicating with surgeons, operating room nurses, biomedical engineers or persons in charge of regulatory requirements. Surgeons may be more concerned with redundancy of tools, nurses cart size and engineers with material compatibility. Although they will all use the same terminology (i.e., sterilization), they differ in perspective. As new fledgling concepts begin to form, creating visual, tactile and verbal cues for communication can have a significant impact on the fidelity of feedback obtained for decision-making.

Cross-functional and Multidisciplinary

All innovation management systems rely on the aggregate power of teams. *Cross-functional* refers to the functional area of focus of the individual, while *multidisciplinary* refers to the educational discipline of individuals. For instance, someone could be an engineer (i.e., discipline) while acting as a technical sales manager (i.e., function). As discussed, the more diverse the team, the more important internal communication using a common language becomes. There is no right or wrong way to select a team. Some of the important points are diversity of knowledge, experience, culture and education. This will be covered in greater detail in Chapter 12.

Once the team is selected, team empowerment and clear direction become the dominant criteria for driving successful outcomes. Team empowerment refers to the ability of the team to make day-to-day decisions with respect to the project. It relies on guidance from management rather than oversight. A good example can be observed in the now-famous IDEO shopping cart video (*IDEO the Deep Dive*, 1997) where David Kelly provides guidance as the team reports their findings. In the video, his team leader states that, "we don't want to tell them what to build or else we take away the benefit of the (process)." Instead, Kelly provides structure to their next steps by challenging them to determine "what needs do they optimize their solution to." Also, critical to their process is team leadership, where the team leader is "good at managing teams," not picked by seniority.

Last, creative team abrasion is also known to be positively related to innovation outcomes. Research indicates that repeat innovation teams lose the ability to challenge each other, resulting in reduced innovation performance (Roach, 2012). Thus, a level of discord in team interaction can be beneficial to the process if managed constructively.

Information Driven, Agile and Effective

All successful innovation systems are structured one way or another around agility. However, agility for the sake of agility can be quite harmful to innovation outcomes. Popularized by proponents of Agile Development, the LS and Concurrent Engineering, "scrums," "hacks" and "rapid development" are often mistakenly used to project agility to stakeholders such as senior management or investors.

Agility should instead be the output of a proper innovation management system, where information is first gathered, assessed and processed into actionable items. This highlights one of the limitations of many of the agile systems, since they tend to be "solution-centric" rather than "problem-centric." Systems that start with solutions (or partial solutions) often fall victim to group think, narrow perspectives and limitations of solution space. As we will discuss later, in the memorable words of Dr. Robert Cooper, there is "no substitution for homework." Proper background work, focusing on trends, problems and issues rather than the often-totted market size, dynamics and growth must be executed first. The importance of this background work should not to be minimized, since it crucially informs the next steps in information gathering.

Remaining agile does however have some significant advantages. For instance, it can allow an enlightened team to remain *flexible* on aspects of the innovation until such a time as uncertainty can be reduced and risk assessed. It can also be helpful to break any "paralysis by analysis" issues often found in repeat innovation teams and/or in highly regulated markets (e.g., medical, aerospace). Also, the agile approach is fundamentally built upon a build–measure–learn feedback loop which when coupled with strong information gathering can yield significant benefits. Rapid deployment of iterations allows the team to gather feedback quickly and adapt their innovation concepts in response to real-time insights.

Requirements and Attributes

Key to any successful innovation management approach is the ability to "do the right things right." This involves establishing early design requirements. This requires a process that (i) systematically establishes needs, (ii) clarifies their nuances and (iii) is open to inputs that add, subtract or refine these constructs. Requirements however are determined by the language of the customer (Griffin & Hauser, 1993). A customer might say that they feel confident using a certain type of golf putter. The innovation management question is "why do they feel that way"? Confidence thus could be a requirement; however, what key attributes of the product produce this feeling of confidence?

Often, attributes are confused either with specifications or with features of the innovation. For instance, a key attribute of a golf putter could be its esthetic design, defined (i) qualitatively and (ii) interpreted subjectively. However, we can probably all agree that this is an important aspect of a putter. What then are the features that deliver this attribute? Features could involve, color(s), size and shape, materials, etcetera. Thus, attributes are what really satisfy needs and must be delivered via features of the innovation. Using our example, specifications quantify features by specifying colors, materials, weight and dimensions.

The other factor is "who"? I often use the analogy of trying to solve a mathematical equation with two unknowns. This can only be accomplished by an iterative approach, where one factor must be held constant, while manipulating the other. In innovation management, the two unknowns are (i) the customer (or the decision-making unit, i.e., who) with the other being (ii) the attributes of the product or innovation itself (i.e., what). Thus, at the FEI, there are always two unknowns: "who" and "what." As will be discussed later, these hypotheses are initially established in the secondary research phase. This then "informs" the primary research phase, where the process of converting customer insights into informed decision-making begins.

Problem Focused not Solution Focused

I am often asked by my graduate students what factors separate individuals that I have employed over the decades from others. The answer is simple. It's their ability to define the correct problem(s) to solve. Once the correct problem is acknowledged, the solutions are often readily apparent. This may appear simplistic but, in my experience, it is far from it. Customers often cannot easily articulate their problems with words. This is why I always counsel innovation teams to be very careful with words since human beings are very complex entities. One of my favourite sayings is "never believe what people say...merely observe their behavior. There are numerous instances where innovation teams have gone astray by taking what customers say verbatim. This is one of the key limitations of the LS, where their approach relies on customers fully verbalizing their needs.

Often, novice innovation teams begin with solutions in search of a problem. In many instances, they contend that they are not solution-centric but have some vague ideas of the innovation in mind. This unconscious bias is not only a beginner's problem but often the unconscious approach of technical teams (e.g., engineers, scientists, and computer scientists). This approach is analogous to "when one has a hammer...everything looks like a nail." In practice, it is almost unavoidable to begin an innovation project without having some sort of concepts in mind. However, all successful innovation management systems understand that problem identification is the key to success. As a result, an innovation management system must provide guardrails to buffer this propensity. This will be covered in the following chapters.

Creativity Enhanced, not Driven

Creativity is often used synonymously with innovation. This can be highly misleading. It is true that all successful innovations involve some form of novelty or creativity. Creativity focused on key problems or issues can be highly effective, while unfettered creativity is often unhelpful to the innovation process. As a result, I prefer to use the term *novelty* since it has better connotations to the field of innovation management. *Finding a novel way to create value for the customer through a differentiated product is the objective of the innovation management process.*

This is one of the limitations of DT since in practice it is often usurped by the ideation (i.e., creativity) process. It tends to create volumes of ideas that must be sorted, assessed and eventually resourced or killed. As a result, best-of-class innovation management approaches concentrate creative activities focused on identified problems.

Relative Value

All innovations will be referenced by users to some neutral point. No matter what problem or set of problems are perceived, users will rank these against their next best option. This can include other products, services or combinations. In the rare occasions where there is no direct solution, users will measure it against the status quo. Regardless, all innovations will be ranked against a real or perceived benchmark.

In most situations, users have solutions for their current needs. These are most often existing products or services, each with unique attributes and features. Users may even create a mental image of a hybrid solution that incorporates the best features of two or more products. This becomes their benchmark for assessing the *relative value* of a new solution. As an example, when individuals think of trying a new restaurant, they may create a hybrid of the best ambiance, service, food type, menu selection and so on. They will then rank a new restaurant against this mental model to determine how they perceive an alternate value offering.

All innovation management approaches rely on *creating value relative to the customer's next best option*. This infers that innovation teams must identify and understand the benchmark from which the target audience determines relative value.

Boundaries

Effective ideation should be based on a process that is more likely to produce value-added outcomes. Free-floating, casually managed, and undirected ideation activities rarely lead to successful outcomes. The perception however is that ideation (or brainstorming) activities must be free from constraints, since these will stifle the creative process and lead to concepts that lack novelty. This myth has been perpetuated by throngs of creativity consultants who mistakenly believe that creativity and innovation are the same construct.

Going back to the origin of brainstorming, it was originally described as "organized ideation" by advertising executive Alex F. Osborn ("Brainstorming," 2024). Although many of the key characteristics that we now associate with brainstorming were present (e.g., defer judgment, push for quantity), he stressed another key aspect. Specifically, that activities should be guided by a *clear statement of the problem*, going so far as to say that sessions addressing multiple questions were inefficient (Osborn, 1963). His approach emphasized refining the problem statement (i.e., narrowing the scope) to make ideation activities more *effective*. Later Dr. Edward de Bono in his seminal book *Lateral Thinking* (de Bono, 1977) established many tools and techniques that are now inextricably linked with brainstorming. Although I will cover these in more detail in Chapter 7, suffice to say that many of his techniques involve restating the problem and narrowing its scope. In the ubiquitous IDEO shopping cart video, the team lead is heard to say "if the solution doesn't nest, then it doesn't work." He was referring to "nesting" which was the team's terminology for how shopping carts must fold into each other for storage. This statement made during the brainstorming session clearly indicates that they had created this *boundary* prior to their brainstorming activities.

All of these approaches stress succinct, clear, and unambiguous problem statements that *narrow the scope* of *what's in and what's out* of the ideation process. Although many DT proponents will argue that this is all part of the process, in practice I have rarely observed the use of boundaries around ideations activities.

Check-in, Check-out

All innovation management approaches have a system of checking-in and checking-out. As discussed earlier, Dr. Robert G. Cooper is famous for his "gate"" concept, which refers to a decision point at each stage of the process. These gates serve as critical junctures where project teams evaluate progress and make informed decisions about whether to proceed, modify or terminate an innovation project.

Under his approach, the decision-making process is based on predefined criteria and evaluation parameters (i.e., check-in). These criteria typically cover aspects that include technical feasibility, market potential, financial viability and alignment with business objectives. The term "gate" implies that the project must pass through this point, and a decision is made before moving forward (i.e., a checkpoint). This provides a structured and disciplined approach to innovation management, enhancing the likelihood of successful outcomes.

Innovation Invariably Collides with the Business Model

Whether a startup, small-to-medium-size enterprise (SME) or a business unit of a multinational corporation, all innovation activities invariably collide with the business model. However, at the FEI, business modeling can be problematic since it is based on assumptions, most of which are non-existent, imprecise and/ or highly subjective in nature.

In larger corporations, this often takes the form of standard cost accounting practices, which estimate the variable, fixed and overhead costs together with revenue projections. Standard metrics are then applied based on best accounting practices. These include (but are not limited to) return on investment (ROI), cost of capital, payback and breakeven to name a few. These are used to eliminate or approve projects. In practice, however, they often suffer from "gaming," since the underlying assumptions can be manipulated to senior management's satisfaction, providing whatever outcome is required at the time. This practice is often exposed during post-mortems when projects that should have been discontinued were consistently resourced by management often pursuing a sunk cost fallacy.[2] This is why leading specialists such as Dr. Cooper state that "there is a time and place for ROI calculations, but not too early in the process."

---

[2]The sunk cost fallacy is a phenomenon whereby individuals or groups are reluctant to abandon a course of action even when abandonment would be more beneficial, because they are heavily invested in the outcome.

More recently the startup community has increased focus on business modeling through such methods as the LS and tools like the business model canvas. In practice, this approach also tends to suffer from limitations since they are often incorrectly used or mistakenly applied. For instance, the popular business model canvas has in practice become a "fill in the blank" exercise, considered necessary for developing pitch decks.

As will be discussed in the following chapters, using these methods and approaches can be very beneficial if managed properly. It will be argued that a pragmatic business modeling approach is required based on a set of heuristics (i.e., rules of thumb). A business model is nothing more complex than a revenue and cost model, where the latter has a fixed and variable component. Most of the business modeling literature (including the Business Model Canvas) involves lengthy discussions of *drivers* of the revenue and cost models. Thus, it will be argued that simple heuristics should be used to establish business model viability. Much like the innovation process itself, once the problem is properly defined, the business model solutions become apparent. Then, gifted entrepreneurs, managers or teams can apply creative solutions to tackle problems.

There is a Project Management Component

I once asked a trusted colleague who had won one of the most prestigious project management awards in Canada to define project management for me. He told me the answer is simple… "it's the ability to look around corners accurately." This definition has stuck with me over the years due to its simple description of a complex topic. What he meant was that there is an art to project management which involves a combination of methods, tools and experience that must work as a system. Without the thoughtful combination of these aspects, projects will invariably hit roadblocks that will result in delays, scope creep and budget overruns.

Unfortunately, much of project management education focuses on the tools, only briefly touching on the "soft skill" aspects of management. Too much attention is given to the intricacies of PERT charts or software tools to minimize the critical path. Although many educators would disagree, the training is also highly focused on predictable projects where there is not a lot of uncertainty within work packages or the aggregate project itself. Although the project management BOK PMBOK Guide thoroughly covers all aspects of project management, in practice few project managers understand or are capable of managing innovation projects. The question is why?

Fundamentally it comes down to requirements definition and uncertainty. Requirements in innovation projects must be extracted from the VoC. These requirements must be (i) discovered, (ii) made tangible in some fashion, (iii) interpreted and (iv) decisions made to manage the next step of the project. This process is fraught with uncertainty since this information is qualitative, hard to interpret and subjective in nature. This sequence of events that forms the scope of the project is nonlinear and iterative in nature, thus strict time management with minimal "slack" between activities is not appropriate. Project managers who are taught to manage the relationship between scope, time and costs feel pressure at the front end of an innovation project not to allow the project to slip on any of these dimensions. As a result, they drive the early stages of an innovation project based on timelines that are frequently unrealistic based on a moving scope. This results in the critical path driving the decision-making process which is damaging at the FEI.

Uncertainty Management

In every innovation project, the prime objective is to acknowledge and reduce uncertainty. There are three levels of uncertainty, spanning technical, market and economic dimensions. Technical uncertainty (i.e., feasibility) encompasses R&D risks and regulatory limitations. It necessitates a systematic approach to identify and mitigate uncertainties in technical, regulatory and intellectual property domains. *Research* endeavors, being inherently unpredictable and complex, often pose challenges, while *development* activities, grounded in established principles, are more predictable.

Market uncertainty (i.e., desirability) differs from the traditional entrepreneurship emphasis on market size and dynamics. Instead, it focuses on understanding adoption barriers and unmet needs in the marketplace. Early-stage information gathering prioritizes user needs, competitive product analysis and market adoption potential. While market size and growth rates are part of the decision-making process, they are often assessed prematurely. They are more geared toward *project selection* rather than innovation management. The primary objective in the early stages is delineating the essential features and benefits of the innovation.

Economic uncertainty (i.e., viability) focuses on assessing the strength of the business model. Entrepreneurs often rely on business modeling for preliminary viability assessment. ROI calculations if applied too early are prone to flaws due to unsubstantiated assumptions. Instead, an effectual approach based on affordable loss models (Sarasvathy, 2001) is advocated for assessing innovation projects at the early stages. This entails estimating revenue and cost models while acknowledging the inherent uncertainty in assumptions.

Conclusion

In summary, there is more than a half-century of methods, systems, tools and techniques related to the FEI. Recent methodologies such as DT and the LS are merely reconfigurations of other approaches albeit with a new flavor and vocabulary. This does not mean that they are not valuable; however, understanding their inspiration should lead to a deeper understanding of their application. Innovation management at its core is an uncertainty management exercise, where the desirability, feasibility and viability of the innovation must be managed until a final solution is attained.

All approaches must also manage the relationship between *effectiveness* and *efficiency*. I argue throughout this book that to be successful at innovation, *effectiveness at each step is the key*. Efficiency can come from doing things better (i.e., being more effective) rather than short-circuiting the process to gain time.

Increasing effectiveness will over the long run result in better outcomes and more efficient use of time and resources. Like an all-star baseball player, becoming the most effective at all the skills is the recipe for success, not speeding through practices to get to the game.

The next chapter will examine the strengths and weaknesses of both DT and the LS. Opportunities for overcoming limitations will be discussed to improve the *effectiveness* of these systems. Further chapters will recommend an innovation management model that is first *effective* and by default *efficient*.

Chapter 2

Limitations of Design Thinking and the Lean Startup

The innovation management process must go beyond merely generating ideas. Over the past decade, sound innovation management practices have been usurped by populist methodologies such as Design Thinking and parallel entrepreneurship approaches such as the Lean Startup. Although there are many benefits to these approaches, both suffer from limitations. Design Thinking approaches the innovation process from an idea generation perspective, where ideation activities overshadow the process. Similarly, the Lean Startup proposes that the business model dominates, and that one can pivot their way from idea to success through a series of hypothesis tests. While both have their merits, generating more ideas further complicates the selection process, while pivoting is often the result of poor planning and execution. This chapter examines these methodologies within the context of robust innovation management approaches.

Design Thinking as a System

A Brief History

In their thorough analysis of Design Thinking (DT), Johansson-Sköldberg et al. (2013) break the construct into two distinct categories, which they call "designerly thinking" and "Design Thinking." The former derives from the design-based literature originating in the late 1960s, with most theory development published in design journals, not management journals as generally perceived. The DT discourse on the other hand took a different path. In an effort to legitimize itself, the design community needed to find a way to talk about design in a way managers could understand and make sense of. This begat semi-academic literature and popular press articles by management scholars in the mid-1980s, followed by the mainstream media at the turn of the century. Articles in management publications (e.g., *Harvard Business Review* and *Design Management Review*) popularized the concept due to their reputation with US executives and managers.

The Innovation Approach:
Overcoming the Limitations of Design Thinking and the Lean Startup, 23–38
Copyright © 2025 by David C. Roach
Published under exclusive licence by Emerald Publishing Limited
doi:10.1108/978-1-83797-799-420241002

This popularity was also largely driven by the publicity generated by IDEO and Dean Roger Martin at the Rotman School of Business at the University of Toronto. It quickly became a "portal for the whole design area to contribute to innovation and (for) Design Thinking enabled innovation to supersede strategic management" (Johansson-Sköldberg et al., 2013, p. 1127).

This conceptualization spilled over into the engineering-anchored innovation domain, which was in dire need of more imaginative approaches. Based on methodologies developed by IDEO and the Stanford d.school, it is now hard to think about innovation without including DT. This conceptualization evolved to include a unique combination of methodologies, creativity, culture and infrastructure. Recently, Carlgren et al. (2016) criticized the soundness of the concept arguing that it is still ill-defined and largely driven by practitioners and advocates. Although growing in importance, they assert that this lack of coherence limits the ability of the concept to be studied by innovation scholars.

Although DT has many proponents and critics, there is no doubt that it has been widely adopted within the practitioner community. It is generally described as a human-centered approach to problem-solving, creativity and innovation. It involves need-finding through understanding user involvement and experimentation with a bias toward user testing (Seidel & Fixson, 2013). Cultural diversity underwrites the entire process by assembling a diverse team with different skills, personalities and capabilities.

Modern Incarnation

The modern incarnation of DT was largely popularized by two sources. First the emergence of the commercial firm IDEO based on a two-part 1997 NBC depiction entitled the Deep Dive, where Stanford Professor David Kelly narrates the development of an innovative shopping cart using IDEO's novel innovation management system (*IDEO the Deep Dive*, 1997). This became the focal point for the integration of the industrial design community with that of the technical or engineering community, each of which had previously treated the other with suspicion. The second was Roger Martin's push to brand the Rotman School of Business at the University of Toronto as the "marquee" DT business school. Based on knowledge developed in the 1990s by such visionaries as Dorothy Leonard at Harvard Business School, he almost singlehandedly brought the concept into business education and practice by endorsing it as a way to solve "wicked" business problems. This resulted in legitimizing "design" with the business community to a level only dreamed of in the 1960s. It also, reset the classic corporate R&D model where technology factions of organizations drove the innovation management process from R&D labs.

The table was thus set for what many considered a revolution in the innovation management process.

What is DT?

Before delving into the strengths and weaknesses of the system, let's review the fundamental tenets of DT.

It is impossible to think about DT without thinking about the product design and development firm IDEO founded by David M. Kelly. IDEO as a commercial enterprise has long championed the DT process as a way for industry to re-align its innovation management activities. It not only promotes the methodology but actively supports it as a business unit through its online IDEOU courses and certificates (*IDEOU Certificate Programs*, 2024). Fundamental to this concept is the narrative of bringing together what is *desirable* from a human point of view with what is technologically *feasible* and what is *economically* viable (see Fig. 2).

To achieve this tripartite relationship, they break down the process into distinct steps. They note, however, that although presented linearly, these frequently overlap as new information becomes available, resulting in an iterative approach. The Stanford d.school further emphasizes a human-centered design approach; however, their focus tends to drift toward solving complex problems rather than creating differential advantage. Their stages include:

Empathize: This stage involves empathetically engaging in an understanding of the problem(s) from the perspective of end-users or customers. Teams gather insights into their needs, feelings and experiences. This empathetic understanding they suggest is crucial for generating meaningful solutions.

Define: Involves distilling observations and insights from the empathize stage to define a clear and specific problem statement. This step helps ensure that the team addresses real and relevant issues.

Ideate: Ideation is all about brainstorming and generating creative ideas. There's an emphasis on thinking outside the box and encouraging a wide range of ideas

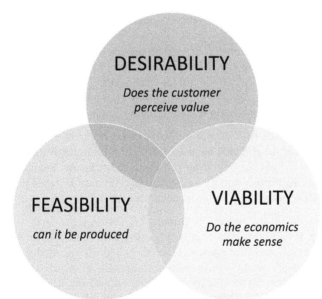

Fig. 2. Adapted from IDEOs Design Thinking Framework. *Source*: https://www.ideou.com/pages/design-thinking.

without judgment. Techniques such as brainstorming and storyboarding are commonly used.

Prototype: Prototyping involves creating low-fidelity representations of ideas or concepts. These can include sketches, physical models, or even rough drafts of digital products. The goal is to quickly turn ideas into tangible forms for testing and communication.

Test: This stage involves obtaining feedback on prototypes from potential users, gathering reactions and insights. This iterative process helps refine solutions based on real-world feedback.

Iterate: Using feedback received during testing, improvements and refinements are made to prototypes. This process is often repeated multiple times until the team arrives at a solution that effectively addresses the defined problem.

Within these overlapping stages, their systems employ various techniques to execute the steps of the process. For instance, one popular approach is customer journey mapping, a technique for the team to systematically walk through the steps a customer faces when interacting with a product or service. Maps are used to explore the problem space, followed by synthesizing learnings from observations and interviews. This not only chronicles the journey but is a powerful team communication technique. Other techniques include rules of brainstorming, mind mapping, etc.

Strengths of the System

There are many strengths of the system but most revolve around the following:

Creative process: At the core of DT is the process of brainstorming, which is highly visible, fun and creative. This process allows for the exploration of ideas and concepts that otherwise would not have been conceived. It relies on the premise that creativity is the key to successful innovation and that even non-creative people can create if given the right environment, training and structure.

A systematic approach: Although presented in linear steps, the process is by nature iterative. Steps can be revisited as new information becomes available or as new learnings come to light. As with most processes, the outcomes are highly dependent on the quality of execution within each step. Care must be taken not to let one step overshadow others in order of importance.

Highly user-centric: The process is empathetic, focusing primarily on end-user requirements. It relies on primary research using both semi-structured "probe & learn" interviewing and observational (anthropological) knowledge acquisition. Both techniques are qualitative in nature, the results of which are highly subject to interpretation. To be effective, it relies on a well-structured, diverse team approach not influenced by hierarchical decision-making. It also relies on a committed management approach that is comfortable with a level of uncertainty in decision-making based on the interpretation of qualitative information.

Tactile and prototype driven: One of the key strengths of DT is its emphasis on vicarious prototyping. Many years ago, when Dr. Robert Cooper investigated best practices in new product development, prototyping was the purview of the R&D department. Their narrow objective tended to be whether the prototype worked as conceived and met specifications. Today, based on companies like IDEO, prototypes are initially "rough-rapid-ready" or what we used to refer to as *focused* prototypes (i.e., focused on a narrow aspect). Prototypes are also used in a broader sense, not only to answer technical questions but also market adoption and business model questions.

Continuous learning: DT relies on the fluidity of process where a culture of continuous learning is embraced. Tools and techniques used to bolster knowledge generation fuel this process, which are then interpreted by a team with broad skills and capabilities. The process is flexible enough to adapt to new information that may challenge preconceived notions, allowing for revisitation of steps.

Weaknesses in Practice

Too great a focus on *idea generation*. This can be positive in the divergence part of the process (i.e., concept generation) but may not address one of the core problems in innovation management – namely the convergence process (i.e., concept selection). In an article published in MIT/SLOAN magazine, managers were surveyed as to where their resources were focused at the FEI and how it matched their requirements (Birkinshaw et al., 2011). In essence, companies spent a considerable number of resources on generating ideas, while their biggest requirement was how to winnow down and select the best ones. The point of the article is that idea generation is fun, builds *esprit de corps* and is highly visible to senior management. The dirty work of selecting the best ideas is difficult, goes unnoticed and is often unmanageable due to the *volume of ideas* to be sorted through. There is also a perception that ideas must be highly creative/new-to-the-world to rationalize the idea generation activities, when in fact, incremental ideas most often win the innovation game. Thus, idea generation and brainstorming are powerful tools if used appropriately, but they must be used with care and attention.

Too much of a focus on *customer empathy* can narrow the focus of the problem space. In practice, the DT process (although not designed this way) tends to be end-user focused rather than decision-making unit (DMU) (Aulet, 2013) focused. In most situations, the end-user may not be where the most critical problem(s) occur. I often use the simple example of purchasing a teddy bear. I ask students "who is the end-user"? After some deliberation, the answer is invariably the child. I then ask, "if we only (or mostly) focused on the child, would we be able to create a commercially or socially viable teddy bear"? Again, after much discussion, the answer is no, because others are involved in the transaction. These include parents, aunts/uncles, grandparents, friends and relatives. There are also actors who influence the process outside of the transaction who often impose other requirements on the process. Thus, although a customer-centric and empathetic focus is commendable, it is *necessary but not sufficient* for the optimum management of the innovation process.

Linearity in a *unilinear approach*. As stated earlier, DT as a system is iterative rather than linear. The question is why? When new information becomes available, steps in the process should be revised since earlier assumptions and decisions may no longer be valid. This has to do with decision-making in the areas of uncertainty. At the beginning of any innovation project, virtually all assumptions are grounded by uncertainty. As information is gathered, uncertainty is reduced. One of the strengths of DT is its ability to make decisions based on qualitative, uncertain and sometimes conflicting information. However, this can also be one of its Achilles heels. In practice, teams often rely too heavily on the iterative nature of the process and fast forward through important steps in information gathering. This weakens problem identification as teams rush to the idea generation phase. They rationalize this approach believing that the quicker they formulate concepts, the quicker they can iterate back through steps to get to their optimum solution. Now there is some validity to this thinking; however, in my experience, it is highly prone to "idea bias" and strays from problem centricity – the hallmark of effective innovation management processes. Don't get me wrong, highly skilled teams or consultancies such as IDEO and the Basadur group tend to manage this process well. However, legions of DT consultants tend to short-circuit this process, ending up with a greater "idea bank" than they had prior to the project. As discussed above, this makes converging on an optimum set of concepts problematic.

Observation to *uncover latent needs*. Dorothy Leonard's seminal 1996 book – *Wellsprings of Knowledge* (Leonard, 1995) ushered in an era of qualitative research in marketing and new product development. She highlighted the use of observational research as a tool to uncover latent (unspoken) customer needs. This approach has proven to be highly effective and, in many cases, led to new insights. However, observational research is a unique skill set not possessed by most team members. Even when non-verbal observations are made, interpreting their meaning is a highly complex process and not within the proficiency of neophyte teams. As a result, the ability to use these observational cues to uncover unspoken needs is a limiting factor for most teams.

DT recommends a *systematic approach* following a defined process. However, in practice, many projects suffer from what Dr. Robert Cooper characterized a lack of "quality of execution." Many DT projects emanate from a creativity core and thus creativity plays an outsized role in the process. DT and to a greater extent Lean Startup (LS) proponents believe that you can start virtually anywhere and iterate your way to a successful outcome. Reflecting to my years of advanced mathematics, an iteration was described as repeatedly applying an operation to a particular input (or starting point) to produce a sequence of values. It starts with an initial value, applying the operation to produce a new endpoint. The endpoint becomes the revised input, and the process is repeated until the result converges on an optimum solution. As a result, the further away the initial assumption, the more iterations are required to get to an ideal state. Part of the art is knowing where to start. In the context of DT and the LS, rushing to an initial solution from which to iterate, often leads to endless (and unnecessary) iterative steps. Unlike mathematics, each iterative step is prone to "drift" (i.e., it is not quantitatively precise) which can result in driving the project in a harmful direction. To put it another way, if you are navigating a course for a sailing ship and you are off by two degrees per step, after relatively few iterations you can be severely off course. Thus, for DT, the quality of execution preceding brainstorming is crucial for staying on course. As will be discussed later, each step must inform the next step of the process to maintain the *effectiveness* of the approach.

User focused rather than *problem focused*. Although they are closely related, the approach taken by the team makes a difference. A myopic focus on the user can be detrimental to the process depending on how it is implemented. In a purely user-focused world view, the team empathizes with the end-user and looks for frustrations, emotional signals and/or overt likes and dislikes of the product or service. These are all fine, but they can suffer from an end-user bias that can impact the quality of the problem space. As an example, in the field of medical devices, observing the end-user's frustration is often only part of the problem. A medical practitioner may want a clinically better, more environmentally sustainable, easier-to-use solution, but the decision-makers (i.e., the DMU) may have different problems to solve. There may be logistical problems (e.g., transportation, storage), business unit budget allocations issues (e.g., savings accrue to one department, but the budget comes from another) and medical practice issues (e.g., standards of care vary between different jurisdictions). Thus, the problem space that may be inferred from the end-users is often a good starting point but is *a necessary but not sufficient* assessment of the problem space. Taking a problem-focused approach based on the entire ecosystem is one of the hallmarks of a best-of-class innovation management system.

The LS as a Methodology

A Brief History

Although touted as a methodology, the LS for the purposes of this book should be considered as a *system* developed by Eric Ries, a serial entrepreneur and author. It focuses on building and launching businesses with an emphasis on efficiency and minimizing waste. It has its roots in the software and technology industry within Silicon Valley and is designed to help entrepreneurs and startups succeed by promoting a systematic and *efficient* approach to building and scaling businesses. Its foundation is built around Lean manufacturing theory and Agile software development.

The approach gained popularity through his book, *The Lean Startup: How Today's Entrepreneurs Use Continuous Innovation to Create Radically Successful Businesses*, which was published in 2011 (Ries, 2011). This book provided a comprehensive explanation of the principles of the LS. It offered a practical guide for entrepreneurs and startups looking to build scalable businesses. The LS has been adapted and applied to various industries and has become an established approach in the world of entrepreneurship. It is often coupled with the Business Model Canvas (Osterwalder & Pigneur, 2010), a visual tool for mapping business models, developed prior to the publication of his book.

Alexander Osterwalder and Yves Pigneur created the Business Model Canvas as a tool for providing a structured way to describe, design, challenge and pivot a business model. While conducting research, Osterwalder recognized the need for a systematic approach to describing and analyzing business models. This led to a collaboration with Yves Pigneur, a professor at the University of Lausanne. Together, they worked to develop and refine the Business Model Canvas, creating a visual representation of core components of a business. In 2010, they published the book *Business Model Generation: A Handbook for Visionaries, Game Changers, and Challengers*. This book served as a comprehensive guide to the Business Model Canvas, becoming a bestseller, widely acclaimed by entrepreneurs, business leaders and innovators. The book not only explained the concept of the Business Model Canvas but also featured numerous case studies and practical examples. The Business Model Canvas gained rapid adoption in the business and startup world due to its simplicity and effectiveness in mapping and communicating business models. It provided a structured way to ideate, design and challenge business models. It is unclear when the LS and the Business Model Canvas became inextricably linked, but it is now difficult to think of one without the other.

Steve Blank, a mentor to Ries in his startup at IMVU, also became closely linked to the LS (Ries, 2011). His 2005 book, *The Four Steps to the Epiphany*, played a pivotal role in laying the groundwork for the LS. While he was not the creator of the LS, his book served as a precursor to Eric Ries' LS principles. Consequently, he is often considered one of its key proponents and thought leaders. He is predominantly known for emphasizing the importance of "customer development" as a crucial component of the LS process. Customer development, he contends is about getting out of the building and interacting with potential customers, validating hypotheses and refining a startup's product and business model based on real-world feedback. He has incorporated the Business Model Canvas alongside the LS methodology into his teaching and advisory work.

What is the LS?

The current embodiment of the LS owes its roots to Ries, Blank and Osterwalder. Although it draws some of its processes from the DT community, its core focus is on a systematic approach to building and scaling businesses. As a result, it has a strong focus on efficiency, validated learning and customer feedback.

Osterwalder's approach is most closely associated with business model innovation. The methodology associated with his Business Model Canvas includes nine building blocks which include: customer segments, value propositions, channels, customer relationships, revenue streams, key resources, key activities, key partners and cost structure. Although not routinely used in practice, he also developed a complimentary *Value Proposition Canvas*, which emphasizes customer segments and value proposition to refine the product–market fit. These contributions provide the essential *techniques* often used in conjunction with the LS system to structure, test and refine their business models and value propositions.

Blank's contribution to the approach emphasizes "Customer Development" in three stages. This initially begins with *Customer Discovery*, in essence identifying target customers and establishing their needs. He advises the use of a structured process of talking to potential customers to understand their problems, pain points and whether solutions address their needs. This is followed by *Customer Validation* a process of validating hypotheses about the customer segments and their problems by testing solutions with real customers and collecting feedback. The next step takes a leap into *Customer Creation* the process of creating and growing the customer base through marketing and sales efforts. The last step involves *Company Building*, which includes expanding the team, optimizing operations and preparing for growth. His key contribution is a structured framework for validating and refining a startup's business model through customer interactions and feedback.

Ries integrated these techniques into his LS system, where he proposed a three-part approach to the startup process. The first part merely defines a *vision* that sets the stage for entrepreneurial management via validated learning. This is executed through a process of refining the definition, learning through fact-finding and experimentation. The next phase is *Steering*, where the entrepreneur or team takes a leap into the unknown and begins the build–measure–learn process using minimum viable products (MVPs) to test assumptions. He stresses an iterative approach where adjustments (what he refers to as pivots) are not only encouraged but stressed. The approach concludes with his third phase – *Accelerate*, which he defines as batch, grow, adapt and innovate. Effectively, he professes how to speed through the build–measure–learn feedback loop as the startup scales. He advocates for lean manufacturing concepts such as the power of small batches and organizational design.

As a result, the steps or components of the LS process can generally be summarized as follows:

Start with a Vision: Begin with a clear vision of what must be achieved through a startup.

Create Hypotheses: Formulate a series of hypotheses about the business model, including who the customers are, what problems the product/service needs to solve and how value will be delivered.

Build an MVP: Develop a minimal version of the product or service that includes its essential features. The MVP is designed to be quickly built and launched to test the hypotheses in the real world.

Measure Key Metrics: It forces the identification of key performance indicators (KPIs) that help evaluate the potential success of the MVP. This may include metrics like user engagement, conversion rates and customer acquisition costs.

Learn from Feedback: It expects that a later-stage MVP will be soft-launched to a small group of early adopters. Data and feedback are collected to assess how the product meets needs and whether the business model assumptions are valid.

Pivot or Persevere: Based on data-driven feedback, assumptions are validated. If positive, the business is ready for scaling. If negative, the team pivots by making changes to the product, target audience and/or strategy.

Build–Measure–Learn Loop: Continuous iterative approach through the Build–Measure–Learn loop. This involves making incremental improvements to the product or business model, measuring results while learning from outcomes.

Validated Learning: Using data and real-world feedback to guide the decision-making process. Validated learning helps avoid wasting time and resources on concepts that don't work.

Accelerate and Scale: Once a product–market fit is achieved, focus can then turn to accelerating growth and scaling the business. This frequently involves raising capital, expanding the team and reaching a broader audience.

The LS process is characterized by its flexibility and adaptability. It encourages startups to remain nimble, iterate quickly and make data-driven decisions. The goal is to reduce the risks and uncertainties associated with starting a new business while maximizing the chances of success. As a result, it focuses on customer listening as its primary tool for information gathering. It relies upon the capability of the entrepreneur or entrepreneurial team to establish the relevant facts and decipher their meaning.

Strengths of the System

It is *Business Model* focused. One of the critiques of DT is that it is light on the business and economic aspects of the developed concepts. As a result, the LS provides more rigor than DT, but at the same time less than the classic business plan model[1]. The strength of the LS is that the business model is front and center from the beginning of the process, resulting in constant evaluation (i.e., viability) as the feasibility and desirability of the concept are established. This mimics to some extent Dr. Cooper's Stage Gate™ approach where he proposes that the economics of the opportunity must be examined at each stage along with technical and marketing aspects.

The Canvas! The canvas is a clever and well-thought-out visual tool for understanding the relationship between drivers of the business model and their impact. It also forces critical thinking as to how each component relates to the other and how the business model works as a system. I was first introduced to the canvas two decades ago at a competition at the Ivey School of Business at the University of Western Ontario. I was impressed by its simplicity and its practical application to understanding business models. It was clearly designed for non-businesspeople (namely engineers and computer scientists) to force them into a box where they had to acknowledge the relationship with aspects beyond their product or service concept. What also impressed me was that it had a "backbone," centered by the value proposition and supported by a revenue and cost model. As I began

---

[1]For more in-depth information, please refer to "New Venture Creation: Entrepreneurship for the 21st Century" originally developed by Jeff Timmons at Babson College (Spinelli & Adams, 2016).

to use it in both practice and academia, I began to refer to this backbone as the "inverted-T," given its visual image. The value proposition links all the other aspects of the business model, which ultimately results in revenues and costs. This mirrors the Babson College approach where a business model is nothing more complex than a *revenue* and *cost model*, where the cost model exists to support the revenue model (Zacharakis et al., 2019).

Eliminates concepts early that do not meet market, economic or technical tests. The LS emphasizes that all aspects of the conceived product or service must result in a viable business model. Thus, simultaneously crafting the product/service value proposition while building and evaluating business viability allows for poor concepts to be systematically eliminated. This reflects Dr. Cooper's vision that progressively increasing market, economic and technical tests are required in any innovation management system to "winnow out" concepts that will not survive contact with the market.

Weaknesses of the System

Customer listening is often poorly executed in practice. Foundational to the LS is the ability to extract key knowledge from end-users and other market participants and understand how this knowledge impacts potential adoption. As discussed earlier, this type of capability is not in the purview of most entrepreneurs or start up teams for two reasons. First, these nascent managers are not trained, nor do they have the propensity, to extract knowledge either through probe and learn or observational methods. Most are engineers and computer scientists who are technically skilled and have self-selected themselves into academic training or jobs that fit their predisposition. If they do have someone on the team who has business training, they often approach the problem from a finance or accounting perspective, neither of which is particularly helpful at the FEI. Second, even if they can adequately execute a customer listening strategy, their ability to interpret qualitative, subjective and often conflicting information is generally highly compromised. As an example, a young entrepreneur once bragged to me about interviewing 115 potential customers in her customer discovery phase. After I probed for more information, she proudly stated that these interviews lasted 10–15 minutes each, conducted with individuals from her extended social network and were based on their perception of her idea. Clearly, this approach was highly biased, relied on her ability to extract and interpret findings and suffered from a lack of training and/or understanding of how to conduct proper customer listening.

Pivoting assumes that the process can start from anywhere and end up in a success. This is one of my key criticisms of the LS methodology. Not because I disagree with the principle, in fact I think it admirably describes the entrepreneurial process. In practice, however, it has acted as a "get out of jail free" card. It gives nascent entrepreneurs and their teams a false sense of security since it provides clemency for not executing the early stages of the process properly. In fact, as I've stated in a recent article, pivoting is a euphonism for lack of (or bad) management of the process (Roach, 2020). Recently I joined an online session with a Babson College professor, who expressed the same serious concern with the practice of pivoting.

His concern was that young entrepreneurs driven by their vision feel enabled to pursue their concept at the expense of the underappreciated hard work of proper background research. Using a metaphor, he stressed that pivoting came from the game of basketball, where athletes keep one foot on the ground as they contemplate and execute their next move. They don't jump arbitrarily to the next position and then decide what to do from there. I found this insightful and happily in line with Reis' introduction to his book where he stresses that a pivot refers to "changing course with one foot on the ground." In practice I have seldom observed a properly executed LS pivot.

The LS begins from a *solution-centric* position, since it relies on the initial intuition of the founders. It is predicated on the assumption that the concept is generally workable and needs only refining and positioning in the market. It essentially short-circuits the innovation process in the "blind faith and hope" that all will be revealed through customer discovery and MVP testing. The approach relies on "force fitting" a solution by eventually aligning it with a problem or set of problems. In defense of the system, this may be why they emphasize perseverance, since this approach is generally ineffective from an innovation management perspective.

It is *business model "canvas"* focused. This is another critique of the LS system it draws too heavily on the Business Model Canvas as a technique. As stated earlier, I am a big proponent of the Business Model Canvas, however in practice, it has become perceived as a necessary fill-in-the-blank exercise for nascent entrepreneurial teams. It is often sold by proponents as the basis for investor "pitches." Consequently, it has lost much of its luster since it fails to deliver the results it was initially designed for. When this occurs, entrepreneurs feel that once they have completed the canvas, their business model in good shape merely requires some fine-tuning. They believe they are then ready to work through the LS process and pivot as necessary as new information becomes available. This usually involves adjusting the target audience and/or the value proposition. What they fail to understand is that the true value of the canvas is how it foresights the impact on the revenue and cost model, the core (or backbone) of the business model. They become surprised later when it becomes clear that although their product–market match "may" be in good shape, they have no plausible business model. Had they concentrated on the revenue and cost model earlier in the process, they would have created alternate hypotheses to test along the way.

It assumes that the *business model* MUST be novel! Nothing could be further from the truth. Driven by the advent of the internet and the popularity of the Silicon Valley approach to business, nascent entrepreneurs are either coerced into producing a novel business model or indoctrinated into this approach. In my experience, most of the "novel" business models held up as shining examples involved cutting out part of the value chain by taking products or service directly online rather than using traditional channels. This worked well in the late 1990s or early 2000s, when the cost of customer acquisition was low. Today however customer acquisition costs in many cases exceeds traditional brick and mortar costs. This is largely driven by the value of data that can be collected and monetized through the online channel and/or customer life time value (LTV) models. What always astonishes me is that most nascent entrepreneurs often do not even consider traditional channels when crafting their business model. Also, selling through an online channel hasn't been novel for almost two decades and in practice it is often poorly costed. Chapter 14 will cover what I refer to as a "heuristic business modelling" using standard assumptions.

The *MVP* tends to be more comprehensive rather than focused. One of the key fundamentals of DT is to produce rough-rapid-ready (triple-R) prototypes. There are many reasons why this approach has stood the test of time. First and foremost, it is a communication vehicle both within and outside of the team. These triple-R prototypes are what Ulrich and Eppinger refer to as *focused* prototypes (Ulrich & Eppinger, 2012). They are designed to communicate narrow aspects of an idea or concept. They are almost invariably used for team communication for such things as desirability, feasibility and viability and are rarely shown to potential users. They are very useful prior to and during creativity sessions to drive the process forward. We know from case studies and research that more and quicker iterations result in a better final solution (*Team New Zealand (A)*, 1997). Thus, from an innovation management perspective, less iterations equals less learning. Second, prototypes are also used for outside interests such as obtaining user feedback. However, this type of feedback generally requires what Ulrich and Eppinger refer to as *comprehensive* prototypes (i.e., looks like – works like). These require more time and effort resulting in less iterations. Thus, the LS methodology tends to drive teams toward comprehensive prototypes to obtain early user feedback, resulting in less input than the DT process.

Finally, *rapid iterations*. Since the LS method was born out of the Lean software development model, it assumes that all products or services can be continually built "on the fly." I remember in the mid to late 1990s at a Harvard lecture, the professor introduced consulting work they were doing with a large software firm. Based on what they termed at the time as "vicarious prototyping" they had gone to minimal daily software builds. They would allow a few hundred downloads at midnight on the West Coast so that when developers began their workday on the East Coast, they had instant feedback on patches, new features, etc. It was groundbreaking at the time but seems old school now since this model has been used for decades. The lecture at Harvard challenged us as practitioners to find ways to apply this technique across our various industries. However, this method integral to software innovation does not necessarily translate across all industries and product categories. For instance, in medical devices, this approach has significant limitations driven by the regulatory process, clinical requirements, complex decision-making process, etc. I don't know how many times I've been invited to "medical hackathons" promoted to be groundbreaking innovation sessions only to find a bunch of aspiring entrepreneurs coming up with another medical application (i.e., App). As a result, the ability to rapidly iterate, prototype and/or pivot does not translate well to tangible products and is highly industry dependent.

Implications

Building on best practices of innovation systems, combined with the strengths and weaknesses of both DT and the LS, some gaps in practice are exposed. These take the form of both processes and techniques. *Processes* refer to a set of inter-related stages of activity, while techniques refer to the activities themselves at each step of the process. Overcoming process limitations requires minor reconfiguration of stages to emphasize (or deemphasize) sequences of activities. Overcoming technique limitations requires adjusting activities to be more effective.

To establish opportunities for improvement in these systems, a gap analysis is performed as shown in Table 1.

In more detail:

Problem focus infers that both systems can drift toward either *user focus* or *solution focus*. User focus can occur when primary research activities are expedited without directional knowledge to inform this process. Solution focus can occur when teams rush to ideation exercises too quickly. These will be covered within the core steps and capabilities section of this book.

Value relatively refers to the human tendency to judge value relative to a benchmark. These benchmarks can be real or perceived, but they are nonetheless valid. Understanding the customer's frame of reference early in the innovation approach makes subsequent activities much more effective.

Latent needs are requirements that are unspoken or poorly articulated by the target audience. They are difficult to gather and even more difficult to interpret. As a result, finding, interpreting and translating them into solutions is a special skill set, rarely available in most teams. Discovering and satisfying these needs is at the core of creating differential value. Techniques will be covered in the advanced tools and techniques section of this book.

Ideation and creativity are at the core of the innovation process. These are the techniques that produce novelty in new products or services. They however must be engaged in the correct sequence (i.e., process) and must be targeted in the correct direction (i.e., techniques). Together they increase the effectiveness of the overall innovation management approach.

Customer listening involves extracting the voice of the customer (VoC). As I've stated many times in my classroom and consulting engagements – *"the voice of the customer is a whisper."* The ability to extract key requirements based on the customer's perception is complex. The capability to interpret this idiosyncratic information for decision-making further complicates this activity. Team composition, probe and learn techniques and training are keys to the effectiveness of this process.

The *DMU* refers to the complex interactions between actors in the adoption process. These actors each have different problems, requirements and perceptions of novel solutions. Understanding early in the innovation process who these actors are, what their role is and how they impact adoption is key. Merely focusing on the end-user is not only ineffective, but often detrimental to the innovation management process.

Table 1. Innovation System Gap Analysis.

	Design Thinking	Lean Startup	Gap
1. Problem focus	Addressed but inconsistent	Not adequately addressed	Increase emphasis on problem definition
2. Value relativity	Value approached through user empathy	Assumes value creation will emerge	Begin from customer's next best option
3. Latent needs	Assumes observation will uncover	Does not adequately address	Increase effectiveness of listening techniques
4. Ideation and creativity	Bias toward unfettered creativity	Bias toward business model creativity	Increase focus and effectiveness of techniques
5. Customer listening	Relies on aggregate skill set of teams	Relies on skill set of founders	Increase effectiveness of techniques
6. DMU	Bias toward end-user	Assumes all DMU issues will emerge	Increase focus on DMU requirements
7. Prototyping	Triple-R for internal and external communication	Comprehensive MVP for external communication	Enhanced prototyping strategy
8. Linearity	Ad hoc approach to nonlinear activities	Pivots drive nonlinear	Separate linear and nonlinear activities
9. Economic viability	Byproduct of value creation	Business model assumes value is created	Base viability on business model heuristics
10. Off ramp	kill switch based on concept attrition	No kill switch	Add kill switch

Prototyping, also referred to as MVPs, are a key activity in all innovation management systems. Prototypes are fundamentally used for two main purposes, namely *internal* and *external* communication. There are also many forms of prototypes each with their strengths, weaknesses, time and resource requirements. Selecting the correct prototype for the correct purpose can increase the effectiveness of this key activity.

Linearity refers to the sequence of activities within a process. Activities can be sequential or iterative depending on what is required at the system level. Systems will often dictate which processes are linear and nonlinear. Establishing which activities to perform chronologically and which require reexamination is one of the cornerstones of effective innovation management systems.

Economic viability is foundational to successful innovation management. Whether commercially or socially driven, both require a viable and stable business model. This necessitates a sustainable revenue and cost model. This is predicated on a differential value proposition from which these models evolve. Understanding basic business model heuristics increases the effectiveness on this process.

Off ramp refers to the ability to eliminate poor concepts early in the process. It allows for scarce resources to be redeployed to concepts that have greater potential. This is a *systems-level* issue impacted by individual, political and group think influences. All best-of-class innovation management systems have systematically embedded an early ability to kill concepts or projects.

Conclusions and Recommendations

In an ideal world, we would design an approach that builds on the strengths of each system while mitigating their weaknesses. Building on these systems, the remainder of this book will focus on *effective* approaches to various aspects of innovation management to optimize results.

In the next chapter, innovation will be first defined to position what aspects need to be managed to create an effective process. This will be followed by proposing a more intuitive model that blends aspects of traditional design and development systems with popular methodologies such as DT and the LS.

Chapter 3

A Complimentary Model of Innovation Management

Peter Drucker famously stated that you cannot manage what you can't measure. Implied in this statement is that you cannot manage what you don't understand. Over the years, many "purpose fit" definitions of innovation have been developed to describe this multidimensional construct. Economists see innovation as a process of creative destruction where innovative entrepreneurs create novel solutions which drive the economic process. Policy advocates see innovation as a tool for growth, while engineers and scientist see innovation as research and development activities. This chapter examines the various definitions of innovation, framing them within their context. It is then argued that a new definition of innovation is required to guide the innovation process in a more fruitful direction. Using this working definition, a complimentary model of innovation is proposed as a more effective approach to managing the front end of innovation.

Introduction

Innovation is ostensibly everywhere. The term has been used to refer to everything from invention to creative approaches to idea generation. I often joke with my students that the word "innovation" is much like the word "quality." I have spoken to hundreds of senior managers from corporate CEOs to early-stage founders and I always get the same response... "...our product or service has outstanding quality." In practice, however, I think most would agree that many products or services have at best adequate quality, while many would be considered poor. The same rhetoric applies to innovation. Every company or entrepreneur I have ever spoken with believes that their innovation is groundbreaking and highly superior to anything the competition can deploy. In practice, most innovation projects end up with serious flaws that make them unadoptable from a market perspective, uneconomical from a business perspective and/or unworkable from a technical perspective.

The Innovation Approach:
Overcoming the Limitations of Design Thinking and the Lean Startup, 39–54
Copyright © 2025 by David C. Roach
Published under exclusive licence by Emerald Publishing Limited
doi:10.1108/978-1-83797-799-420241003

What Is Innovation?

After reading dozens of books and hundreds of academic and practitioner articles on innovation, it has become clear to me that the term innovation is so broad that it has become unusable. Why is this? The core of the problem emanates from the direction or lens from which the construct is approached. Whether coming from an economic, technical, creative or business approach, I believe it is important to understand the varied definitions of this term. Once understood, it can then be framed in a way that it becomes practical for managing projects at the front end of innovation (FEI). As will become clear, there is some common ground from which to build upon. Once properly defined, innovation can then be managed appropriately.

Next is a summary of many of the classical interpretations of term "innovation."

From an Economics Lens

From an economics perspective, innovation is described in terms of efficiency, productivity and economic growth within society or industry. Through the creation and implementation of new ideas, technologies, products and/or processes, it involves the application of knowledge to transform resources into new or improved goods and services. Innovation, it is argued, is a critical driver of economic growth, leading to increased competitiveness, job creation and higher standards of living.

The roots of innovation theory are often attributed to Joseph Schumpeter (1934) and Frank Knight (1921), both of whom see innovation broadly an as approach to market equilibrium/disequilibrium. Schumpeter stresses innovation, while Knight emphasizes uncertainty as preconditions for entrepreneurship (Brouwer, 2000). Schumpeter emphasizes the role of innovation in the process of "creative destruction," where new innovations disrupt existing markets and industries, leading to overall economic progress. His later work emphasized the concept of "creative reaction" as a driver of innovation (Antonelli, 2015). He contends that firms will react either creatively or adaptively based upon the context in which they find themselves, but that innovation can only occur through a creative process. Knight on the other hand asserts that entrepreneurs' profits are directly related to uncertainty, which arises from unmeasurable risk.

From an economics perspective, innovation comes in various forms which include the following:

Product innovation: The development of new or improved products with advanced features that deliver benefits to the end-user.

Process innovation: This refers to the development of systems or techniques that generate more efficient ways to produce goods or deliver services often linked to reduced costs.

Market innovation: Relates to identifying new markets or market niches for existing products or services and/or finding novel ways to reach and serve customers.

Organizational innovation: Involves improving internal processes, management practices and/or structures within companies or institutions, leading to increased efficiency and improved resource allocation.

Business model innovation: Involves altering how a business creates, delivers and captures value.

In essence, economists see innovation as improvements in efficiency, productivity and economic growth within countries, societies or industry.

From a Creativity Lens

From a creativity perspective, innovation is seen as a process of generating novel and valuable ideas, concepts or solutions. It involves creating positive change or improvement in domains such as art, technology, business or society. It emphasizes the role of original thinking, imagination and the ability to connect seemingly unrelated concepts to create something new and impactful. Although it acknowledges the Schumpeterian view of creative reaction, this worldview highlights the importance of creative thinking in the innovation process and how creativity can be nurtured and harnessed for innovative outcomes.

Some of the drivers of innovation from a creativity perspective include:

Novelty: Innovation involves the creation of something new or the combination of existing elements in a unique way. It goes beyond routine or incremental changes.

Value: Innovations should bring value to individuals, organizations or society. This can be in the form of improved products, services, experiences or solutions to problems.

Creativity: Creativity involves challenging conventions and exploring unconventional ideas. Creative thinking can be fostered through techniques such as brainstorming or lateral thinking.

Implementation: Innovation is not just about ideas but includes creating solutions that solve problems. This often involves overcoming barriers and adapting to changing circumstances.

Impact: Innovations should have a positive impact, whether by addressing a pressing societal issue, enhancing efficiency or providing new forms of artistic expression.

Although this perspective does not fully align with the economist's societal outlook, it does align in many respects. These include the role of creative reaction to markets, the role of implementation and the implied requirement of a functional business model to support the innovation process.

From a Strategic Management Perspective

From a strategic management perspective innovation is understood to be a driver of competition. Built upon the economist's model, it is often defined as a set of systematic processes for developing and implementing new ideas, products, processes or business models that create a competitive advantage. It is a driver of strategic success, allowing companies to adapt to changing markets, stay ahead of competitors and achieve long-term growth and profitability.

Some of the key elements of innovation from a strategic management viewpoint include:

Strategic focus: Innovations should align with the organization's overall strategic goals and objectives. They should contribute to the company's mission and vision.

Competitive advantage: Innovation should give the organization a competitive edge. This can be achieved through improved product features, cost structures or market positioning.

Resource allocation: Innovation requires careful allocation of financial, human and technological resources. It involves prioritizing and investing in innovations that have the greatest potential for success.

Risk management: Strategic management involves assessing and managing risks such as market uncertainties and technological challenges to minimize negative impacts.

Long-term viability: Strategic innovation involves creating a culture of continuous improvement and adaptability within the organization.

Like the economist's view, innovation is about products, processes, services and market innovations. It goes beyond the industry or societal views and focuses on the enterprise itself. It stresses the importance of aligning innovation efforts with the organization's strategic goals to achieve competitive advantage. As a result, it is also about efficiency, risk management and the viability of the business. From a creativity lens, it does not endorse any specific methodology but recognizes systems such as Design Thinking (DT) as approaches to innovation that support the strategic goals of the organization.

From an Entrepreneurial Standpoint

From an entrepreneurial perspective, innovation is the foundation of any early-stage enterprise that intends to compete in the marketplace. It involves a process of identifying, crafting and exploiting new opportunities (Shane & Eckhardt, 2003). It is based on products, services or business models that cater to unmet needs, solve problems or disrupt existing markets. It is considered an essential driver of entrepreneurial success where differentiation from competition is achieved through value *creation* and *capture*.

Key elements of innovation from an entrepreneurial viewpoint include:

Opportunity recognition: This is foundational to entrepreneurship. Successful entrepreneurs are skilled at identifying gaps or opportunities in the market that others have overlooked. Innovation starts with recognizing these opportunities for creating something new.

Uncertainty management and *risk-taking*: Entrepreneurial innovation involves a willingness to be comfortable with uncertainty until calculated risks can be assessed. In this way, entrepreneurs can allocate resources into unproven ideas or ventures, often based on an affordable loss perspective (Sarasvathy, 2001).

Customer-centric approach: Successful entrepreneurial innovation is often customer-centric, focusing on meeting the latent needs and preferences of target customers. It involves developing a deep understanding of customer problems, pain points and desires.

Iterative: Entrepreneurs recognize that innovation is an iterative process. It may involve multiple adjustments and learning from failures before achieving success. The popular view is that pivoting is essential to success.

Business model innovation. In addition to product or service innovation, entrepreneurial innovation can also involve creating new business models or rethinking how value is delivered and monetized.

From an entrepreneurial perspective innovation emphasizes the role of opportunity recognition, customer focus and risk-taking in the process of creating value and building successful ventures.

Innovation Defined

Over the years I have often begun my innovation management classes with executives, graduate and undergraduate students by asking a simple question – what is innovation? The results are curiously similar between these seemingly disparate groups. Although participants bounce around quite a bit, key themes (many of which are described above) begin to emerge.

Novelty always leads the way. Participants feel that there must be something new in the product, service or approach for a concept to be considered an innovation. Participants often throw around terms like breakthrough, radical or disruptive innovation, believing that for something to be innovative, it must be new to the world. When pressed, participants often cannot come up with good examples of these types of innovations, falling back to the usual examples such as the Post-It™ note or Tesla. This begets a discussion on the merits of sustaining or incremental innovations, which form the majority of innovations.

It is often conjoined with *creativity*. Participants spend a lot of time talking about creativity, to the point that some see innovation and creativity as synonymous. Unfortunately, many academics and practitioners often fall into the same trap. When I then ask "is creativity innovation?" – this prompts a debate about the relationship. As the two sides trade logic, the term *novelty* will often re-emerge. When I ask what the relationship between creativity and novelty is, the class generally agrees that novelty is the output of the process, while creativity is required to create something novel. Thus, the conclusion generally circles back to *novelty* as part of any definition of innovation.

Success is not far behind. I sometimes ask my executive class to bring examples of what they consider good and bad innovations. We then spend some time pouring over the merits and failings of each example looking for common themes. I then ask the class to step back and reflect on our discussions and assess whether anything stands out. I seed this reflection with the question – what differentiates good innovation from bad innovation? Someone (often sheepishly) raises their hand and states that all innovations were successful, while all poor innovations invariably failed. Thus, the consensus is that *success* must be an intrinsic component of innovation.

This invariably leads to a discussion of *for whom*. Some innovations they contend are adopted by certain types of individuals while not by others. This opens a pandora's box of issues from "what is value" to "who" the customer might be (e.g., the end-user or the purchaser). The discussion of value invariably focuses on how value must be relative to some benchmark either real or perceived. The latter (i.e., who), leads into a discussion on the end-user, the purchaser, the influencer, etc. Thus, for whom the innovation resonates is much more complex than it appears to the uninitiated. However, all agree that it should be an integral component of any definition of innovation.

Expanding upon the construct of value, the term *solution* is always a dormant notion lurking in the background. If value must be perceived by a certain group of individuals, then it stands to reason that any innovation must provide a "delta" in value relative to the next best option. The next best option could be a competing product or service, some do-it-yourself (DIY) combination or merely the status quo. When asked how individuals chose between these options, participants routinely bring up the concept of a solution (i.e., their preferred choice must solve their problem better than the next best option). Theodor Levitt – the marketing guru at Harvard in the 1960s famously stated that individuals hire a product (or service) to "do a job" effectively solving their problem (Levitt, 1984). Thus, we typically come to agreement that at the core of value is the concept of the problem (or problems). A solution implies that the problem(s) have been identified and that the solution fits. Thus, the concept of *solutions* should form part of the broader concept of innovation.

There is a lot of discussion around terminology. For instance, popular constructs such as disruptive innovation frequently arise, as does product, process, organizational and business model innovation. These refer to types of innovation and are at the periphery of the core concept. As a result, I have over the decades concluded that a new definition of innovation is required in order to manage the FEI process. To be succinct, here is my working definition of innovation:

> Novel solutions that are successfully adopted by the relevant DMU (decision-making-unit). (Roach, 2020)

Although this definition appears simplistic, it encompasses all the important aspects of what must be managed at the FEI. An innovation must have some *novel* component, whether it be from a technological, marketing or business model perspective. This novel *solution* must address the breadth of problems that a product or service must meet, relative to the next best option. It must be *successful* in its ability to be *adopted* in the marketplace. Finally, the term *decision-making unit*, first coined by Bill Aulet (Aulet, 2013), encompasses the often-complex relationships between actors in the decision to adopt innovations.

Of note, however, are the omissions from this definition.

- Nowhere does it refer to technology. Technologies at best are enablers that deliver attributes of innovation.
- It does not include the term idea or invention. As discussed, the myth of someone waking up with a fully formed brilliant idea that revolutionizes the world is the property of fairy tales. From an innovation management perspective, it is rarer than winning the lottery.
- It does not include the term creativity. Creativity may be a driver of novelty but is meaningless unless used systematically within the confines of a proper process.
- It does not include economics or policy. Much of the literature around innovation is driven by economics or policy but has little to do with developing innovations.
- It does not include open innovation. Open innovation has been popularized over the past few decades as a way for organizations to use knowledge outside of the boundaries of the firm (Chesbrough, 2003). From an entrepreneurial perspective, it encompasses drawing from knowledge outside of the team. In this book, I will argue that all innovation is open.
- It does not include the term sustainability. Even though I am a strong proponent of sustainable development, I have strategically omitted the term from this definition. Approaching an innovation project from the "get go" from a sustainability perspective, clouds and biases the process and limits the success rate. I will devote a full chapter on sustainable innovation and how to integrate it into the innovation management process.

Thus, for the purposes of this book, I will focus on managing the key aspects of this definition. The remainder of this book will focus on how to overcome the shortcomings of otherwise strong systems such as DT and the Lean Startup (LS) to successfully create *novel solutions* that can be *successfully adopted by the relevant* actors within the *decision-making unit*.

Innovation and the Business Model

Success, whether commercial or social must be supported by a viable business model. Much like the definition of innovation however, there is much confusion about the notion of the business model. Although there are many characterizations, most are focused on *aspects* of the business model, rather than the business model itself.

Peter Drucker defined the term simply as "assumptions about what a company gets paid for" within the context of his theory of business. He stresses that it answers the age-old questions of "who is the customer" and "what does the customer value" (Ovans, 2015). Alex Osterwalder, famous for developing the business model canvas, frames the business model as a set of hypotheses. His nine-part business model canvas is organized to lay out assumptions about various drivers of the business model. His approach is anchored by the *value proposition, revenue streams* and *cost structures*. Together these describe the rationale of how an organization creates, delivers and captures value.

The business model however should not be confused with the business plan. A business plan is a blueprint that lays out the strategy for managing aspects of the business model including resources, risk management and financial requirements. The business model lays out the approach, while the business plan concentrates on the execution of the strategy. Confusion around this relationship often leads novice entrepreneurs to confound business modeling with financing, since they often rely on their proposed business model to *pitch* for early-stage financing. One of my favorite pieces of advice to nascent entrepreneurs is to "never mistake the pitch for the business." They can pitch a business model, but they must be prepared to execute the business plan.

In any event, for the purposes of this book, it is important to separate the business model into its two main components, namely *value creation* and *value capture* (see Fig. 3).

Value creation is the process of creating differential advantage vis-à-vis the customer's next best option. This is effectively what this book is all about. The innovation approach is firmly grounded in the belief that *a poor concept can rarely be converted into a commercial or social success*.

For this value to be "successfully adopted" it must be structured in such a way that value can be economically *captured*. This involves iteratively crafting a viable business model that, in the words of Dr. Scott Shane can be "exploited" (Shane & Eckhardt, 2003). By exploitation, he merely refers to successful implementation.

The *techniques* highlighted in Fig. 3 are simply the tools that transform plausible ideas into viable products or services thus creating value.

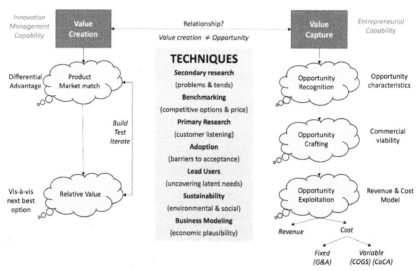

Fig. 3.   The Business Model.

The often-used terminology of *business model innovation* refers to novel approaches to value creation, value capture or both.

The innovation approach which will be examined throughout the remainder of this book is primarily about value creation delivered through FEI activities. This value creation cannot be developed in isolation from the ability to capture value. Thus, innovation management can be thought of as the precursor to business modeling although they must be developed in unison.

The Innovation Approach

Over the decades I have consistently refined my approach while keeping the same general methodology. The objective of successful innovation management is to execute an *effective* system while maintaining *efficiency*. In a nutshell, there are certain parts of the system that must be linear and sequential, while others can be nonlinear and iterative. Also, there are *natural phases* to the FEI process that channel the activities toward a robust concept that is desirable, feasible and viable.

The approach consists of four core linear activities which include *secondary research, benchmarking, primary research* and *ideation*. In this *cycle of innovation*, each step in the process informs the next step, making each ensuing step more *effective*. This information transition process acts by creating a set of boundary conditions around the innovation activities, keeping the team focused on "doing the right thing right" (Cooper, 1986). Although a significant amount of knowledge is transferred between steps, it is summarized in a revised or enhanced *problem statement*. The problem statement becomes the touchstone of team focus, establishing what is *in* and what is *out* of scope. As each activity builds upon the other, it eventually results in a robust body of knowledge infusing the ideation process. The ideation process and subsequent converging activities ultimately result in a team-based "fledgling" concept that is ready for more vigorous analysis. This analysis involves tests for desirability (i.e., do customers see value), feasibility (i.e., are there any technical challenges) and viability (i.e., are the economics plausible). This is where the concept (or concepts) are subjected to the critique of users or others involved in the decision-making process. This process is displayed in Fig. 4.

Once the fledgling concept has been evaluated and feedback has been interpreted, many areas of uncertainty will be discovered. This begins a new cycle of core activities that require a reevaluation of initial findings, beginning with secondary research and moving through the same steps. This is where the process presents as nonlinear and iterative, while at the same time maintaining enough structure to remain effective. What is perceived as a nonlinear approach is in fact a transfer from one phase to another. What is assumed to be a "step back" (or pivot) to reevaluate the process is in fact forward progression through a planned set of activities. What is understood as a pivot, is in fact what it was always meant to be; holding one foot on the ground while rotating to create space for an alternate play.

This pivot is the transition point (or phase change) between natural innovation cycles. The first and initial phase is what I term the *discovery* phase. This phase begins with a vision of what the project might be. In a corporate setting,

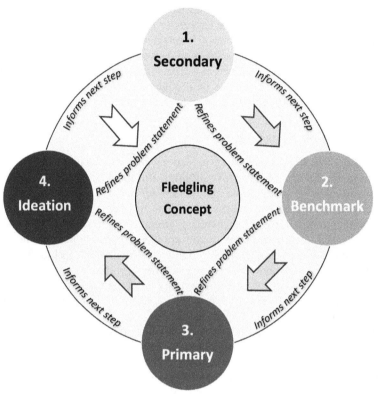

Fig. 4.   Cycle of Innovation.

this could come from business unit strategic planning activities, while in an entrepreneurial setting, this could come from the founder's vision. Following a linear set of activities described above, a fledgling concept will emerge from this initial phase. Invariably the fledgling concept will have limitations and the initial target audience is frequently in need of modification. A common issue at this stage is the need to increase the relative value (i.e., desirability) of the concept. This is where the transition to the next natural phase begins, which I refer to as the *adoption* phase (see Fig. 5).

The fledgling concept at this stage has some novel aspects, a unique selling proposition (i.e., differential value) and other appealing features. This is the point where it should be viewed through an "adoption lens," where fundamental principles of adoption theory are brought to bear on the process. This engages a new cycle where additional secondary research is required focusing on *how* and *why* individuals adopt products and why many products fail due to adoption shortcomings. This in turn requires a re-examination of benchmarks and a renewed round of primary research. At each portion of the cycle, the problem statement is refined to reflect this renewed direction. For instance, one of the adoption principles is visibility. The problem statement for example might be refined to read "how might we increase the *visibility* of our value proposition of our concept..." This

IDEA   ALPHA

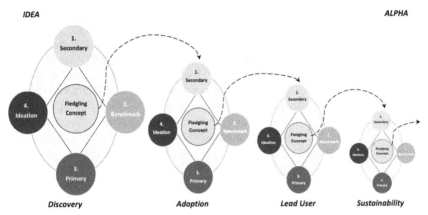

Fig. 5.   The Innovation Helix.

becomes the focal point for ideation activities leading to revised and sometimes completely new concept(s). Between each phase, a renewed round of desirability, feasibility and feasibility testing occurs which reduces but does not eliminate uncertainty. Armed with these new inputs, a third phase begins which I refer to as the *lead user* phase.

This phase may appear controversial to some, but lead users as defined by Eric von Hippel are individuals that have "extreme needs that cannot be satisfied by existing products or services and are thus forced to innovate" (von Hippel et al., 1999). What they bring to the innovation approach is twofold. First, they highlight potential latent (unspoken) need areas that have not been addressed. Second, they have created their own solution to satisfy their needs. In effect, they have redefined the innovation problem and have foresighted a plausible direction. By pursuing this line of inquiry, an entirely new approach and set of questions kicks off an innovation cycle concluding with refocused ideation activities. Fledgling concepts regularly emerge from this cycle with highly differentiated features that provide significant value to the users. Now some will argue if this is indeed the case, why not start with lead users from the beginning to save time and effort (i.e., it will be more *efficient*). I reject this proposition since in my experience lead user input is great at refining otherwise robust concepts but can take the innovation process drastically of track if used too early. This will be discussed in greater detail in Chapter 10.

The approach then ends with a final phase which I term the *sustainability* phase. The primary input to this phase is a robust, highly differentiated concept with a unique selling proposition and relative value to the end-user. I always examine sustainability as the last phase of the innovation approach which is often contentious. Critics argue that sustainability must be at the forefront, driving the project with a clear vision of how innovation is a catalyst for a more sustainable world. They argue that a more sustainable product will create great value in the marketplace and as a result will be adopted and replace existing products. Although I wholeheartedly agree with this sentiment, based on decades of study and practice I respectfully disagree. Value is relative to perceived gains and losses. Losses are coded by users 2.25 times higher than gains (Soman, 2014). Thus, the aggregate total of gains and losses results in the perception of value. As a result, the innovation approach must start from a position of creating superior and differentiated value relative to the customer's best option (i.e., their benchmark). Only then can the concept be improved using principles of sustainability to become *as sustainable as possible*. Steven Eppinger, a product design and development expert at MIT, after decades of frustration, was interviewed for an insightful article where he made a convincing case for why only incremental sustainable innovations have the potential to solve the world's problems (Hopkins, 2010). His argument is that grandiose sustainability projects almost invariably fail, resulting in discouraging others from ever trying it again. Incremental changes that move the sustainability agenda forward are much more likely to succeed. They are more likely to gain adoption and condition the market to accept the next generation of sustainable products. This is a much more *effective* way to succeed at sustainable innovation which will be covered in Chapter 11.

Key to the transition between cycles is the governing role of the *problem statement*. It informs the next steps within each of the innovation cycles, providing a bridge to the next phase of the innovation approach.

Problem Statement

Central to the innovation approach is the concept of the problem (or product) statement. When I was first introduced to this concept several decades ago, I mostly dismissed it as a nice but unnecessary step. Surely, team members immersed in an innovation project generally understood the vision, direction and key requirements of the project and this seemed like a needless exercise. Later I understood the concept as not only helpful but a necessary part of the process.

Having an evolving problem statement creates a "touchstone" from which developing concepts can be assessed (Ulrich & Eppinger, 2019). This iterative approach to concept development is an *inductive process*, since the problem statement impacts fledgling concepts, while these concepts impact the problem statement. They are symbiotically related where one cannot be separated from the other. The problem statement continues to be modified as the team cycles through each innovation cycle, culminating in fledgling concepts. As these concepts are examined at the end of each phase for desirability, feasibility and viability, invariably issues arise that can impact the problem statement. Also, as the innovation approach transitions between phases, the problem statement should adapt since the innovation cycle is now examined through a different lens (or prism). For instance, when transitioning from the adoption phase to the lead user phase, the focus of the innovation cycle changes in its priority.

There are many approaches to defining, refining and prioritizing problem statements. The most prominent ones include approaches from the domains of project management, product development and DT (and to a lesser extent the LS).

Project management begins with a *scope definition*, which becomes the basis for what is commonly referred to as the project charter. The scope definition provides direction for the project, while the charter establishes the details. The scope generally includes the, *what, who, how* and *why* objectives of the project. The charter expands upon this by concentrating on the *how* and *by whom* aspects of the project. It also expands on what is in and out of scope, essentially creating boundaries around the project. Stakeholders in the process are also acknowledged. Under this approach, the scope statement and project charter tend to be stagnant documents.

Traditional product design and development takes a similar but tangential approach, sometimes referred to as the *mission statement*. This one-page document describes the product's vision (i.e., what), the target audience (i.e., who) and the benefit proposition (i.e., why). Ulrich and Eppinger (2019) also emphatically stress that the statement cannot have an embedded solution. Like the project management charter, the mission statement outlines assumptions and constraints (i.e., boundaries) as well as stakeholders in the process. The mission statement requires periodic updates as critical information is uncovered.

DT uses the terminology of the actionable *problem statement*. It promotes an iterative approach (i.e., periodic reframing) to developing an emergent problem statement. It must be broad enough as not to stifle the solution space, while narrow enough to keep the team focused (i.e., creates boundaries). A typical problem statement begins with the simple phrase "how might we..." It then must include an emphasis on the user (i.e., who), what needs it hopes to resolve (i.e., what), importance of solving the problem (i.e., why) and constraints on the solution space (i.e., how). The team must avoid building-in a solution into the statement and must remember that needs should be verbs and be open to new insights as the process unfolds (*Design Thinking Bootcamp Bootleg*, 2010).

The common ground between all of these perspectives includes:

- It must include the who, what, why and how queries
- It must not include an overt solution
- It must evolve with project learning
- Alterations should be developed by the team, documented and have an impact
- The statement must be actionable
- It should be accompanied by more detailed documentation

For the innovation approach, the problem statement should be revisited within each innovation cycle and again between cycles as the process moves from phase to phase. For instance, at the beginning of the discovery phase, the initial problem statement should be formulated in conjunction with secondary research activities. This transforms the initial vision statement (the inspiration for the innovation project) into an actionable problem statement. After benchmarking and primary research, the problem statement should be updated to reflect learnings prior to ideation activities. Ideation activities should focus on the problem statement, resulting in fledgling concepts ready for evaluation and transition to the next innovation cycle. In this case, the next innovation cycle is the adoption phase where the problem statement is revisited, reframed and readjusted to align it with the objectives of the specific phase. The process continues throughout subsequent innovation cycles.

In Practice – Problem Statement

Using an example that will be expanded upon in Chapter 4 – benchmarking, let us examine the evolution of the problem statement from phase to phase using the example of creating a novel golf putter.

The format should generally include the following: (i) what is the problem, (ii) who does the problem impact, (iii) why does the problem exist and (iv) how can it be solved (i.e., solution space)

Phase 1: Discovery:

The discovery phase began as an inspiration to develop a new putter. This was translated into a raw and vague statement that *golfers would like a new putter that is appealing, adjustable and uses state-of-the-art materials*. This vision fails the test of a product statement at many levels, including that it includes solutions, is vague about the target audience and does not frame the problem.

It was partially refined after secondary research but was reframed after benchmarking and primary research into the following:

> *Putting accounts for nearly half the score (WHAT) of most recreational golfer's (WHO) based on quality of their technique (WHY) in conjunction with the limitations of their technology (HOW).*

This became the theme for ideation activities.

Phase 2: Adoption:

Following ideation, fledgling concepts were proposed and evaluated leading into the adoption innovation cycle. The statement was partially updated at the beginning of the cycle when examined through the prism of adoption factors. These include *advantage, compatibility, complexity, trialability* and *observability*. As more information was gathered prior to ideation, the problem statement was reframed into the following:

> *Putting is one of the most important actions in golf (WHAT). Serious recreational golfers (WHO) continually seek to improve their technique (WHY) using the best available equipment (HOW) which gives them confidence.*

This reframing considered several of the adoption requirements by including the concepts of fundamentals (i.e., compatibility) and advanced equipment (i.e., advantage and observability). It also refined the target audience – *serious* recreational golfers and included the key emotional construct –*confidence*. These became the themes for ideation activities.

Phase 3: Lead user:

Entering the lead user phase, the problem statement was further refined to reflect the various aspects of lead users. Specifically, lead users in the *market, attributes* and *analogs*. The problem statement was reframed as:

> *Confidence in putting ability (WHAT) is the key for serious recreational golfers (WHO) who want to improve their score (WHY) through pride in their equipment and endorsed techniques (HOW)*

This highlighted the prominence of confidence, pride and endorsement. Confidence and pride are *attributes* that the user derives from the product, while endorsement refers to the perceived vetting of techniques by celebrities, experts and influencers. The latter can be examined in the market or analog categories. This guided the ideation process to focus on lead users that had developed solutions to increase confidence and pride of ownership in both market and analog categories.

Phase 4: Sustainability:

The final innovation cycle further refined the problem statement around the sustainability of the product.

> *Confidence in putting ability (WHAT) is the key for serious recreational golfers (WHO) who want to improve their score (WHY) while maintaining pride in the satisfaction that their equipment, golf course and influencers promote sustainability (WHAT)*

Many serious golfers have expendable income and vote with their dollars. They drive to the golf course in their electric vehicles and are concerned with minimizing fertilizer use at their course. They are open to sustainable products if it does not compromise their score. This statement links pride with sustainability and became the touchstone for ideation activities.

The Innovation Helix

I visualize the innovation approach as a helix. In both Latin and Greek, helix has been defined as a "spiral-shaped thing" or a curve that lies on the surface of a cylinder or cone. I think this best describes a visual of the innovation approach. Each cycle spirals into the next almost like water spiraling down a drain. I envision it as cone shaped since at each phase the problem space narrows and becomes more focused. In the discovery phase, the problem space is broad and the concepts are wide-ranging. At the end of the process, the problem space is narrow, and the concepts are focused.

Linear activities take place within each cycle, while iterative activities occur at the transition from one cycle to another. At the transition points between cycles, desirability, feasibility and viability are tested and uncertainty in each category is reduced. Within cycles, prototyping is mostly used for team communication, while between cycles prototyping is used to elicit user reaction (e.g., MVP testing). Feedback from this testing process adds to the increasingly robust body of knowledge, translated through a refined problem statement as it enters the next phase. Each phase challenges the team to approach the innovation problem from a different angle, resulting in stress testing (and by default improving) fledgling concepts.

Conclusion

Innovation must be understood before it can be managed. How the definition of innovation is approached, establishes the baseline for what must be managed in an effective FEI process. This process is both linear and nonlinear based on the phases of the process. A repeatable series of linear activities referred to as cycles of innovation form the foundation for subsequent nonlinear or iterative activities. These transitions between cycles serve to evaluate and improve fledgling concepts until such a point as they become desirable, feasible and viable.

Section II

Core Steps and Capabilities

Chapter 4

Secondary Research

As Dr. Robert Cooper once stated "individuals learn early in life that homework is not a lot of fun." However, conducting proper background research is essential to successful innovation management. When examining successful systems, they all tend to rely on intense secondary research at the front end of the process to inform next steps. This disciplined approach is best managed by a multifunction team that can approach the subject matter from many perspectives. Through these various lenses, the innovation space becomes more clearly defined and boundaries set, leading to a deep focus on the situation at hand. This focus defines the problem(s), perceptions, offerings and solutions in the space. Innovation teams must remember that picking attractive markets is a project selection exercise, while creating differential value is the purview of innovation management. This chapter focuses on the multidisciplinary process of conducting secondary research at the front end of the process.

Introduction

All innovation or entrepreneurial pursuits begin with an inspiration. These inspirations come from a variety of places ranging from personal experiences with products or services to strategic initiatives within firms or business units (Liedtka, 2018). Regardless of where inspiration comes from, it is the genesis of the innovation management process and the first stepping stone to success. This chapter will focus on the process by which this inspiration can be better understood, refined and crafted.

What Is Secondary Research and Why Is It Important?

The most significant conflict I have encountered over my career is the difference between the entrepreneurial approach and the innovation management approach. This fundamentally comes down to "project selection" versus "project management." From an entrepreneurial perspective, selecting the right project is essential and involves choosing project A, versus projects B, C, etc. All entrepreneurial projects involve different considerations and carry unique profiles. As such, much of the front end of the entrepreneurial process involves establishing the *opportunity profiles* of alternate options. These range from industry dynamics to market

The Innovation Approach:
Overcoming the Limitations of Design Thinking and the Lean Startup, 57–71
Copyright © 2025 by David C. Roach
Published under exclusive licence by Emerald Publishing Limited
doi:10.1108/978-1-83797-799-420241004

competition (Spinelli & Adams, 2016), however, this process has often been dominated by metrics such as market size, compound annual growth rate (CAGR) and total available market (TAM). These metrics are good for project selection, but *poor at providing the inputs for successful innovation management.* As the theory goes, markets with the most attractive size, growth and customer base should be selected over less attractive options. Notionally this is correct, but it fails to appreciate the distinction between the entrepreneurial and innovation management characteristics of the process. Weak competitors, poor products or underwhelming quality (to name a few) can create an environment where a superior innovation can succeed in the marketplace regardless of market dynamics. The reverse is also true - a market with appealing characteristics may not be an attractive place to innovate. Thus, from an innovation management perspective, *project selection* (or inspiration) should be separated from *project execution* since they are two distinct endeavors. Once a project has been selected, the innovation management system should kick in to create value in the category in question. Once the value proposition is established, project selection can then be confirmed during the business modeling phase which will be discussed in Chapter 14.

Why does this make a difference? From a project selection perspective, teams should pick markets with attractive characteristics. However, secondary research or information gathering has significantly different characteristics when applied to the innovation management process. Much of what is required to make selection decisions is quantitative in nature, market-centric and relies on data based on analysts' forecasts. The information required for innovation management purposes is mostly qualitative, customer-centric and based on trends, problems and needs information. Thus, innovation management teams (and their financial backers) need to understand the difference between these two types of information-gathering activities.

These differences have a significant impact on the secondary research approach since this is the first interaction between now popular approaches such as Design Thinking (DT) and Lean Startup (LS). It also overlaps with traditional market research approaches which come from a slightly different perspective. As a result, these three approaches will be examined in the next section to establish commonalities and areas of focus.

Perspectives of Secondary Research

Secondary research is a systematic examination and interpretation of existing data and information from various sources, such as academic publications, industry reports and government publications. It involves the analysis of pre-existing materials and information to gain insights, corroborate findings and inform decision-making. Secondary research can be approached from multiple perspectives and plays a pivotal role in accessing valuable knowledge for team decision-making and informing the next steps in the process. These perspectives include (i) entrepreneurship, (ii) marketing research, (iii) technology management, (iv) DT and (v) LS. For example, understanding market dynamics, consumer behavior, competitor strategies and technological advancements are important in the front end of innovation (FEI). Each perspective varies in its endpoint with differing emphasis on the type of information to be gathered. An examination of each perspective follows with an emphasis on best practices for innovation management.

Market Research Perspective

A marketing research perspective involves a systematic and comprehensive analysis of secondary data. The objective is to gain valuable insights for strategic decision-making, new product introductions and their supporting marketing strategies. Although one of its objectives is to establish the viability of new products or services, it is largely used to establish positioning strategies, trend analysis, economic attractiveness, pricing policy, market segmentation and competitor strengths and weaknesses. As such, it is often more of a *project selection* process than an exercise in *relative value creation*. Below are some of the key characteristics of this approach.

Market analysis begins with a focus on selecting relevant sources of *secondary data* including government publications, industry associations, trade publications, competitor reports and market intelligence databases. This establishes an understanding of the current state of the market, historical trends and key factors influencing it.

Industry trends and forecasting identifies and quantifies industry trends used for forward-looking predictions about the market. To corroborate the accuracy and reliability of this information *data validation* is often performed by cross-referencing information from multiple sources to confirm its credibility and/or triangulate data sources to legitimize findings.

Competitor analysis focuses on gathering information about competitors, including their market share, product offerings, pricing strategies and customer reviews. This analysis provides valuable insights into the competitive landscape; however, it normally does not involve a deep dive into the features and benefits of each competing product in the category.

SWOT Analysis (Strengths, Weaknesses, Opportunities, Threats) relies on secondary data to assess a firm's *internal* strengths and weaknesses as well as *external* opportunities and threats in the market. It is often considered a "must have" in any market research report but has little value as an innovation management tool.

Consumer behavior analysis aids in examining consumer preferences, buying patterns and demographic information. This knowledge is considered essential for the development of effective marketing campaigns.

Segmentation involves establishing demographics of the customer, geographic profiles to understand regional variations and psychographic characteristics to establish such things as values, desires, goals, interests and lifestyle choices.

Secondary research is generally considered a more cost-effective solution than collecting primary research. It also is generally the precursor to establishing gaps in the knowledge base that can be filled through primary research. By leveraging existing data, firms can save time and resources while still gathering valuable insights into the market. Its primary use from a market research perspective is to establish the market opportunity and establish strategic direction. Although it does have some focus on qualitative aspects of the market (e.g., trend analysis), its primary objective is to collect available quantitative data to support marketing decisions.

Entrepreneurship Perspective

From an entrepreneurial perspective, secondary research plays a crucial role in informing and shaping business strategies. Like market research, this type of secondary research involves the analysis and interpretation of existing data, obtained from various sources such as market reports, academic publications, industry analyses and government publications. As such, some of the key characteristics of this approach involve the same criteria as for market research which include *market analysis, industry trends and forecasting, competitor analysis* and *segmentation*. It however has a slightly different emphasis toward opportunity assessment, business viability and operational execution.

Additional areas of concentration not covered in marketing research include:

Market *trends and opportunities* are of particular interest in the entrepreneurial realm where current market trends and specifically emerging opportunities are the key to success. This information aids in making informed decisions about product development, target markets and potential growth areas.

Risk assessment is also a significant factor in entrepreneurial ventures that can be disproportionately impacted by external environmental factors ranging from market turbulence to industry challenges. By understanding the context and challenges faced by similar ventures, entrepreneurs can use secondary research to proactively develop risk mitigation strategies.

Regulatory compliance can also have a large impact on early-stage ventures since entrepreneurs often do not have deep industry or product knowledge. Secondary research is instrumental in understanding the legal, regulatory and registration landscape within which the business must operate.

Intellectual property (IP) is also of major concern for early-stage ventures since it provides a time-limited monopolistic position leading to differential market advantage. IP comes in many forms including patents, copyrights, trademarks and trade secrets. Understanding this landscape has two significant advantages for entrepreneurial ventures. First, they inform the team about possible areas of opportunity based on IP. Second, it can inform the team as to areas to avoid where the fledgling venture may encounter limitations to their *freedom to operate.*

In summary, a thorough and strategic approach to secondary research empowers entrepreneurs with the insights needed to make informed decisions, mitigate risks and position their ventures for success in a competitive business landscape.

Technology Management Perspective

Innovation has often been confounded with the concept of technology development and/or commercialization. When approaching secondary research based on a techno-centric approach, other areas of investigation tend to take a more conspicuous role. Although many aspects of secondary research exploration follow the market research and entrepreneurship approaches, some aspects gain more prominence when focused through a technology lens. These include:

Industry and technology assessment. This involves scanning existing technologies and industry developments. It often focuses on technology trends, foresighting and futuristic applications. This helps identify emerging trends, breakthroughs and potential areas for innovation.

Benchmarking and best practices. By studying competitors and industry leaders through secondary sources, innovation managers can benchmark their products against the best of class. This aids in identifying gaps and opportunities for improvement in product, service or process innovation.

Collaboration opportunities through identifying potential collaborators, research partners or external innovation sources. This can also involve an examination of open innovation platforms or existing technologies that can be levered for the purposes of commercialization.

Data analytics available from secondary sources are often used to gain additional insights into market trends, customer behavior and emerging patterns. This data-driven approach enhances the decision-making process for innovation initiatives.

In summary, a technology management perspective emphasizes the importance of leveraging external knowledge and insights to drive creativity, identify opportunities and manage risks. This approach fosters a culture of open innovation and adaptation within the organization.

DT Perspective

In DT, the secondary research process plays a crucial role in understanding existing knowledge and context relevant to a design challenge. It involves gathering information from various sources to gain insights that can inform the design process. During this phase, designers aim to comprehend the problem space, identify patterns and explore existing solutions. This research helps frame the problem and provides a foundation for subsequent activities prior to ideation. Secondary research allows designers to leverage the collective knowledge available and ensures that their solutions are informed by a comprehensive understanding of the subject matter.

Secondary research for the DT process typically includes:

Gaining *user insights* through understanding the needs, behaviors and preferences of the end-users. This may involve establishing user personas, analyzing user feedback from existing products or services or evaluating user behavior.

Establishing market *trends* involves determining current trends and dynamics in the market related to the problem at hand. This can involve analyzing industry reports, market research studies and competitor analysis.

Exploring the *Technology Landscape* to establish current technologies that may be relevant to the design challenge. This helps in understanding technological constraints and possibilities.

Investigating the historical *context* of the problem to identify any patterns or recurring issues that could be important in addressing long-standing challenges.

Understanding the *regulatory and compliance* framework based on legal, regulatory and industry standards that may impact the design.

Learning from *case studies* of similar projects or solutions to learn from both successes and failures to provide insights into what works and what doesn't.

The methods used to gather this information vary and may include literature reviews, online research, reviewing interviews and/or surveys and expert consultations. Designers may also leverage databases, academic journals and other reputable sources to extract relevant data. The goal is to compile a rich set of information that informs the design process and guides the development of the innovation. There is little emphasis on quantitative information and most of what is gathered is quantitative in nature. *Any quantitative information is a byproduct of the process rather than the focus of the activity.*

LS Perspective

The LS emphasizes business modeling using build–measure–learn feedback loops. In the context of secondary research, the methodology places importance on obtaining relevant information quickly and efficiently. The secondary research process generally involves the following:

Begin with *hypothesis generation* driven by a proposition about who forms target market, customer needs and potential solutions. Secondary research is used to gather data and insights that can assist with developing hypotheses.

Swift *market analysis* is conducted to understand the competitive landscape, identify potential customer segments and assess market trends. Data is gathered on market size, growth and competition without investing significant resources upfront.

Customer segmentation is conducted to understand the target audience through demographic and psychographic information. This may involve accessing consumer reports and segmentation studies.

Industry *best practices* involve learning from successful industry practices and understanding common pitfalls, mostly focused on business models. This involves case studies, success stories and lessons learned from similar ventures.

Regulatory and Compliance involves identifying any legal or regulatory constraints that may affect the viability of the project. This involves researching industry regulations, standards and compliance requirements.

Technological Landscape is examined through existing technologies relevant to the startup's product or service. This includes staying informed about the latest advancements and potential technological challenges.

From an LS perspective, the objective of the secondary research phase is to understand the market and its dynamics. This high-level assessment is the core of their approach leading to customer discovery through primary research. From this perspective, the innovation activities take a back seat to the business model since it is assumed that the "idea" or "concept" is sound and that the market opportunity is of the utmost importance. It believes that as information is gathered and validated through hypothesis-driven minimum viable product (MVP) tests, aspects of the product will eventually become apparent. This iterative learning they contend is a necessary part of the innovation process. They argue their agile system is naturally hedged since fundamental changes to the product are accomplished through pivots.

In summary, the LS views secondary research as a means to quickly acquire relevant information that informs the business process.

What Secondary Research Information Is Important for Innovation Management

As discussed in the introduction to this chapter, innovations can succeed in marketplaces that may or may not be attractive. In the preface to this book, I highlight that a poor concept can rarely be crafted into a successful product or service. Thus, innovation teams must remember that picking attractive markets is a *project selection exercise*, while creating *differential value* is the purview of innovation management. Consequently, while approaching the secondary research phase of a project, some methods and sources should take priority over others. For instance, sources and techniques at the *customer–product interface* are where secondary research should be concentrated and must take priority over *market-product* secondary research activities.

The objective of secondary research is to make the process of primary research more effective, *focused* and *broad-based*. Thus, the team needs to engage in a process that highlights issues such as trends, problems, likes/dislikes, behaviors, obstacles, environments and opportunities. These are mostly qualitative in nature and although are often supported with quantitative information, the objective of this phase is to identify these issues to inform subsequent primary research activities.

Guiding Models

Before delving into secondary research approaches and how it informs the primary research phase, let us first examine two fundamental models that influence these combined activities.

The KANO Model

At this point, I often bring in some theory to direct the team prior to conducting secondary research. One theory that I bring to the table is the KANO (pronounced Kah-no) model. This model has often been associated with the quality function deployment (QFD) movement. It is used to highlight the common notion that customers don't really know what they want, when in fact there are certain needs that they can't easily express verbally. This *practitioner's theory* developed by Professor Noriaki Kano in the 1980s classifies customer preferences into three categories based on their impact on customer satisfaction (*What Is the Kano Model?*, 2023). The model was developed to help businesses understand and prioritize features or attributes of their products based on needs categories. While the KANO model is not widely used today, it has not entirely lost its relevance.

The first set of needs are *basic* (i.e., must-haves) needs, which are essential features that customers expect to be present in any product or service. The absence or failure of these features quickly leads to dissatisfaction, while their presence does not significantly increase satisfaction. They are often considered prerequisites for a product or service to be viable in the marketplace. Since these are expected in any product or service in the category, they are most often not verbalized by the customer since they are considered mandatory. As an example, if the product/ service offering was to provide coffee at a conference, no one would verbalize that they would not want a leaky cup.

Next are *expected* performance needs which are features that, when present, enhance customer satisfaction. The more and better execution of these features – the more satisfied customers will be. These features are easily verbalized and commented on by customers and satisfaction tends to follow a linear path. Using the coffee example above, customers will verbalize things like their preferred coffee bean selection, the aroma and their condiment preference (e.g., cream versus milk). Almost any primary research tool can uncover these needs.

Delight (i.e., excitement) needs are unexpected features that, when present can lead to high levels of satisfaction. Customers may not be explicitly looking for these features, but their inclusion can create significant value and enhance their overall experience. Since customers don't know that they can have these, they are unable to verbalize something that they cannot conceive. Going back to our coffee example, a customer would not verbalize that they want a robot to deliver their coffee exactly as they like, directly to their chair, accompanied by their favorite snack.

The KANO model also considers that customer expectations evolve over time. What was once considered a delight or exciting feature may now be perceived as a basic expectation. Delight features become expected features as the category matures and expected needs drift into basic needs. As an example, mobile phone cameras when first introduced were delight features, however over time these have become basic needs, since it is impossible to think of a mobile phone without one. The dynamic nature of consumer preferences and technological advancements shift as the category matures.

Although there is a KANO survey instrument, in my experience it is of limited use. The KANO model, as displayed in Fig. 6, in my opinion, is *best understood as a conceptual model* that effectively highlights that most of what customers really want cannot be easily extracted using traditional research techniques.

From an innovation management perspective, the objective should be to create differential value relative to the product or service category. As such, concentrating on *expected* and *delight* needs should be the focus of research activities, while basic needs must be addressed later in the process once more comprehensive concept testing can occur. As will be discussed in Chapter 5, expected needs can be extracted using a myriad of primary research techniques, while delight needs require more advanced tools and techniques which will be expanded upon in Chapter 10.

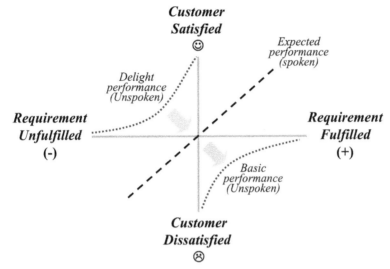

Fig. 6. KANO Model.

While the KANO model may no longer enter contemporary discussions, its fundamental principles have left a lasting impact on how businesses approach customer satisfaction and product development. It remains a valuable tool for businesses to understand customer preferences and prioritize features to maximize customer satisfaction.

The User-centered Model

The next important model to understand is the user-centered model. I ran across this model many decades ago which emphasizes that usability can only be established by the end-user. Unless you understand the user's environment and the task they are trying to perform, you cannot design a desirable product or service. This model was developed as the basis for designing usability tests, however, I have used it as the basis for how to integrate the voice of the customer (VoC) into the innovation process. One of the objectives of the secondary research phase is to begin the process of (i) identifying the user, (ii) establishing the tasks (or set of problems) they confront and (iii) beginning to understand the environment within which they operate. This becomes crucial for subsequent primary research activities when observational and probe and learn techniques are employed. One of my critiques of both DT and specifically the LS is that observation is not necessarily conducted in the user's environment resulting in an incomplete understanding of these relationships. Fig. 7 emphasizes the interaction between the human, their task and their environment. Segregating one aspect from the remainder risks interpreting issues out of context.

In the past few decades, there has been an explosion of material on user-centered design (UCD) or user-driven development (UDD) emphasizing that

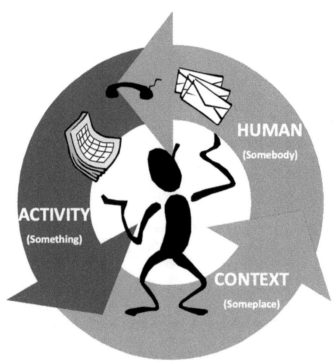

Fig. 7. User-centered Model.

development must include the user as the center of focus. Although UCD specifically has a focus on customer learning, most of the material tends to be focused
on how to determine or test whether the product or service is usable. It is important to understand however that the origins of UCD are often linked to Donald
Norman's seminal book entitled *The Design of Everyday Things* (Norman, 1988).
Here he explains in detail the human-product-environment relationship and how
to design a product that people find usable, esthetically pleasing and desirable.
This and his follow-on book entitled "Emotional Design" (Norman, 2004), I consider mandatory readings for any design team. In practice, I find that teams tend
to rush to the "design" portion of UCD or UDD before truly understanding the
nature of the individual-environment-task framework.

The user-centered model will be discussed in more detail in Chapter 6 "Primary Research".

Secondary Research in Action

In my graduate classes and executive courses I often use the ubiquitous IDEO
shopping cart video as an example of design-centric innovation (*IDEO the Deep
Dive*, 1997). I was first introduced to this video by Dr. Stefan Thomke at Harvard
Business School who had just written the first case on IDEO product development

(*IDEO Product Development*, 2000). This case was the first to put DT on the business academic map. Together with the NBC Nightline video entitled *The Deep Dive*, they were mostly responsible for the popularization of this approach to innovation management. Since this was years before the advent of online video sharing, Dr. Thomke generously mailed me a VHS tape which I still have in my office. I have been using the video ever since as a critical thinking instrument about the process of innovation management.

The video begins with a vignette of creative people bucking the status quo and challenging preconceived notions of innovation in a playful environment. The video goes on reinforce these themes throughout its 22 minutes of playing time. It appears to the average observer that these are the keys to successful innovation management and that replicating the environment, culture and flat organizational structure is the missing link and barrier to successful innovation. However, a more critical assessment exposes a different story. IDEO is more than environment, culture and management; it also has a very systematic approach to managing the innovation process. Although I will revisit this video throughout this book, when it comes to secondary research I have included my observations in the following case example.

Case Example – IDEO Deep Dive (Secondary Research)

The NBC Nightline video – The Deep Dive (*IDEO the Deep Dive*, 1997), is probably the most famous description of what is now considered DT. David Kelly, the founder of IDEO, narrates the video as he describes to the audience their innovation process. To illustrate this, he agrees to take an everyday product – the shopping cart – and redesign it in five days.

First, the team leader acknowledges early in the video that executing a project even as seemingly simplistic as a shopping cart within a week is "insane." He infers that the activities that the audience is about to see would take place over multiple weeks or months. It has been compressed to a five-day period to fit a weeklong segment for NBC. Thus, the depth of activities that are executed during the secondary research phase of the project are relegated to portions of a two-minute segment after the introduction portion of the video. However, when those two minutes are unpacked, they reveal a significant amount of information.

First, is the *within-team* communication where tangible artifacts are used to express everyone's thoughts. Most prominent in the video is the classic shopping cart itself. They use it as a focal point for this multifunctional team of MBAs, linguists, psychologists, biologists and marketers to focus-in on a common language to describe constructs. They briefly highlight their psychologist describing her secondary research where she emphasizes key themes which include safety and theft. Importantly, although she does highlight some statistics, these are only presented to support the argument that these themes are real and are significant enough to warrant attention from the team. This begins a rigorous team discussion to clarify, expand and challenge these themes. The purpose is to create a group understanding and buy-in of the constructs that will need to be clarified during subsequent primary research. This segment is so short that most people only take away the snippet where David Kelly (IDEO's founder) mocks the "caution statement' on the shopping cart that reads "Be Safe." This tends to reinforce the cultural aspect of IDEO but not necessarily their process. Then, almost imperceptibly, the project leader says in the background *"I think we ought to start making a list about the types of questions we are going to ask."* This simple sentence carries a lot of weight. First, it highlights that the purpose of their secondary research was not to determine the viability of the market but to focus the next steps on understanding the themes unrecovered through this process. Second, it reinforces the buy-in from the team on how to approach questioning the underlying themes identified. Third, although not explicitly stated, they are developing a set of directional "probe & learn" questions based on a semi-structured open-ended approach. Fourth, they are developing a general understanding of the target audiences for consideration during primary research. Lastly, these questions will be used to drive observational (anthropological) activities where the investigator does not directly interact with the subjects.

NOTE: In the video, the team does not expand upon the sources of secondary research, however it is extensive and broad based. Also, they engage directly with the competitor's product(s) as a form of benchmarking.

The key takeaways from this critical examination include:

- Secondary research should identify key themes related to the project at hand
- Concentration on problems, trends, obstacles, environments and likes/dislikes are key
- This information must be shared, discussed, understood and assessed by the team
- The underlying drivers of these themes should form the basis of primary research activities
- Establishes hypothesis of target audiences for primary research activities

This results in a set of open-ended questions developed by the team to inform the direction of their primary research activities. I will cover the development and synthesis of these types of questions in Chapter 6 – Primary Research.

Informing the Next Steps

The process of secondary research is iterative and should not be under-resourced from a *time* or *content* perspective. A good rule of thumb is to challenge each team member to conduct an initial a two-to-three-hour review using whatever sources they prefer. The objective is to establish any issues associated with the project at hand. Next, the team should gather and share this information in a collaborative environment using whatever artifacts they need to stimulate understanding of key constructs. The group should emerge from this session with a list of issues to be further examined with each team member taking away an investigation area. This next step should also be limited to two to three hours with team members concentrating on qualitative aspects of the project rather than quantitative. The group should then reconvene to share in greater detail aspects of the initial themes and any other emerging themes or sub-themes generated from this exercise. At this point the team has a reasonably good idea of the direction they are planning to take, however, I always recommend one last individual task assignment prior to beginning the process of interview guide development for primary research. In this last session, I recommend that themes championed by one team member be assigned to a different team member. This reduces bias and may uncover other issues associated with the theme. Also, the team should review the various sources of information available and highlight any sources that may have been overlooked. For instance, nascent teams often have a heavy focus on internet searches and social media activity. They often ignore sources where they are less comfortable such as patent databases, academic journals or regulatory requirements. When the team reconvenes to share their final thoughts, they are ready to begin the process of building their list of open-ended questions in preparation for their primary research activities. This process will be covered in more detail in Chapter 6.

Additionally, as this secondary information is gathered the team should in parallel begin to develop a profile of the target audience. This should be grounded by the information gathered during this activity, rather than team members' "intuition." Rather than building personas, I recommend profiling based on classic segmentation information (e.g., demographic, geographic and psychographic characteristics). These are more useful to the process since they are used to identify individuals who are generally representative of the target audience. These are the individuals who will need to be interviewed during the primary research phase. The term target audience includes both primary and secondary target audiences, the former being most likely to use the product or service, while the latter is closely related but of lesser initial importance (Zacharakis et al., 2019). Personas are helpful for internal team communication, but *not very practical* when determining "who" to examine during primary research. Personas are often built around psychographic profiling which is difficult to assess when selecting interview candidates. Finally, the decision-making unit (DMU) should be examined since there are frequently many individual roles influencing the target audience. These include but are not limited to the economic buyer, champion, influencers and veto power and their relationships (Aulet, 2013). For the DMU I am fine with initially building personas, since the team will need to model their transactional roles in the product adoption process.

One last note. Throughout this process, teams will inevitably come across products or solutions used by customers to solve problems. At this point, these solutions should be set aside so as not to bias the primary research question development process. In the next chapter, I will cover benchmarking where products are examined based on their attributes, features and benefits. This additional secondary research activity will result in adding to the list of open-ended questions in a fashion that optimizes feedback without biasing the process.

Conclusion

In practice secondary research activities are often misguided, incomplete or poorly executed. Many innovation teams miss the mark for a variety of reasons, but mainly they fail to understand the difference between the *customer–product interface* and the *market-product* interface. However, if managed properly this activity has a disproportional impact on *all of the subsequent activities* of the process.

The focus of this book is on managing the innovation process to create differential value within a competitive category. As discussed at length, many nascent teams misunderstand what is required from this activity and either collect the wrong type of information, bias the activity or effectively short-circuit the process by going directly to customer discovery or even worse – idea generation. There are many reasons for this, but both the DT and the LS suffer from different symptoms. If followed properly, DT is intended to systematically use secondary research to inform primary research activities. In practice, however, DT tends to rush toward ideation activities without the rigor brought about by secondary research. The LS on the other hand in its quest to be agile very often systematically short-shifts this activity preferring to go directly to customer discovery, believing that all will eventually be revealed. Why waste time on secondary activities when you can go directly to users and have them tell you their issues? This perspective is at best naïve since we know from the KANO model that customers can rarely articulate their wants and needs. Uninformed customer discovery activities with inadequately trained team members often results in a very biased viewpoint. The LS method can also become misdirected due to the seductiveness of the market opportunity rather than concentrating on how to create value in the category. In practice, they confound *project selection* activities with *innovation management* activities, resulting in under-resourcing the latter.

In any event, how does managing secondary research activities impact either of these methodologies? Allocating the appropriate amount of time and resources toward *customer–product* inquiry results in a much more focused approach to subsequent primary research activities. When managed appropriately, it informs the next step of creating a refined list of issues to be explored during the primary research phase. This focus increases the *effectiveness* and *fidelity* of the information gathered through customer listening exercises and eliminates much of the bias encountered using unguided probing exercises. It also rallies the team around key constructs that need to be explored by creating a shared language and an understanding of often complex paradigms. As the process evolves, this shared understanding reduces vagueness and ambiguity, paying dividends throughout the life of the project.

From an innovating management perspective, DT when executed properly tends to outperform the LS approach, however, both tend to rush this phase to their detriment later in the process. Following the approach described in this chapter, secondary research should be performed by a multifunctional team, taking a customer–product-centric approach, executed in distinct steps and based on a team understanding of key issues. This process should allocate approximately 2.5 working days per team member assigned over a one- to two-week period to allow for the synthesis of information (see Chapter 13 – Project Management Essentials). Following this approach teams should be well prepared to undertake the next steps of the process – the focus of the next chapters.

Chapter 5

Benchmarking

Benchmarking is the process of understanding what solutions consumers use to solve their problems. Solutions are often products or services that provide perceived benefits; however, they may also involve substitutes or do-it-yourself (DIY) solutions. If consumers have a problem or need, they have likely found a preferred solution and have performed, at some level, a comparative assessment of the features and benefits of the alternatives. Building on secondary research where solutions are discovered, this chapter focuses on a benchmarking assessment where features and benefits of various solutions are established.

Introduction

I was first introduced to benchmarking in the mid-1990s while attending an executive training course recommended by my employer. At the time, many organizations were interested in building capability in Total Quality Management (TQM) and benchmarking was the "flavor of the day." This two-day working seminar advocated that "if you benchmark any of your practices against the best-of-class alternative, most of your corporate problems will be resolved." As with many of these packaged methods that came before and after, it did not deliver the results management hoped for. Despite much of the thinking being sound, as with most populist programs, the outcomes were simply new twists on conventional management tools.

In parallel, the Quality Function Deployment (QFD) movement was waning due to the complexity of its House of Quality visualization instrument ("Quality Function Deployment," 2024). At the core of this tool was a matrix where product features were listed with a crosstab association to user needs. Each feature was then ranked on a scale from 1 to 5 based on the importance to the customer and order of importance. This was complex enough, but it was then cross-referenced to other relationships that included competitive positioning, interaction between features, technical ability, target specifications and various others. These horribly complex relationships, promoted by engineers, were never implementable and were mostly rejected as tools for benchmarking and innovation management. The QFD system also relied on a belief that everything could be quantified to a point

The Innovation Approach:
Overcoming the Limitations of Design Thinking and the Lean Startup, 73–85
Copyright © 2025 by David C. Roach
Published under exclusive licence by Emerald Publishing Limited
doi:10.1108/978-1-83797-799-420241005

where innovation decisions could be made accurately. Although there are still zealots that use this technique, this approach failed miserably as an effective tool for managing the front end of innovation (FEI).

Although I attempted to use both approaches for innovation projects, neither was very useful in practice. One feature that stood out was the embracement of subjective (or qualitative) measures within the benchmarking portion of the system. Scale ratings were invariably based on subjective evaluations of best practices. The attempt to link user needs to product features was also of interest. There were other aspects of benchmarking that I believed were not addressed by these approaches but gained prominence through the work of Dr. Eric von Hippel at MIT. His innovation management approach, which he called Lead User Research, highlighted the concepts of "attributes" and "analogs" as key constructs that must be understood in any innovation project. In the advanced tools and techniques chapter, I will discuss Lead User Research, however, I will make the case below that attributes and analogs must also be investigated as part of the benchmarking exercise.

Benchmarking is a *special type of secondary research* and deserves to be discussed as a separate method. Its primary purpose is to develop a deep team understanding of the product category under investigation, with all its nuances and specific language, including features, attributes and benefits. In most organizations, this is an ad hoc process with little structure or rigor. Thus, I will argue that this should begin during the secondary research portion of the process and be used to inform subsequent primary research activities conducted by the team. Then, what I will refer to as a *benchmark orientation matrix* can be created as a touchstone for the team to refine and update as more information becomes available.

However, before we go down this road, let's first examine how customers make purchase decisions when it comes to products or services.

Consumers' Relationship to Products

One of the primary considerations for consumers is the *perceived* value of a product. This involves weighing the benefits offered by a product relative to its cost. In its purest sense, consumers seek to maximize utility and satisfaction while minimizing expenditure. As a result, they rely on factors such as quality, features and brand reputation as a guide for how they assess value. However, anyone who has ever been involved in sales management will tell you that customers "buy emotionally, then justify rationally." Consumer purchasing decisions are influenced by a myriad of factors that encompass both rational and emotional elements. Understanding this complex process is crucial for innovators aiming to develop successful products or services. Thus, the goal of the innovation management process should be to create a set of features and benefits that allow the customer to make what they perceive as an *informed choice, but in fact is based on emotional triggers*. Once this emotional attachment has been solidified, the customer can then be provided with the information they need to *rationalize their decision* based on the features of the product.

One of the issues that I frequently hear from both students and practitioners is the concept of brands. For the purposes of managing the innovation process,

I will argue that a brand is a high-level "attribute" of a competitive product that plays a significant role in the decision-making process. Consumers often develop attachments (read: emotional attachment) to brands based on positive past experiences, perceived quality and the brand's alignment with their values. But from an innovation management perspective, what is a brand? A brand can be defined as a unique and identifiable combination of tangible and intangible attributes. Intangible attributes include an overall impression or perception about a company, product or service, while tangible attributes are delivered through the product's features. Thus, for the purposes of benchmarking, we will ignore for the moment the brand effect and concentrate on the tangible aspects of the product or service. We can then revisit the brand effect when we make adjustments to the business model.

Many psychological factors also contribute to consumer decision-making. Perception, motivation and attitude all play roles in shaping preferences. For instance, a consumer's perception of a product's quality (read: attribute) can be influenced by advertising, packaging and personal experiences. Motivations, whether utilitarian (meeting practical needs) or hedonistic (providing pleasure or emotional satisfaction), also guide consumers toward specific products. Cultural values, norms and societal factors further contribute to the complexity of consumer choices. Thus, these factors will need to be pursued during the primary research portion of the process, however, they must be guided by an appropriate benchmarking assessment.

Category Features and Benefits

Although there are many factors that influence the consumer decision-making process, the objective of benchmarking is to develop a set of features that intuitively resonate with the customer. These are the tangible aspects of the product or service that unlock perceived benefits and value.

In the context of products, *attributes, features* and *benefits* are distinct elements that contribute to the overall understanding of a product. For our purposes, I will define them as follows:

Attributes are the inherent characteristics or qualities of a product. They are the fundamental building blocks that define what a product comprises and its overarching set of traits. They are regarded as characteristic or inherent parts of something although intangible in nature. Examples include quality, style, esthetics and/or novelty to name a few.

Features are the specific functionalities or capabilities that a product offers. They represent what the product can do and how it delivers certain tasks. Examples include things like size, weight and functionality.

Benefits are the positive outcomes or advantages that customers gain from using a product. They address the "what's in it for me" question from the perspective of the consumer. Examples include cost effectiveness, time management, convenience, speed, pride of ownership, etc.

In essence, attributes are the basic characteristics, features are the functionalities and benefits are the positive outcomes that make a product appealing to consumers. When marketing any product, firms tend to communicate all three aspects to their audience to highlight their value proposition and meet the perceived needs of potential customers. In essence, they communicate what is widely touted as their unique selling proposition (USP), advocating for the *attributes* of their product by highlighting their distinctive set of *features* and *benefits*. Thus, by examining competitors' communication and publicity materials, the relationships between attributes, features and benefits can be established. When several products are aggregated together in a structured way, it is possible to develop a set of criteria that describes the product category. I will refer to this as *benchmark orientation matrix*.

Systematic Evaluation

Assuming the product category has been identified, the next step of the process involves information gathering from a wide range of sources. These include competitors' websites, brochures, packaging and promotions. It should include product reviews, YouTube videos, social media publicity, input from key opinion leaders (KOLs) and celebrity endorsements to name a few. Team members on their own should gather this information and summarize it in a one-page product summary table format (see Table 2).

Table 2.   Product Summary Table.

SUMMARY TABLE
Image: One to three images highlighting the product.
Strengths: Outlines in a short paragraph the strengths of the product or service offering.
Weaknesses: Outlines in a short paragraph the weaknesses of the product or service offering.
Unique selling proposition: Outlines in a few concise sentences the overt value proposition.
Primary target audience: Describes the psychographic, demographic and if appropriate geographic characteristics of the target market.
Key features: Outlines in bullet form the key product features being promoted.
Key attributes: Outlines in bullet form the key attributes of the product or service.
Key benefits: What benefits does the product provide to the end-user.
Price: Outlines the retail price range of the product or service.

This individual research activity should take no more than three to four hours initially. Each team member should be challenged to examine three competitors' product using the above framework. It is important to emphasize that this exercise is *highly subjective* and that there are no wrong interpretations. When reporting back to the team, these assessments are based on everyone's *opinion*. Invariably there will be overlap between team members' chosen products, which is not only expected but encouraged. When the team meets to share their findings, the objectives are (i) to agree on the four to five products that best represent the category (no more than six) and (ii) agree on the features and attributes of each of these products. This may involve one additional round of fact-finding, concluding with *revised summary tables* reflecting the teams' aggregate assessment. Once this initial process is complete, the team is then ready to begin organizing this information into a structure format that can be used for assessing the category. A summary table example is highlighted below in the In Practice section.

In Practice: Summary Table Example

Creating summary tables is initially an individual exercise that is completely subjective. These documents are then shared and discussed within the team where decisions are made concerning which products best represent the *breadth* of the product category.

INPUTS
Secondary research

PROCESS
The following is an example of a summary table examining the golf putter category.

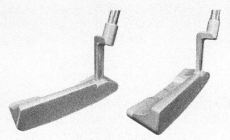

Fig. 8.   Titleist Scotty. Cameron Newport 2 Plus.

	Description
Strengths:	Top brand position; leading design and engineering; multiple customizable options
Weaknesses:	Perceived as not differentiated enough from less expensive competitors
Unique selling proposition:	Prestige; style; summed up with a quote from Scotty Cameron *"…the putter…when it's finished, should look like it melts into the ground. It should appeal emotionally, as well as physically."*
Target audiences:	High net worth male golfers; competitive female golfers
Key features:	Tour-inspired shape; 303 stainless steel; solid milled face; aluminum sole plate (anodized clear and engraved with the line's graphics); weight to perimeter; high MOI; stability; sight line; customizable SS sole weights; line's shaft band; headcover; textured Pistolini Plus grip; RH/LH; Lengths: Loft; Lie; Neck; Toe Flow; Offset
Key attributes:	Styling; quality craftsmanship; superior performance; celebrity endorsement; feedback/feel; alignment; balance;
Key benefits:	Status; pride of ownership; accuracy
Price:	$630 pricing controlled by manufacturer

OUTPUT

In this example, individual team members came back with a total of 11 different putters, some of which were repetitive. The team then needed to aggregate duplicate findings into one summary table per product. Five products were then selected by consensus to initially represent the product category.

As can be observed, in any product category, teams will encounter category-specific *terminology* coupled with competitor-specific *jargon* normally used for marketing or promotional purposes. In our example, jargon such as "textured Pistolini Plus grip" and "anodized clear and engraved with the line's graphics" are highlighted as differentiating features of the company's product. Category terminology includes terms such as moment of inertia (MOI), loft, lie, etc. For the purposes of the summary table, these descriptions are fine since these will drive interesting conversations within the team about exactly what these terms mean and what benefit they actually provide to the customer.

This summary table becomes one of several communicated to the team, often in the form of slides of a PowerPoint deck.

Benchmark Orientation Matrix

The benchmark orientation matrix shown in Table 3 is nothing more than a visual way to organize competitive product information in a structured format. The objective is to create a document that highlights attributes, features, benefits and price in one record. The general structure of the matrix is previewed in the table.

Each reference product is itemized in columns, with rows broken down into three distinct aspects, namely *attributes, features* and *benefits*. For the moment let's ignore the two categories of *complementor* and *analogs* as these will be covered at the end of this chapter. Although not apparent at this point, features are then ranked using a three-point scale from low, medium to high. Even though some features are categorical, the team must use their best judgment to rank them on a hierarchical scale. Using the summary tables developed by the team, the matrix can begin to be populated starting with attributes of the product. This normally begins a rigorous team discussion about what differentiates attributes from features. As a general rule, attributes are intangible while features are tangible. Once attributes are entered, the team can then begin to allocate features to the appropriate attribute category. Again, this is a very subjective exercise, and certain features may belong to two or more attribute categories. This is where the aggregate judgment of the team comes into play, since together they will have enough insights to make generally good predictions as to where they belong. I always caution teams not to spend too much

Table 3. Benchmark Orientation Matrix Structure.

ATTRIBUTES	FEATURES	Product A	Product B	Product C	Complementor	Analog	BENEFITS
Attribute A	Feature 1						
	Feature 2						
	Feature 3						
Attribute B	Feature 4						
	Feature 5						
	Feature 6						
Attribute C	Feature 7						
	Feature 8						
	Feature 9						
	PRICE (low)						
	PRICE (high)						

time ruminating over which category features belong, since exactly where they are placed will resolve itself later in the process. Another word of advice is that once the feature has been entered, I strongly advise that they be ranked before the team moves on to the next feature. This also includes itemizing the benefits related to each feature. Again, as additional products are assessed on each feature, there will be ample time to adjust previous rankings. In the end, this creates a better assessment since each product is ranked relative to the next in a comparable fashion. In my experience, if the team leaves the ranking of all features until the matrix is fully populated, the ranking exercise tends to be rushed resulting in the latter features being short-shifted as the team suffers from matrix fatigue.

Invariably, this process will highlight additional information to be gathered, reveal uncertainties within the team about which products best represent the category and disagreements on rankings. This is to be expected, but the team needs to be pragmatic and do their best to complete the matrix based on their best guesstimates. I recommend that teams take their time with this process and allocate a continuous three-to-four-hour session. If this is not possible, this process can be broken up into two sessions following the steps presented above.

Benchmarking Example

As the team begins the process of populating the matrix several things begin to take shape. First, there are normally more products to examine than is reasonable to assess. Each team member should have researched three products and begun the process of attribute finding and feature breakdown. The team next needs to go through a process of establishing which products best represent the category in question. This process can often lead to vigorous debates about the scope and direction of the project. This "creative abrasion" is a necessary part of any innovation management process and should be embraced, not resisted (Roach, 2012). Of course, vigorous debate should be a constructive process, not a winner-takes-all approach. In most cases, the initial work on establishing a diverse team structure (see Chapter 12) should have boosted this process so that conflicts are minimized. The second issue that becomes clear is that (i) not all team members will use the same terminology for attributes and/or features and (ii) some products may have features that others don't. For the latter, this is one of the key strengths of this approach since it highlights potential gaps in the category. For the former, this creates a forum for discussion leading to a shared understanding of the constructs in question.

Examining our golf putter example (see CASE EXAMPLE section), we can see this process in action. First, the team came back with a total of 11 different putters. As discussed, to create an effective benchmarking orientation matrix the team should ideally limit their assessment to four to five products, but no more than six. Thus, the team had to discuss which products to include and which to exclude. In order to be confident that the category would be well represented, several issues came to light. These included what style of putter, which quartile of pricing, brand representation, breadth of features, etc. Without going into detail, the team came to the consensus that it would be good to have brand representation, that a "blade style" putter was within their scope and that the top half of category pricing should be targeted. The team was confident that this would cover the range of features of the category. To accomplish this, seven putters would have to be examined and one major brand would have to be dropped. Against my advice, it was decided to keep all seven products in the assessment until the orientation matrix was completed. The team then winnowed down their matrix to five representative putters which resulted in the matrix presented in Table 4's CASE EXAMPLE.

Case Example: Benchmark Orientation Matrix – Golf Putter

The benchmark orientation matrix creates a structured and visual representation of competing products. Its purpose is to summarize team learning with respect to the product category to understand the relationships between attributes, features, benefits and price. Although some benchmarking activity is normally conducted by innovation teams, often it is ad hoc, poorly executed or is treated as a spillover of primary research activities. If approached consistently, the benchmark orientation matrix can reveal innovation opportunities that may be overlooked. It also turbocharges subsequent primary research activities, making probe and learn exercises much more *effective*.

INPUTS

Secondary research
Summary tables

PROCESS

Table 4 summarizes background research activities and the team's subjective assessment of the golf putter product category.

Attributes are considered higher-level constructs which are supported by features of the product that deliver them. They are intangible by nature.

Features are the tangible aspects of the product that the consumer can touch, feel and use to deliver the benefits they require from a product. They are tangible by nature.

Table 4. Benchmarking Orientation Matrix.

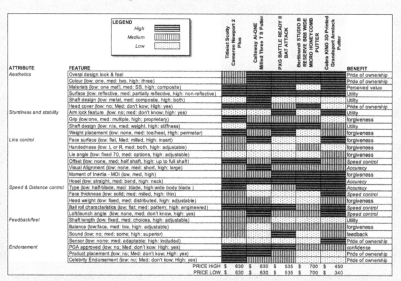

ATTRIBUTE	FEATURE	Titleist Scotty Cameron Newport 2 Plus	Callaway Ai-ONE Milled Three T S Putter	PXG BATTLE READY II BAT ATTACK	Bettinardi STUDIO B RESERVE B8B WIDE MICRO HONEYCOMB PUTTER	Cobra KING 3D Printed Grandsport Armlock Putter	BENEFIT
Aesthetics	Overall design look & feel						Pride of ownership
	Colour (low: one, med: two, high: three)						Pride of ownership
	Materials (low: one mat'l, med: SS, high: composite)						Perceived value
	Surface (low: reflective, med: partially reflective, high: non-reflective)						Utility
	Shaft design (low: metal, med: composite, high: both)						Utility
	Head cover (low: no; Med: don't kow; High: yes)						Pride of ownership
Sturdiness and stability	Arm lock feature (low: no; med: don't know; high: yes)						Utility
	Grip (low:one, med: multiple, high: proprietary)						forgiveness
	Shaft design (low: n/a, med: weight, high: stiffness)						Utility
	Weight placement (low: none, med: toe/heel, High: perimeter)						forgiveness
Line control	Face surface (low: flat, Med: milled, High: insert)						forgiveness
	Handedness (low: L or R, med: both, high: adjustable)						forgiveness
	Lie angle (low: fixed 70, med: options, high: adjustable)						forgiveness
	Offset (low: none, med: half shaft, high: up to full shaft)						Speed control
	Visual Alignment (low: none, med: short, high: large)						Accuracy
	Moment of Inertia - MOI (low: low, med, high)						forgiveness
	Hosel (low: straight, med: bend, high: neck)						Accuracy
Speed & Distance control	Type (low: half-blade, med: blade, high:wide body blade)						Accuracy
	Face thickness (low: solid; med: milled, high: thin)						Speed control
	Head weight (low: fixed, med: distributed, high: adjustable)						forgiveness
	Ball roll characteristics (low: flat; med: pattern; high: engineered)						Speed control
	Loft/launch angle (low: none, med: don't know, high: yes)						Speed control
Feedback/feel	Shaft length (low: fixed, med: choices, high: adjustable)						Utility
	Balance (low:face, med: toe, high: adjustable)						forgiveness
	Sound (low: no; med: some; high: superior)						feedback
	Sensor (low: none; med: adaptable; high: included)						confidence
Endorsement	PGA approved (low: no; don't kow: High: yes)						confidence
	Product placement (low: no; Med: don't kow; High: yes)						Pride of ownership
	Celebrity Endorsement (low: no; Med: don't kow; High: yes)						Pride of ownership
	PRICE HIGH	$ 630	$ 830	$ 535	$ 700	$ 450	
	PRICE LOW	$ 630	$ 830	$ 535	$ 700	$ 340	

LEGEND: High / Medium / Low

Benefits are what the customer "hires the product to do" (Levitt, 1981). They form the basis of how the customer perceives value.

Price is the economic value derived from the product. It is the marker of the perceived value of the product.

NOTE: In the benefit column, only one benefit is highlighted. This is intentional since the team is tasked with subjectively picking the most prominent benefit connected to the associated feature.

Now, critics will argue that this assessment of the category is very subjective and that these forced rankings are at best arbitrary and should not be used for decision-making. I can agree to some of this sentiment; however, I would argue that they have missed the point. There are two main objectives for creating a benchmark orientation matrix. The primary objective is to get the team to congeal around a common language for attributes, features and benefits. These three parameters are often used interchangeably and even if used appropriately often differ in understanding from person to person. The team exercise of agreeing on what is a feature, how it relates to attributes and what benefits these likely deliver is priceless for informing the next steps of the innovation management process. The secondary objective is to turbocharge the upcoming fact-finding (i.e., primary research) portion of the process. This makes these next steps an *order of magnitude* more *effective*. At a system level, this exercise must be conducted in conjunction with the secondary research phase *prior to primary research* or as the Lean Startup refers to it – customer discovery. Extracting what was historically known as the Voice of the Customer (VoC) (Griffin & Hauser, 1993) is only as effective as the ability to systematically *probe and learn*. Proper benchmarking has a profound effect later in the process when developing interview guides that direct the primary research process. This will be discussed at length in the following chapter on primary research.

Evaluation and Analysis

There is one other significant advantage to this structure. It begins the process of understanding the basic category requirements, potential gaps and/or opportunities. Examining the matrix, many observations can be gleaned from this document. I recommend looking at the matrix from three perspectives. First, at a global level...what information initially jumps out for the team? Second, examining it horizontally for what can be learned across competitive products? Finally, scrutinizing columns for what can be learned "within" products that could inform the process.

Looking at our example from a global perspective, we can see that three products are competing for the top end of the market. Titleist and Callaway (the two strongest brands in our assessment) both are priced relative to each other although competing on slightly different features. The third – Berttinardi is priced at roughly a 10% premium although feature for feature our assessment indicates that it should be inferior to the brand leaders. One product that does stick out is Cobra, which feature for feature should likely command roughly the same price as the brand leaders but seems to be priced at a discount to the category. It also appears that the brand effect is roughly $150–$200. Now, I will not bias this assessment but merely state that the team should discuss why they think these discrepancies exist and how it may influence their upcoming primary research activities.

Next, looking horizontally across products, two observations tend to stand out (i) what are must-have features for the category and (ii) are there gaps that could potentially foresight opportunities. For the former, it appears that features such as materials, surface, hosel and ball roll characteristics seem to be a basic requirement for any putter. From an attribute perspective, it appears that esthetics (look and feel) is the dominant attribute category and will require deeper investigation. This seems to be further confirmed by the high ranking of the three premium putters in this attribute category. Looking vertically across features can also provide distinguishing profiles. There appears to be a cluster of features for the non-premium products within the line, speed and distance control attributes. This perhaps foresights where these brands think they can gain an edge in the category relative to the category leaders? Another question that requires investigation is whether there are features that can be improved for the overall category? Features such as handedness, lie angle, shaft length, head weight and balance do not appear to have any category leaders in our group. The connecting theme appears to be adjustability. This could potentially be a point of differentiation since adjustability is a common theme for other golf clubs such as drivers[1].

Analogs and Complementors

Although we will discuss these in subsequent chapters, *analogs* and *complementors* should also considered as the project unfolds. Analogs are products or services that are used in the *same environment* or for the *same purpose*. For instance, a kettle and a microwave could be considered analogs. They are both used in the same environment (i.e., the kitchen) and can also be used for the same purpose (i.e., boiling water). In our golf putter example, analogs could be ball retrievers (adjustable length), drivers (engineered materials) or a pool cue (directional ball striking). Analogs will also become very useful during the lead user phase of the innovation approach, which will be discussed in Chapter 10. Complementors on the other hand are products or services that complement the product category. In our golf putter example, there are many companies supplying third-party grips. Other examples could be putting practice devices, laser alignment attachments or digital stroke recording devices. All have different attributes, features and perceived benefits. As a result, their value to the benchmarking process is that they can add to the feature set of the category, often in areas overlooked by competitors. As the process unfolds, the team should be tasked with uncovering both analogs and complementors during initial primary research. These can then be updated within the benchmark orientation matrix as appropriate.

Conclusion

In summary, the benchmark orientation matrix, even as subjective and imperfect as it is, does deliver a high-level evaluation of the category. It provides multiple benefits to the innovation management process, primarily a deep understanding of the attributes, features and benefits of the category and their relationships. It focuses the team on aspects of the product and more importantly it creates a forum for the team to come to a mutual understanding of the terminology they are likely to encounter when they begin their primary research. It allows for a holistic evaluation of the category and begins the process of determining the hierarchy of attributes, must-have features and potential areas of differentiation. Most importantly it informs and focuses on the next step in the innovation process of primary research, where customer learning and discovery begins.

During primary research, such as interviews, customers will speak in the VoC. They will communicate about many aspects of the product, their environment, their perceptions, their biases along with their likes and dislikes. They will not communicate the differences between attributes or features, nor will they give the

---

[1]Interestingly while reviewing his chapter, VLS Golf launched what they claim is the *first adjustable putter*. https://vlsgolf.com/products/vls-g-track-putter

team a clear understanding of their needs or the benefits they hope to garner from the product. Although we will discuss how to elicit these requirements in the next chapter, the important takeaway is that benchmarking allows the team to dive deeper, to more effectively identify the root causes of issues. Benchmarking, along with proper secondary research as highlighted in Chapter 4 form the required *background research* necessary for effective primary research.

Chapter 6

Primary Research

The "voice of the customer is a whisper", thus customer listening requires particular attention in the field of innovation management. Eliciting end-user requirements is not a trivial task, since they can only articulate what they know and understand. Much of their requirements are thus unspoken and must be extracted through non-standard methods. These include observation, probe and learn techniques and confirmatory methods which are first informed through effective secondary research and benchmarking. This chapter focusses on developing a systematic approach to information gathering focusing on problems, trends and solutions, rather than often espoused market size, compound annual growth rate (CAGR) and attractive trends.

Introduction

This chapter focuses on the role of primary research within an effective innovation management system. The results of primary research are directly related to the quality of background research that precedes this activity. This results in an informed and focused approach, where the team can probe and learn in areas that are more likely to bear fruit. This chapter will highlight an approach to best practices examining various types of primary research.

Approach to Primary Research

For the purposes of managing the innovation process, primary research can take many forms. Although I will cover an approach to collecting primary research, the initially focus will highlight the various classical approaches which include:

The *Marketing research* approach describes a broad process of market information gathering involving both secondary and primary research. Historically it has been responsible for the development of many of the tools and techniques used in primary research. These techniques are both quantitative and qualitative.

The *Industrial design* approach is the established design-focused process in product development. It is primarily interested in human factors – the relationship between the user and the product or service. As a result, it is most focused

The Innovation Approach:
Overcoming the Limitations of Design Thinking and the Lean Startup, 87–105
Copyright © 2025 by David C. Roach
Published under exclusive licence by Emerald Publishing Limited
doi:10.1108/978-1-83797-799-420241006

on the interface between the product and the humans. Their tools and techniques are generally qualitative.

The *Design Thinking* (*DT*) approach in its purest form mimics the industrial design process since it empathically seeks to understand the relationship between the product or service and the individual. It relies on a combination of observational research and customer listening, using artifacts as focal points. As a result, the tools and techniques employed are generally qualitative. For the purposes of primary research, DT and Industrial Design will be considered synonymous.

The *Lean Startup* (LS) approach is primarily driven by its focus on business model development. It employs a combination of interviews, observation and prototyping to accomplish its objectives. Although it relies on both quantitative and qualitative techniques, its focus is primarily on the former to quantify information for decision-making.

All approaches use slightly different research techniques to accomplish their aims. Depending on their philosophy, each will tend to favor some techniques over others.

Types of Primary Research

Primary market research involves collecting data directly from the source. There are several types of primary market research techniques, each with its own advantages and limitations. The following are some commonly used techniques:

Surveys and Questionnaires are cost-effective and generally easy to administer. They work well when there is a known and large enough audience to query. This method has limitations in the type of information that can be captured since it is restricted by its instrument design which can suffer from response bias. Online surveys (the dominant method) can also suffer from sampling an unqualified or unrepresentative population. In my experience, this type of primary research instrument is often poorly executed and frequently used during the wrong part of the process. In practice, this type of research is often driven by management early in the process in support of developing their business case (i.e., a project selection activity). This can result in faulty outcomes, since they are often based on "intent to buy" and/or "pricing" questions which are difficult constructs to establish even at the best of times. More worrying are the results of qualitative and/or open-ended questions, where management tends to "quantify the qualitative," naively believing that they can improve their decision-making through numerical values. Thus, as a primary research tool, surveys have a place later in the process (i.e., the back end of innovation - BEI) to confirm key decisions. Many an innovation project has been harmed by using this method as a front end of innovation (FEI) tool.

Interviews provide an opportunity to collect in-depth information directly from customers while providing opportunities for clarification. The key objective of interviews is to understand from the customer's perspective their relationship with the product or service. What used to be referred to as the voice-of-the-customer (VoC) (Griffin & Hauser, 1993) is nowadays referred to as customer listening or customer discovery. However, what we have known for over three decades is that the "voice-of-the-customer is a whisper" (Roach, 2006). Customers can only communicate a limited amount of information verbally and only in an environment that is amenable to information sharing. As a result, this technique can suffer from limitations including interviewer bias, overly structured or ambiguous questions and interpretation of information. Therefore, caution must be exercised when using this technique, since poorly executed interviews can lead to poor results. There are multiple approaches to conducting interviews which will be discussed later in this chapter.

Focus Groups are historically a favorite tool of market researchers where an artificially generated forum creates an environment for group discussions from diverse perspectives. This technique is led by a moderator who facilitates a discussion on broad topics. These sessions typically last about two hours, should be limited to six to eight participants and involve no more than four topics. Often, they are conducted behind one-way mirrors (or video links) where team members and management can obtain raw feedback in real-time, with the opportunity to suggest follow-on questions through the moderator. Although they can be instructive, they can be highly influenced by moderator bias, the "alpha" syndrome (where dominant voices prevail) and surface-level responses. As a result, they have routinely been criticized by management as ineffective, time-consuming and expensive. For instance, if you compare an eight-person, two-hour focus group to a 90-minute one-on-one interview, the contrast is stark. The focus group has approximately 120 minutes available, however, moderator interaction can easily take up 20 minutes. Assuming three broad topics restricts the discussion to roughly 33 minutes per topic. Assuming a focus group of eight individuals, this further restricts input to around four minutes per individual, per topic. This leaves virtually no opportunity to gather an in-depth understanding, exposing only surface-level issues. In practice, however, two or three individuals often dominate the conversation, resulting in narrow conversations (or debates) on limited aspects of the topic. When compared to a 90-minute one-on-one interview, even accounting for interviewer interaction, each topic should receive roughly 25 minutes of attention, allowing for a deeper understanding of the issues at hand. Consequently, focus groups are now universally considered inadequate as a customer listening technique. Thus, they will not be explored in any greater detail in this chapter.

Observational Research provides firsthand insights into the behavior of users, preferably in the environment where they are performing their activities. Championed by Dorothy Leonard in her seminal book – *Wellsprings of Knowledge* (Leonard, 1995), it is a preferred approach for both industrial designers and DT enthusiasts. It also has limitations ranging from observer bias to subjective interpretation of information. Observational research has been lauded by the DT community as the key to uncovering unspoken (latent) needs. Although I agree wholeheartedly with this belief, relying solely on this method to develop value-added innovations is naïve and often fails to deliver suitable results. The primary reason is that observational research is a methodology that requires aptitude, skill and experience. Observations are highly qualitative, and their interpretation is highly subjective. Most DT teams are not properly equipped to conduct this type of research, resulting in either missing key observations or misinterpreting their meaning.

I am still however a big fan of observational research as a primary research tool but not as the only technique to uncover latent needs.

Field Trials (or product-in-use studies) are also a significant primary research tool. They are very effective for scrutinizing real-world applications of products or services by revealing authentic user experiences. Since these are conducted in the users' environment while performing tasks, they are excellent at uncovering both spoken and unspoken needs. By design, they tend to be a combination of observational research and interview techniques. They allow the opportunity for intervention, permitting the subject to verbalize the "what," "where" and "why" questions as they are encountered. It also allows for the subject to express their emotions more clearly, often the core of value creation opportunities. The downside of this type of research is that they are time-consuming to set up, often expensive and resource-intensive. As a result, they are more effective once the innovation team has developed an early stage "alpha" prototype, rather than at the beginning of the process. In Dr. Leonard's research, her team went into the field with an unnamed company (likely L.L. Bean) to live the outdoor experience over a wet and cold weekend. As she has said, there is nothing like a team member stepping up to their knees in mud to understand the limitations of boots and pants. In any event, this type of primary research has one main advantage over pure observation. Although it is qualitative in nature, the interpretation of results is often less subjective, leading to better decision-making.

Conjoint analysis is a specific type of market research survey used to understand how people evaluate and make decisions about products or services. It helps researchers uncover the preferences and priorities for different attributes of a product or service. It is widely employed in marketing, product development and strategic decision-making. Teams can test features, pricing, brands or any other characteristic that may influence consumer preferences at different levels. It is particularly good for establishing tradeoffs (e.g., cost/benefit per feature), product positioning and customer segmentation. Although a powerful tool, it is not recommended for the FEI, although I have used it in limited cases. For instance, at key junctures of an innovation project, it can be useful for quantifying the value of certain features for management to consider. It can also be used to break decision log jams between the innovation and business factions of the organization. This quantitative method is time-consuming, expensive and must be designed and executed by professionals.

Metaphor elicitation technique is a primary market research tool that elicits both conscious and unconscious thoughts through the exploration of an individual's non-literal or metaphoric expressions (Zaltman, 2003). This technique assumes that people think visually and are often unable to communicate their thoughts either verbally or in writing. Using visual stimulus allows for a focal point from which hidden knowledge can be unlocked. This creates opportunities to get to issues people "don't know that they know." In this approach, participants are asked to bring to an interview a set of pictures that represent their thoughts and feelings about the topic of interest. The interviewer then uses these artifacts to probe participants to uncover profoundly held, often unconscious, thoughts and feelings. Although most often used to help marketers develop marketing communication campaigns, it is nonetheless a powerful tool to elicit the hidden voice of the customer (VoC) input at the FEI. I first became aware of this technique when a colleague in the MIT corridor recommended Dr. Zaltman's 2003 book – *How Customers Think* (Zaltman, 2003). In this book, he goes into great detail on how individuals process information and why much of what they want, and feel cannot be garnered using traditional market research techniques. Unlike many academics, he proposes two practical tools that can be used to extract and codify key information. I've used his *metaphor elicitation technique* quite successfully and am a real proponent of including this method in any innovation management process. The other tool he proposes is a form of *construct mapping*, where cognitive processes and their relationships are charted. I will expand on both approaches later in this chapter.

In summary, choosing the right methods depends on the research objectives, budget and the type of information needed. Combining multiple methods can also enhance the overall reliability and validity of the research findings.

Primary Research Best Practices

Now that we have reviewed the various approaches to primary research, established the types of techniques available and recognized that most of the inputs required are not easily extracted using traditional techniques, let's examine best practices.

In my assessment, there are three approaches to gathering primary research that are most effective at the FEI. Each approach is qualitative and subjective, and can be executed independently of the others, or in combination. These include:

1. Interviews
2. Observation
3. Artifacts

Although the first two may seem intuitive, how these are executed can have a disproportionate impact on the quality of results. Artifacts on the other hand (my preferred terminology) are where I differentiate between prototyping and providing focal points for enhanced learning during information gathering. Most frequently these three approaches are combined into one – often using the interview as the focal point for implementation.

Once the relevant information is gathered, this qualitative data must be sorted, qualified and interpreted. For this to occur, internal systems must be in place to understand, visualize and properly communicate aspects of what has been learned prior to (and in support of) decision-making.

Developing, Executing and Analyzing Interviews

Interviews are a ubiquitous technique in the execution of primary research. However, as an innovation management technique, it comes in many forms, configurations and philosophies. There are some basic principles however that cut across all forms of interview techniques.

Prior to the advent of DT and the LS, one of the most thorough approaches to customer interviews was attributed to Edward McQuarrie in his influential book – *Customer Visits* (McQuarrie, 1998). Lauded as an A-to-Z approach to preparing, designing and executing customer discovery exercises, his approach rested on the fundamental principle that good planning will result in good (and actionable) information. Also, coming out of the 1990s was a seminal article written by Abby Griffin and John Hauser entitled VoC (Griffin & Hauser, 1993). In this article Drs Griffin and Hauser quantitatively evaluated the ability to extract customer needs based on interviews and focus groups, resulting in a systematic approach to integrating the customer's voice into product development. Combining both approaches, namely the rigor of McQuarrie and the methodology of Griffin and Hauser, provides a strong foundation for the execution of customer interviews.

Beginning with the latter, Griffin and Hauser were interested in understanding the approach and boundaries of activities required to efficiently extract customer needs at the FEI. First, they made a strong case for *interviews* rather than *focus groups* for assessing customer needs. Their research found that focus groups had limitations since (i) most of what was uncovered were surface-level issues (rather than deep-rooted causes), (ii) they uncovered expected needs but not delight needs, (iii) they are time-consuming and expensive to execute and (iv) they introduced an additional level of bias through moderator influence on the process. On the other hand, interviews were not without their flaws. They also suffered to a lesser extent from interviewer bias and were also time-consuming and resource-intensive. However, judging by the cost per customer interview hour, interviews were much more efficient, dwarfing the focus group method. What they concluded was that (i) interviews are much more efficient from a time and cost perspective than focus groups, (ii) 20–30 interviews per customer segment resulted in 95% of expected needs being identified and (iii) no major expected needs were missed. Reviewing their data, it appears that stopping their process at between 17 and 20 interviews was likely a more realistic target. It was later recommended that interviews be conducted by pairs of interviewers from functionally different backgrounds and analyzed by several individuals (i.e., a team). As a result, this approach has often been coined the 2–20 interview method. However, given that interviews were conducted in isolation (i.e., one did not inform the other), many now believe that ten interviews are adequate at the initial stages of the FEI. More on this topic is covered in the IN PRACTICE section.

Edward McQuarrie's approach to interviews and customer visit advises a systematic approach based on best practices. He includes many caveats within his book which he appropriately describes as "pitfalls, traps, dangers and risks." He describes step-by-step instructions on how to effectively use these techniques along with how to select the right number and kind of customers to visit. He explains in detail how to develop a discussion guide and provides practical advice on how to develop appropriate questions and conduct face-to-face interviews. His steps include:

Step 1 – Objective setting referring to the type of information the team hopes to collect

Step 2 – Sample selection referring to types, segments and number of customers

Step 3 – Team selection referring to team structure, disciplinary functions and roles
Step 4 – Discussion guide development referring to topics, questions and sequence
Step 5 – Conducting interviews based on roles, interactions and environment
Step 6 – Debriefing team learnings, adjusting and informing subsequent interviews
Step 7 – Process of analysis, dissemination and interpretation of qualitative
information

Although these steps seem unassuming at first glance, in practice there are
indeed many pitfalls, traps, dangers and risks. In practice, qualitative customer
interviews can result in missteps, misdirection and/or misinterpretation. Although
I will not explain in detail how to conduct interviews (for those interested I
would highly recommend reading his book), in practice several areas should
be of particular focus to innovation managers. His methodology first relies on
the development and enhancement of a problem statement, segmentation (or
persona identification) and team configuration. This solid foundation provides
the backdrop for the most important steps of (i) discussion guide development,
(ii) conducting interviews and (iii) interpreting results (i.e., STEPS 4–7).

Discussion Guide

Discussion guide development is not a trivial task. Many primary research activities have been driven off course through inadequate attention to interview guide
development. Often this process is rushed in the guise of efficiency or the false
sense of urgency to get to creativity activities – confusing action for effectiveness. First, the guide must be informed by adequate background research. Proper
background research should uncover trends, problems and issues related to the
category, which become the foundation of the discussion guide. It should provide
some consistency across interviews while acting as a rough agenda for starting
conversations. One criticism of the LS method is that founding teams, usually
heavily weighted with technical people, often feel most comfortable with precise,
highly detailed scripts that they believe will increase the precision of their work.

Discussion guides are *not a set of survey questions* but a framework for information gathering. As such, they should be based on top-level themes garnered
from background research as agreed upon by the team. A discussion guide should
be perceived like a roadmap for a journey. Much like any road trip, there are several ways to get from destination A to B. Along the way the terrain changes, interesting sites reveal themselves and the traveler may just need to do some exploring.
The most efficient path from A to B often is the least interesting and least informative. This is why discussion guides must provide flexibility for interesting detours
where the road is less traveled, and the destination unclear. The traveler must
also be comfortable with the potential risk of getting lost along the way. Hence,
discussion guides must be constructed in such a way as to allow for what is often
referred to as "probe and learn" interview techniques.

For a detailed overview of interview guide preparation, I refer students and
clients to Chapter 6 of Edward McQuarrie's book – *Customer Visits* (McQuarrie,
1998). Here he reviews the rationale for design, tips for constructing good

questions, as well as appropriate and inappropriate questions. He also covers techniques to keep interviews flowing seamlessly by suggesting such things as natural transitions. If executed correctly, the interviewer should effortlessly provide a segue from one topic to another. As an example, see IN PRACTICE section.

In Practice – Probe and Learn (Part 1)

The following outlines a typical approach to probe and learn interviews.

Ice breaker question (example)

> *Q. How long have you been doing this kind of work? What is your background and how did you come to be here?*

Introduction question (free range question)

> *Q. As you're aware we are here to talk about XXX, what are your general thoughts about the industry, the products, the competitors, etc.*

> *(NOTE: often this type of question will highlight one or more of the team's topics providing a segue. Thus, teams should take cues from the interviewee on which topics to pursue in what order)*

Topical Questions (3–5 recommended based on results of secondary research)

   Topic A
   Topic B
   Topic X

Wrap up question (used to summarize discussion)

> *Q. Puling all that we have discussed together, what are your main recommendations, concerns or issues that you would want us to take away?*

Assuming three to five topics, general time frames should be between 10 and 20 minutes each, with introduction and wrap up roughly five minutes each. This is interviewee dependent, where some topics may be more noteworthy than others. The rule of thumb is that root causes rarely reveal themselves in the first 10 minutes. Interviewers should thus strive to keep the conversation fluid as long as appropriate. It becomes abundantly clear when a topic has been exhausted, so interviewer judgment is part of the art of probe and learn interview technique.

Conducting the Interview

Conducting interviews should be about *effectiveness* and *efficiency* of information gathering. There is always very limited time with each interviewee and the objective should be to get deep as soon as possible to uncover root causes of underlying issues. DT and the LS tend to assume that interviews, observation and prototyping will uncover deep-rooted issues which can be used to create features that will delight the customer. DT tends to rely too heavily on observation, while the LS tends to take what Dr. Robert Cooper often refers to the "fire-ready-aim" approach to collecting the VoC. These methods are neither effective nor efficient at uncovering delight needs. Thus, the objective of conducting interviews is to get beneath surface-level answers (effectiveness) while at the same time uncovering the breadth of needs in a timely fashion (efficiency).

The first step is to conduct interviews based on the 2–20 interview principle. The "2" stands for having two individuals conduct the interview, from different functional backgrounds, each taking notes throughout the discussion. Using two individuals is key since each will interpret the interview through their own filter and unconscious biases. The key to executing this method is to have each interviewer summarize their findings (and interpretation) separately, immediately after the interview. This eliminates any groupthink and allows for a raw interpretation of events. As soon as possible they should each present their findings to the team, initiating a discussion. Inevitably, these individuals tend to agree on most findings, however, the real magic is where they disagree or recall issues differently. For instance, the marketer may recall that the customer was unhappy with the size and feel of the product, while the engineer heard specifications. These areas can lead to highly productive team discussions and often become focal points for future probe and learn exercises. The "20" portion of 2–20 interviews refers to the number of interviews that should be conducted to obtain more than 90% of expected needs. As per our earlier discussion, if conducted properly initially ten interviews are sufficient to extract key information from customers at the FEI. This approach also employs a semi-structured, open-ended, probe and learn approach executed over a 60–90-minute time period. This timeframe is important since it allows sufficient time for the interview to go beyond surface-level issues. The semi-structured, open-ended approach should have been established through proper discussion guide development, while the probe and learn aspect is associated with how the guide is delivered. For tips on how to conduct a probe and learn approach see the IN PRACTICE – Probe and Learn (Part 2) section.

Critics (specifically LS enthusiasts) often say that this approach is impractical since it slows their "agile" process down…and besides – their quick and dirty approach will *eventually* uncover all these issues. Moreover, their push for volume will leave no stone unturned. This often results in getting team members to conduct interviews with dozens if not hundreds of customers. From an efficiency perspective, this is akin to the sledgehammer approach. One typical example I recall was a young entrepreneur who was delighted to tell me about their brilliant idea that had been validated with 115 customers. When I asked about the interview process, they told me that they asked random individuals about their idea over a 10–15-minute conversation. They had "pushed for volume" and believed they had received invaluable feedback, which I'm sure at some level they did. However, this approach was ineffective, inefficient and unreliable as a process. I then asked about their next steps which was unsurprisingly "pitching to investors." They confessed that they were disappointed at the lack of interest, but they intended to "pivot and persevere" …I wished them well…

DT proponents on the other hand often rely too heavily on observation by untrained individuals, conducting one-on-many style interviews combined with observation. This approach has many merits but is often ineffective. As stated earlier, observational research can be a very powerful tool, but has limitations when executed by untrained, neophyte teams. Having observed professionals trained in this area over the decades, I have full confidence that they will uncover significant latent (i.e., unspoken) issues using this technique. They also have the training to interpret these observations and understand their meaning. As a test, I gave an assignment to my undergraduate class to observe YouTube videos of golfers using putters and tell me what they observed. Some observations such as aligning the putt were identified by many of the students and interpreted correctly. However, the most blatantly obvious one eluded them all. In each video, virtually all professional putters do the same thing…they wipe the blade of the putter, align the ball with the putter face then wiggle their feet until they are ready to strike the ball. Now, I'm still not sure how to interpret this observation, but it would certainly be one that I would probe during interviews. Out of more than 40 students, remarkably none had observed this. Thus, relying on observation as your primary tool for extracting delight needs, for most teams is akin to shooting darts at a blank wall. There is still a place for observation in primary research, however blind adherence to this technique can have significant consequences.

In Practice – Probe and Learn (Part 2)

Probe and learn has often been associated with the "5 whys" methodology, largely attributed to the Toyota Motor Company as an approach to getting to root causes of problems. In practice, asking "why" five times comes across quickly as a prescriptive exercise, thus it is not recommended as such. However, this probing approach to uncover root causes is appropriate if executed properly.

INPUTS

Secondary research
Benchmarking
Profile of the Primary Target Audience (PTA) and associated Decision-Making Unit (DMU)

PROCESS

To accomplish this, I always recommend more effective segue prompts. In practice, I have always found that once you get the interviewee's initial response to a question, the most effective approach is to have them project responses on a third party. This allows them to remove any inhibitions about being judged, since they will very often project their beliefs on others. This allows in the limited time provided during interviews to *"go deeper more quickly."* As a result, I always recommend to *"project 'why' on someone else."*

Below are a few examples of transitions that can be used instead of using the word "why":

Projecting "why" on someone else.

Q. Given what you have just told us, can you think of a colleague (or anyone) that would disagree (agree) with you?

Follow-on: Why do you think they have this position?
Follow-on: What do you think is driving them?
Follow-on: Do you think this position is shared by others?
Follow-on: What do you think is needed to pull these disparate positions together?
Follow-on: Who is doing the best job at trying to bridge these gaps?

NOTE: the golden keys to successful probe and learn interviews is to only prompt when the conversation drags. Otherwise, it is best to keep quiet.

OUTPUTS

As you can see, the term "why" is not required to probe and learn and maintains a conversational style with the interviewee. It very often reveals the interviewee's real opinion allowing them to say what they really think without judgment.

Observation Within Interviews

Observations are best used within the user centered model framework (See Chapter 4, Fig. 7), the core of what is often referred to as user-centered design (UCD). Although much has been written about UCD, I find at the early stages it is best to keep it simple. As a result, I tend to look at it through two lenses.

First is Dorothy Leonard's approach of living with the product, in the customer's environment performing their activities. In this "user-centered model" approach there is an emphasis on gaining tacit knowledge to discover context-specific information that cannot be easily articulated. By witnessing individuals at work, one can gain insights into their processes, interactions and problem-solving approaches that may not be evident through traditional primary research techniques.

This contributes to a more comprehensive and holistic understanding of the customer experience from their perspective. Her approach does not recommend observation as a primary tool but as part of a set of ethnographic techniques. She refers to these as "shadowing," namely a combination of observation and in-depth (i.e., probe and learn) interviews, followed by documentation and analysis. Observation is a component of her shadowing process and is used as trigger points for probing in real time.

Second is the "design" part of UCD. UCD is an iterative design process in which the needs, desires and limitations of end-users are considered in the development process. The primary goal of UCD is to create products or systems that are intuitive, efficient and satisfying for users to interact with. Much of the popularization of UCD can be accredited to Donald Norman's seminal book entitled the *Design of Everyday Things* (Norman, 1988). Here he explains in detail the human–product relationship and how to design a product that people find usable, esthetically pleasing and desirable. This and his follow-on book – *Emotional Design* (Norman, 2004), I consider mandatory readings for any design team.

Combining Leonard's and Norman's approaches can be very powerful during primary research. Leonard allows for the determination of "what" the customer requires, while Norman's approach provides the boundaries for "how" these can be satisfied. Having an understanding from a design perspective of how customers interact with products can (and should) help form part of what the team endeavors to uncover during the primary research phase. This is why industrial designers are often very skilled at uncovering unspoken needs, since they approach their observations and probing techniques from a deep understanding of a human–product relationship.

In practice, I find that teams tend to rush to the "design" portion of UCD before truly understanding the nature of the individual–environment–task framework. One of my critiques of both the LS and to a lesser extent DT is that observation is (i) not based on an understanding of a human–product relationship and (ii) not necessarily conducted in the user's environment executing their tasks. This results in an incomplete understanding of these relationships, limiting the "triggers" that can be used for probing.

Thus, observation when used within the correct framework, for the right reason (i.e., as a probing prompt) and at the appropriate time can be a very powerful primary research tool. It has the potential to highlight unspoken (latent) needs, which "can" lead to creating delight features – the core of creating differential value. In a later chapter, I will explore other techniques that can enhance this type of activity.

Case Study – Observation

Years ago when we developed a world-leading handheld GPS device that used a micro display rather than a screen, I remember asking my developers whether we should incorporate a dimmer feature into the display.

Their response was "Why would we do this" since the display was bright and readable under any sunlight conditions. This was one of our main unique selling propositions (USP). Many months later, the team participated in a 24-hour search and rescue competition to stress test the device. Upon their return, they gained many insights, one of which was the requirement for a dimmer. When I asked what changed their thinking, the team leader confessed that he had almost lost an eye by walking into a tree at night due to night blindness. This is a classic example of issues that can only be understood by examining the individual–task–environmental relationship.

Another example came from a long-term client in the blood diagnostic business. The company supplied specialty diagnostic products which were uniquely better, in an industry that was notoriously cost-conscious. To better understand the individual–environment–task framework they visited client sites to observe and discuss how testing took place. What they observed was that these large testing laboratories were more akin to high-tech sweatshops. Individuals were under pressure to deliver 100% accurate results, under tight time frames at the lowest costs. "Reworks" were frowned upon. What they realized was that lab technicians wanted *anything* that would make their task less stressful, while the lab managers wanted anything that gave them confidence in the results. As a result, the company focused its products and marketing activities on ease of use and confidence in results.

Artifacts as Focal Points

Although both the LS and the DT are strong advocates of prototyping, it is important to note that they may not always be the best tool for eliciting customer input at the FEI. As a result, I prefer to use the term *artifact* as the basis for primary research. I define artifacts as tools of communication that are aimed at eliciting feelings. As such, they act as triggers for expressions of human thought and provide a focal point for meaningful discussion.

As discussed earlier, Gerald Zaltman in his seminal book *How Customers Think* (Zaltman, 2003) suggests what he refers to as the *Metaphor Elucidation technique*. In this technique, he makes a strong case for why customers think visually and that most of their needs are buried in their subconscious. He also speaks loosely of efficiency when he argues that interview time is always limited, stating that one-hour interviews should be the minimum. The objective must be to quickly get below surface-level responses, which require the use of triggers to prompt interviewees into disclosing their core feelings early in the conversation. In his method, he asks interviewees to bring copies of images that best describe a *metaphor* about their feelings on the topic at hand. He suggests that they concentrate on core feelings of happiness, sorrow, frustration, etc., within the *task* and *environment* in which they are executing their work. Although his primary use for this technique is for brand development, the core concepts can be applied to primary research for innovation management purposes. This is where both the DT and the LS's focus on prototyping for eliciting customer needs can benefit by refocusing on the concept of *artifacts*.

In practice the logistics of getting individuals to show up with images based on metaphors is problematic. First, it presents a hassle to the individual who has already agreed to give up their time. Second, it goes under the presumption that people truly understand what a metaphor is. Often individuals show up with last-minute images based on pet peeves hastily downloaded from the internet minutes before the interview. Lastly, for the purposes of innovation management, this approach can easily derail a carefully constructed interview guide, effectively losing control of the purpose of the interview. Although a powerful tool to elicit deep customer needs, in my experience the Metaphor Elucidation technique loses its power due to delivery problems. As a result, I suggest that upon completion of the interview guide, the team endeavors to find images that relate to the topics they have agreed upon. Agreeing upon which ones are appropriate is a good team exercise, which I consider part of the interview guide development. These images can then be brought to the interview in a folder and used as appropriate during the interview. These artifacts can be used strategically to push the interviewee into a deeper conversation about specific issues or for probing purposes. Unlike rough prototypes, these artifacts often lead to emotional triggers rather than a discussion on "features and benefits."

Interpreting Results

Interpreting results is a difficult task. Verbal, non-verbal and observational data must be subjectively assessed, organized and interpreted. This activity is highly dependent on the make-up of the team, their aggregate skills and their ability to collaborate. In the end, it is an incomplete and imperfect exercise that must be attempted before ideation exercises can begin. Consequently, many techniques and approaches have been developed and advocated over the years to aid in this journey. However, all are based on helping the team understand the context within which they will need to ideate.

Customer Journey Mapping

Customer journey mapping is primarily an *internal communication tool*. It is one of the many tools often associated with DT. Others include (but are not limited to) storyboarding, stakeholder mapping and empathy maps (Lewrick et al., 2020). In practice, I find that customer journey mapping, if done correctly, incorporates most of the pertinent information from the others.

Customer journey mapping is often used to put ideas into context for the team to gain insights into customer behavior, preferences and pain points through interaction with a product, service or brand. This visual tool can help identify opportunities for improvement, customer satisfaction and/or optimize the overall customer experience. Typically, it involves creating a visual representation of the customer journey, outlining key stages (e.g., before, during and after use), touchpoints and emotions associated with each step. It should also include the customer's interaction with other stakeholders in the system.

In essence, customer journey mapping is a valuable technique within the broader framework of DT and to a lesser extent the LS. Its ultimate purpose is to provide a structured way to understand the user experience as part of an iterative design process. In practice, users of DT tend to execute this technique reasonably well, since their process is highly user-centric and empathetic. With their emphasis on agility, waste minimization and business hypothesis validation, the LS practitioners tend to develop ad hoc maps on the fly (if at all).

Although a powerful team communication tool, journey mapping relies heavily on the quality of inputs from the interview process. As the adage goes…garbage in – garbage out. Thus, teams should use this tool with some caution as it may unintentionally divert the early part of the innovation process in an unfavorable direction, which can have detrimental effects on outcomes[1].

In practice, I've developed a "love–hate" relationship with journey mapping since I find that it is often unconsciously used to rationalize the team's vision of who the customer is. When it does reflect the "customer's" viewpoint, it often does so without understanding the complex relationships between other actors involved in the decision-making process. As an example, in my undergraduate and graduate classes, apparently all customers are "Gen Zers"[2] who remarkably behave like an aggregate of the class. In my executive courses, the customer takes on the air of the "dream" customer who is value-conscious (i.e., not price sensitive), wants every feature available and is easily reached by traditional methods. As a result, I find that other tools such as cognitive mapping (see next section) can act as a buffer to this groupthink limitation.

Cognitive Mapping

The Oxford reference defines cognition as *"the mental action or process of acquiring knowledge and understanding through thought, experience, and the senses"* (Cognition, 2024). Cognitive mapping is merely a tool to visually represent the customer's experience through their perceptions, judgments and memory (International, 2023).

Cognitive mapping (a form of mind mapping) is a sporadically used visual tool whose purpose is to put customer thought patterns into context for the team. It differs from journey mapping since it takes a cognitive approach to understanding dominant thought processes and more importantly their relationships (Zaltman, 2003). Cognitive maps serve as a shared visual representation of customer thinking, facilitating communication within a development team. It helps

---

[1] A concise resource for customer journey mapping is the *Design Thinking Toolbox: A Guide to Mastering the Most Popular and Valuable Innovation Methods* from Wiley (Lewrick et al., 2020).
[2] "Gen Z" is the commonly used term for the generation following Millennials. They are characterized by their digital nativism, diverse perspectives and a strong connection to social issues.

team members proactively agree on cognitive constructs and their relationships. The process of building these maps also assists in understanding each team member's perspectives and contributes to a more cohesive approach to customer needs assessment. Unlike other types of maps that are hierarchical, cognitive maps are more free-form.

Cognitive mapping is all about the visual identification of themes and patterns based on the core sentiments and beliefs of respondents. It creates a cognitive road map to how innovations will fit into the customer's mindset. Although qualitative in nature, it establishes not only the key mental constructs but forces the team to consider their relationships. As a result, this analysis tool can often uncover drivers and the strength of these relationships for use in unlocking higher-level (or gateway) constructs. Consequently, it can unearth strong themes and avenues for exploration before team ideation exercises. This technique is also very useful for markets where there may be a limited pool of experts available to interview or where small sample sizes (8–10) are available (International, 2023).

Why this approach? It provides a forum for the team to not just walk in the customer's shoes (i.e., journey mapping) but to journey through the customer's mind. It allows the team to see the world through the emotional, often illogical and messy biases of the customer to understand their decision-making processes. Once understood, this technique creates a focal point for subsequent ideation exercises and provides the basis for more advanced tools and techniques which will be discussed in subsequent chapters.

In practice, when individuals report back on their primary research findings, I ask them to summarize their thoughts and observations based on key cognitive constructs. As they present their findings, I often interrupt by asking "Given what you have just reported, what do you think are the cognitive processes at work"? We then put all of these on Post-it™ notes and begin to build a "straw man" version of the cognitive map. This is analogous to the d.school method of "saturate and group" (*Design Thinking Bootcamp Bootleg*, 2010). This leads to refining and grouping these "like" constructs and establishing their relationships. As more interviews are conducted, often the map almost appears to develop itself. It creates an interesting forum for discussion between interviewers who may interpret results differently. Once all interviews have been reported, a final review of the cognitive map provides a forum for feedback and refinement. This results in a collective understanding of insights. I then summarize by asking "So, what problem are we really trying to solve." Invariably, it is different than what the team began with. A case study for this is presented in Fig. 9.

Case Study – Handheld GPS

Many years ago, I led a multifunctional team charged with developing a high-end handheld GPS device. The company was in the aerospace business and had developed a significant amount of mapping technology and wanted to move from military applications into the consumer market. The mapping technology was state-of-the-art and far ahead of any consumer applications at the time.

The company's position was that its technology was so advanced that it would practically sell itself. Although there was some truth to this, in reality, customers wanted an "experience" that fit their mental model. The target customers were "outdoor enthusiasts" and "hunters and fishers"; the latter affectionately known as the "hook and bullet" segment. These segments cared as much about the look and feel of the product as the advanced technologies inside. After various forms of information gathering, we constructed a cognitive map; a simplified version looked something like this:

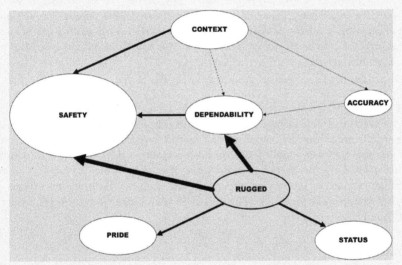

Fig. 9. Cognitive Map for Handheld GPS. *Source*: Entrepreneurial Techniques Across Disparate Industries, Management Roundtable, December 8, 2004, San Francisco, CA.

Once the map was agreed upon and examined, several things became clear. First was that the construct which represented "accuracy" (a source on which the firm prided itself) was of minimal importance and had mostly weak relationships within the mind of the customer. Without context, they felt like they were *lost with infinite precision*. What was more interesting was the construct described as "rugged" which had several strong relationships to higher-level emotional constructs. One of these constructs (i.e., safety) was by far the most dominant, since most customers stated that the only reason to take a GPS to the wilderness was for added safety (NOTE: we heard many horror stories). As the cognitive map highlights, rugged was clearly a gateway (or feeder) construct which could unlock other higher-level constructs.

Customers perceived that the more rugged the product was perceived, the safer they felt, the more pride of ownership they experienced and the more it enhanced their status within their community.

This was the point where the team had to ask themselves the tough question "What problem are we really needing to solve." As a result, the project and subsequent ideation exercises were refocused on creating the most rugged handheld GPS on the market, rather than improving accuracy and mapping features. Using the customer's mental association with other rugged products (i.e., benchmarks), the project was refocused on increasing the rugged look and feel.

Note: From an innovation management perspective, this map was created based on qualitative information gathered by the team. The impact (i.e., size) of each construct, their strength and directional relationship were all arbitrarily arrived at by team consensus using a simple heuristic approach (i.e., low, medium and high).

In practice, I always begin with cognitive mapping rather than storyboarding or customer journey mapping. The reason is quite simple – storyboarding or journey mapping should focus on how customers *think* and how this leads to *behavior*. Once the team agrees on a cognitive map, it may be helpful to create a storyboard or journey map for increased team buy-in. In my experience, a cognitive map creates a much richer and more useful schema to focus the ensuing ideation process.

Conclusion

This chapter outlines the approach to organizing, conducting and analyzing primary research. This process is first and foremost informed by properly executed background research which concentrates the team's efforts to be both *effective* and *efficient*. This plots the direction of inquiry allowing the team to concentrate on the central issues and keep them from drifting early in the process. Without this level of focus, many teams tend to lose control of the direction of these activities.

Background research then drives the team's development of a team-based interview guide grounded on the simple principle of *probe and learn* interviews. These types of interviews are open-ended, semi-structured and should be conducted by two team members from different backgrounds. They should be scheduled for 90 minutes (no less than 60 minutes) and preferably executed in the interviewee's environment. Interviewers should come prepared with agreed-upon visual cues depicting scenarios related to the topics at hand and used thoughtfully to probe for root causes. The results of the interview should be transcribed separately, directly after the interview and prepared as a crisp presentation for the team. Each interviewer should present their findings and with the help of the team, come to general conclusions on what the interview discovered and what the focus of the next interview should be. Adjustments and enhancements to the interview guide should be made as necessary in preparation for subsequent interviews. The team should then begin the process of cognitive mapping by highlighting discoveries from the interview using Post-it™ notes on a whiteboard. Preliminary groupings into "like" constructs and relationships can begin but should be limited at this point. Each interview should also be mapped to a specific color of Post-it™ notes for easier interpretation later.

As additional interviews are reported, the team can spend more time beginning the process of analysis. I highly recommend sticking to populating the cognitive map rather than other forms of storytelling at this point. Very quickly dominant and supporting themes begin to emerge and relationships begin to clarify themselves. It also becomes quite clear whether gathering more information from subsequent interviews will yield additional or new information. A good rule of thumb is to pause this process at 8–10 interviews and complete the cognitive map for analysis. At this point, the team may feel the necessity to create an additional visual in the form of a journey map if it helps them focus their thinking. At the conclusion of this process, the team should ask each team member one question – *What problem are we really trying to solve?* Once everyone has had their say, the *problem statement* should be adjusted to reflect this new learning. The team is then ready to enter the diverging (or ideation) part of the process[3].

---

[3]NOTE: In my experience, teams that find little reason to adjust their problem statement or merely make minor modifications, invariably fail to create any value-added innovations.

Chapter 7

Concept Development

Concept development is the most straight forward of all the innovation management processes. It is often linked with brainstorming, since there is a creativity component involved. Brainstorming itself has also become the most visible activity. Advocated by the proponents of Design Thinking, much attention has focused on the tools and techniques of conducting brainstorming sessions. Many of the effective techniques however can be traced back to Dr Edward de Bono and his seminal book on lateral thinking. He argues that brainstorming is merely a forum for ideation, and that team-based training is mandatory prior to any ideation activities. In addition, concept development must be viewed within a broader context since the objective is not to merely rely on generating novel solutions. Innovations must provide a differential advantage – they must be uniquely better than the customer's next best option(s). This chapter focuses on how to manage concept creation towards the development of uniquely better products or services.

Introduction

Concept development is the visible and exciting part of the innovation process. This is where creativity is employed to create something "novel." It is stimulating and often a strong team bonding exercise. Brainstorming (the most well-known ideation approach) has become the go-to technique for concept development. This has been driven mainly by the publicity of the IDEO Deep Dive video (*IDEO the Deep Dive*, 1997) and the subsequent advent of the Design Thinking (DT) movement. Most everyone is familiar with the classic rules of brainstorming – one thought at a time, don't critique ideas, build on other's ideas, etc. These are correct and considered a "must" for this type of activity. However, there is a deep-seated perception that creativity must be unfettered and free of constraints to avoid limiting ideas and concepts. Although generally correct, this can create its own set of problems unless the team is aware and committed to managing this process.

Brainstorming activities need to focus on superior value creation, not novelty for the sake of novelty. DT enthusiasts will argue that without crazy ideas, the

The Innovation Approach:
Overcoming the Limitations of Design Thinking and the Lean Startup, 107–120
Copyright © 2025 by David C. Roach
Published under exclusive licence by Emerald Publishing Limited
doi:10.1108/978-1-83797-799-420241007

team will never reach breakthrough concepts, since they won't have enough ideas to build upon. Although I agree with this sentiment, in practice what I often observe are teams believing, through either groupthink or poor management, that concepts must be "new to the world." This approach drives the process away from value creation, often in an irreversible direction. Even more concerning is the rush toward creative activities before (or based on incomplete) fact-finding activities from secondary research, benchmarking and primary research. This approach mostly results in the creation of an "idea bank," only tangentially related to the market category, with limited value creation for the end-user or decision-making unit (DMU).

This is not only a DT concern but extends to the Lean Startup (LS) approach as well. The LS, through its emphasis on business model innovation, tends to further short-circuit these activities. This results in marginal value-added concepts, combined with a rush to create a novel industry business model. They argue that incumbents are slow, lazy and out of touch, and through clever social media promotion combined with ICT technologies, they can replace traditional business models. Again, there is some merit to this argument, however as I will discuss in a subsequent chapter, there are heuristics (i.e., rules of thumb) that must be followed to assess the viability of any business model.

This chapter will discuss how to approach to concept development (i.e., diverging processes) and concept winnowing (i.e., converging processes).

Tools and Techniques

The ubiquitous IDEO Deep Dive video is an influential behind-the-scenes look at the front end of innovation (FEI) (*IDEO the Deep Dive*, 1997). In it, they popularized the concept of brainstorming to a point where it has become intricately linked with DT. It has also created a perception that creativity and innovation are synonymous.

I've been involved in concept generation and ideation since the late 1970s when I was introduced to it by a young engineering professor. In those days I considered myself an "innovative" person and generating a bunch of cool ideas was, in my opinion, the key to successful innovation. The more the better...the stranger the better...creativity was the key! I soon found out through the school of hard knocks, that ideas are a dime per dozen and that successful innovators rarely credit the *creativity of the idea* for their success. Since those early days, I literally embarked on becoming a scholar in the field.

Brainstorming

Concept *development* and *selection* are generally considered FEI activities. Concept development is a *diverging* activity, while concept selection is a *converging* activity. These activities involve more than creativity and the generation of numerous ideas. An article that caught my eye several years ago in the MIT Sloan Management Review summarized a lot of my observations of the FEI. In this article, the authors interviewed 54 senior managers across a wide spectrum of organizations (i.e., a heterogeneous sample) (Birkinshaw et al., 2011). They found expected issues ranging from the myths of the eureka moment to support for the bottom-up approach. However, it was the context that intrigued me. What they found was that companies were quite proficient at generating ideas inside and outside the organization and really didn't require help producing more. Interestingly however, they spent a significant amount of their resources at the FEI on idea generation. This raised two questions, namely "why" do they feel the need to do this and "where" should they be spending their capital? Their conclusion was that ideation and creativity exercises are highly visible and are perceived by senior management to be moving their innovation agenda forward. Where they needed help was winnowing down ideas – turning them into products or services and diffusing them throughout their organizations. Thus, what most companies were doing was *systematically bloating their innovation process*, creating an uncontrollable downstream problem. This not only plugged up their systems but became perceived by participants as management ignoring their hard work. This resulted in alienating the very people needed to conduct the critical follow-on work. Conclusion: generating more ideas *does not increase the efficiency or the effectiveness* of the innovation process.

One lesson I learned in academia was to examine the original source to fully understand any concepts. Almost invariably there are nuances, misinterpretations and in some cases wild claims that may or may not have transitioned to present-day understandings. Before doing research for this book, I had always gone back to my early source – Edward de Bono, most famous for the term "Lateral Thinking" (de Bono, 1977) and his later book entitled *The Six Thinking Hats* (de Bono, 1985). What I liked about his interpretation of brainstorming was his analogy of picturing the human brain as a mountain. Over millennia mountains become creased with rivers and waterfalls as the weather shapes the paths of precipitation. This is analogous to the brain, where over time based on tendencies, socialization and culture, people tend to follow well-worn paths when they make decisions. Their thought patterns will literally "waterfall" from a high level to a lower level almost instantaneously. What de Bono argued was that like water on a mountain, if you break the trajectory of the river, the water must go somewhere else, in essence creating new rivers and waterfalls. Using this analogy, he coined the term "Lateral Thinking" to inspire individuals to break away from traditional thought patterns and explore new perspectives. Both "Lateral Thinking" and to a lesser extent the "Six Thinking Hats" contribute to the divergent thinking process in brainstorming. They provide tools to expand the range of ideas, explore different angles and overcome cognitive biases that might limit creative thinking. This is why techniques like brainstorming work, since they are good at breaking ingrained patterns of thought, allowing for new areas to be explored that would otherwise not have come to the fore.

Digging deeper into brainstorming, it appears that the origin of the concept is attributed to advertising executive Alex F. Osborn who invented the technique to creatively solve advertising problems. He developed group thinking sessions which he termed "organized ideation." Participants later coined the term "brainstorm sessions" based on the use of "the brain to storm a problem" ("Brainstorming," 2024). In this rudimentary approach, Osborn stressed deferring judgment while striving for quantity. This necessitated withholding criticism and acceptance (if not encouragement) of wild ideas. Once the ideation portion of the session is complete, the next phase is to combine and improve upon generated ideas. He stressed that these activities should be guided by a *clear statement of the problem*, going so far as to say that sessions addressing multiple questions were inefficient if not inappropriate (Osborn, 1963).

Today, brainstorming has become the de facto standard for ideation and creativity exercises, but its power is only as good as its inputs and overall management. The standard rules today are generally attributed to IDEO who assembled their own set of principles and guidelines for creative collaboration and brainstorming. These include (not an exhaustive list and in no order) the encouragement of wild ideas, deferring judgment, building on the ideas of others and staying focused on the topic. This was combined with a culture of failing often to succeed sooner and iterative prototyping. Although these are good guidelines for group behavior, they don't delve into the inputs and management of the process itself. In my experience, inputs are often limited to team-based communication exercises (e.g., storyboarding), while management frequently presents as no management at all (i.e., little training, boundaries or constraints on the process). This results in a rush to ideation based on gratuitous inputs, followed by an open-ended creativity session. This is not a recipe for effectiveness.

DT enthusiasts will argue that there is a wealth of information that would refute my observations. They argue that properly trained team leaders, who follow the process and are collaborative and open-minded can use brainstorming to successfully generate creative ideas. Besides, there are many ways to conduct ideation and other effective means of generating concepts. All of this is correct but in practice the temptation of rushing to ideation exercises seems to be too seductive to pass up, resulting in undirected brainstorming in the guise of innovation. See the CASE STUDY – IDEO DEEP DIVE as an example of this process.

Lateral Thinking and Diverging

In my experience, successful brainstorming has three critical characteristics. First, the *problem must be properly defined* through a series of iterations before attempting any ideation activities. Based on informed background research, the problem statement must be refined (and redefined) until it is clear, succinct and targeted. Second, the participants in these sessions must be at least nominally trained in creative thinking techniques. This not only gives them tools from which they can approach idea development but can also be used by team leaders to direct the process within these sessions. Third, most participants should have been involved in the fact-finding activities generated through background research. This allows them to build upon the entire body of knowledge, bringing added fidelity to the process. These characteristics are where lateral thinking and brainstorming intersect.

According to Dr. de Bono, brainstorming is a type of *formal setting* for the use of lateral thinking (de Bono, 1977, p. 131). He emphasizes that it is not a special technique, but a *special setting* that encourages the application of lateral thinking.

Lateral thinking is primarily an individual endeavor, whereas brainstorming is a group activity. Brainstorming sessions provide a forum for cross-stimulation in a non-judgmental formal setting. In brainstorming, participants provide stimulation to others while at the same time receiving it. He believes there is a *skill set that must precede any formal setting* and that this can be taught through practice. Unfortunately, as he states, "such practice ought not to await formal organization but it very often does" (de Bono, 1977, p. 56). He also stresses that the purpose of the session is not actually to find "new" ideas, emphasizing that novelty is not necessarily what should be strived for during ideation sessions. Current ideas that are repurposed or merely improved upon are more often where novelty is created. He believes that groups who perceive that they are charged with coming up with new-to-the-world ideas, often result in failure. In summary, brainstorming is *only as effective as the ability of team members to employ proper ideation techniques.*

de Bono's remedy is to apply the various techniques he emphasizes which leads to lateral thinking. He breaks these down into two categories, namely *backward* and *forward*-thinking processes. Backward thinking involves generating alternatives and challenging assumptions. This stresses the rearrangement of activities while establishing a quota of alternatives. Forward-thinking processes refer to challenging status quo conventions by asking "why" to "known answers." Both processes are grounded by analysis of the problem space, or as he states, "ways of looking at things" (p. 93), rather than concept generation activities. He highlights several skills and techniques that he believes are necessary for *effective* innovation using these backward and forward-thinking processes. I will not list them all but will highlight the ones that I have found to be particularly useful in practice.

Dominant ideas refer to commonly accepted thoughts, assumptions or approaches that individuals tend to rely upon. Related are *crucial factors* which are the key variables considered critical within a given context. Dominant ideas are the organizing themes, while crucial factors are the tethering points around which dominant ideas are built (i.e., they are the drivers). In lateral thinking, the goal is to break away from the constraints of dominant ideas and crucial factors by engineering a different path. If one cannot pick out the dominant idea, one will be dominated by it (p. 108). In practice, teams before ideation should take the time to acknowledge the dominant ideas and what crucial factors underpin them. This can then become the theme for the brainstorming session. In practice, I have often used this approach in what I call "logic breakdown." Often when dealing with scientists, engineers or managers, I carefully listen to the linear (or vertical) approach to their logic chain. I then stimulate them by removing and reinserting a piece of the logic chain. With open-minded individuals, this can allow them to more comfortably go to a lateral logic chain which often reveals fruitful areas for innovation.

Fractionization is about breaking a problem into subcomponents. This may sound simple, but in practice, it can be more difficult than it appears. Ulrich and Eppinger (2019) recommend a version of this technique by breaking incumbent products into "chunks" of architecture. They then recommend ideating around these subcomponents or rearranging them into a unique configuration. Fractionization is not limited to tangible components but can be applied to needs, users or even perceptions. However, it is not always clear where to fraction ideas. de Bono recommends challenging the team to merely break any concept into two halves. Once this is accomplished, challenge them to break each half into two components. This quickly disassembles the problem and creates new avenues to guide ideation activities. One technique that I have successfully used is to challenge teams to only generate concepts that can be assembled from existing (off-the-shelf) components. When concepts are then assessed, it clearly highlights areas of uncertainty and where to concentrate the next steps of the process. For an example, see the CASE STUDY – IDEO DEEP DIVE later in this chapter.

Reversal is a well-recognized and useful approach to ideation activities. I am however always surprised by how little it is used and how poorly it is applied. It allows for flipping conventional thinking by considering the opposite of accepted ideas or reversing the normal sequence of events to generate new perspectives. de Bono uses the example of a swimmer pushing off against a bulkhead to make a turn. The swimmer uses the bulkhead to produce an equal and opposite force. This provides power for the swimmer to create momentum. By reversing how the problem is perceived (i.e., the bulkhead provides the force rather than the swimmer), new alternatives can be envisioned. This is probably the most useful tool I have used over the decades to move teams from traditional linear thinking to a parallel (i.e., lateral) path. As an example, we developed a groundbreaking technology used in general anesthesia to remove CO_2 from the patient's re-breathing circuit. The "dominant" process was anchored by a "crucial factor" known as absorption. By reversing the problem from absorption to filtration, the solution became evident. The solution was to sequester expensive and ozone-depleting anesthesia vapors, rather than binding CO_2 using a chemical reaction. I can say without reservation that reversal works virtually every time and invariably has led to aspects of concepts that have created superior value.

Analogies are simple stories or descriptions of situations designed to provide movement in the ideation process. As an example, de Bono uses a snowball rolling down a hill as an analogy for how a rumor spreads. Once a simple analogy is created, alternate viewpoints can be brought to the table. For instance, what if there isn't snow, what if one could get out of the way, etc. Analogies provide renewed direction to the brainstorming process and can often unlock alternate paths that would otherwise go unexplored.

Entry point refers to how the problem is approached or the first point of entry. It stimulates creativity by introducing unrelated concepts or ideas into the problem-solving process to stimulate fresh thinking. It refers to the part of the problem (usually the most obvious) that must be attended to first. It relies on patterns of established memory which are not conducive to restructuring linear patterns into lateral thinking. He provides several examples related to geometry; however, other examples are more pertinent. In more practical examples he goes out of his way to highlight "missing information" which can include the story, the picture or the context. I have always relied upon the usability model to determine the entry point based on the environment, task or the individual. For instance, if the logical entry point is the individual, I will reframe the entry point as the environment. This is one of the shortcomings of DT since in practice most entry points are based on the individual given its user-centric approach.

Lastly, de Bono emphasizes the role of what he calls the "chairman," which we now refer to as the "team lead." The chairman's responsibility is to find new ways to approach the problem using different lateral thinking techniques to stimulate the group. The role must include pulling people back to the central problem statement, otherwise the group may drift in a totally different direction. He stresses that *how* the problem is formulated can make an enormous difference in the outcome. The problem must be concisely stated at the beginning of the session. This often leads to incremental clarification during the session. He stresses that these sessions should be roughly 20–30 minutes in duration but no more than 45 minutes. Since people often have ideas post-session, there also needs to be a way to incorporate these prior to concept selection (p. 137). This is why he stresses that evaluation sessions should never be held on the same day as the brainstorming session! He breaks the evaluation process down into four components: directly useful, interesting approach, further examination and discard. But more on that later.

de Bono highlights many other skills including random provocation, stimulation, polarization and aspects of design. However, the five listed earlier I have found to be the most practical. All of these are designed to create movement in the ideation process that is traditionally associated with brainstorming. These techniques aim to break free from traditional linear thinking and encourage individuals to explore unconventional paths to problem-solving. The brainstorming process however is only as effective as the skill level of the team members, the clarity of the problem to be addressed and the ability of team leadership to manage the process in a positive direction. Lateral thinking techniques are designed to align all of these challenges, providing momentum to *move the ideation process forward*.

While writing this book, I re-read many of the chapters in his book and it occurred to me that I've been applying Dr. de Bono's lateral thinking principles almost unconsciously for most of my career. I very often interject in group brainstorming activities and challenge the team to explore different approaches to ideation when things are drifting. One aspect that I will improve on is preparing teams by employing "warm-up" exercises to get them to think laterally as de Bono suggests. This is something I will adjust on my next project.

Case Study – IDEO Deep Dive

The NBC Nightline video – The Deep Dive (*IDEO the Deep Dive*, 1997) is probably the most famous description of what is now considered Design Thinking. David Kelly, the founder of IDEO, narrates the video as he describes to the audience their innovation process. To illustrate their process, he agrees with NBC to take an everyday product – the shopping cart and redesign it in five days. He and his team are quick to point out that they would never put that kind of timeline on a project, but they would agree for demonstration purposes.

When I ask my students what they observe by watching this video, I invariably get the same set of responses. They see a "cool" work environment where everyone gets along. They love the counterculture philosophy and the apparent playfulness. They see a supportive boss who doesn't punish people for failures. When I ask about their process, they focus directly on the brainstorming session where people are coming up with wild ideas, drawing, building objects and shooting Nerf balls. When I ask them what else they see, they jump directly to the final solution seeing any interim steps as an extension of the brainstorming process. I then ask them to watch the video again with a critical eye concentrating on their process. We then have a lengthy group discussion summarized as follows.

As discussed previously, their process starts with background secondary research. Although they do show some statistics (e.g., number of accidents involving shopping carts), they are more interested in problems, trends, issues and challenges. Statistics are used to support these findings rather than support market size and growth rates. They also do a rudimentary form of benchmarking by examining a competitive shopping cart where David Kelly jokes about the child seat where it says "be safe" (NOTE: safety becomes one of their key focuses). They then conduct primary research where they employ probe and learn interviews, combined with observation. These activities are guided by their background research which *informs and directs* their investigation. For instance, they probe into the theme of safety with the maintenance person, while others anthropologically observe "native" shoppers in their environment while performing their tasks. They then return to headquarters with what they refer to as the "golden keys of innovation" and share their knowledge with their peers through verbal and non-verbal means (e.g., rough prototype descriptions or drawings). These are for internal communication rather than outside feedback and to the naked eye resemble a continuation of the initial brainstorming session. In some ways it is, but in other ways it is different. This knowledge-sharing becomes a building block for improving initial ideas. The team then uses what can only be described as a qualitative and subjective voting system where team members vote on concepts using Post-it™ notes while suggesting improvements. Although it likely occurs off-camera, these concepts are then lumped together into "like" categories, since many have similarities. This is the transition from *diverging* processes to *converging* processes where concepts enter a refinement stage. At this stage, David Kelly and a team of "grown-ups" gather to determine how to guide (i.e., create boundaries) around the next phase. They agree that sub-teams will each take on a "needs" area as the focus of developing their concept into a comprehensive (i.e., integrated) prototype. Importantly, they did not create boundaries based on technology, consumer segments or the best ideas but on focused *needs*.

Our exercise often lasts over an hour as we discuss and review critical sections of the video. Students later comment that there is much more to IDEO's process than they thought and that there is a systematic way to approach creativity, ideation and concept development. I ask them whether they think the environment/culture or process has more to do with the success. The results are mixed, but they all invariably agree that the process is a major part of IDEOs success. Finally, I ask them how long this type of process would usually take in practice. They tend to gravitate toward 12–16 weeks – coincidentally roughly the length of their semester.

Note: This examines the IDEO process over a compressed timeframe and does not do justice to the iterative nature of their system. As more information is gathered and new evidence is accumulated, it is not unusual to revisit steps in the process.

Converging

Converging on concepts is probably the most difficult step in the FEI. There are several reasons for this which range from small-p political issues, difficulty in selecting the "best" concept, transitioning from ideation to product, dearth of customer input and so on. As stated earlier, ideation is the fun and overt part of the process, but it must eventually come to an end. The question is how and when, while trying to eliminate structural bias.

All innovation projects can suffer from what is kindly referred to as the "alpha dog" (or Alpha) syndrome. These are charismatic individuals who are assertive and have strong leadership propensities. They often take initiative, drive the team forward and are not afraid to take risks or share their opinions. These qualities are essential in the *diverging* process but can often be counterproductive in the *converging* process. These individuals frequently have a strong belief in their own solutions and are effective at marshaling allies in the direction they want the project to go. Their dominant personality can overshadow more introspective members who feel that their input is immaterial since the decisions are a "fait accompli." If the Alpha solutions are selected, they pour themselves into *their vision* of the outcome. If their solutions are not selected, they tend to covertly grumble and check-out or be disruptive to the next steps of the process.

Next is what is often referred to as paralysis by analysis. This slang phrase is used to describe the inability to make decisions due to overthinking a problem. It often happens when dealing with too many variables while continually searching in vain for perfect solutions rather than acting. The nature of the FEI as stated repeatedly through this book is fraught with uncertainty and vagueness. The front end is a systematic process of reducing uncertainty to the point where risk can be assessed. Risk is the quantification of uncertainty based on probabilities and impact. Risk-averse teams are not comfortable with uncertainty and are intolerant of decisions that they cannot quantify. This is why the exploration of entrepreneurship became so receptive to the theory of effectuation (Sarasvathy, 2001). Effectuation is at its core an uncertainty management approach, where risk is structured from an affordable loss perspective, rather than a traditional causational approach (Ryman & Roach, 2024).

Closely related is the perception of the dearth of customer input. Advocates of this approach fail to understand the nature of the FEI. They are often the business-related members of the team who align with marketing, finance or general management. This has both functional and historical related aspects. Historically, finance gets involved at the project *selection* stage, where they review project budgets and conduct return on investment (ROI) calculations. They seek to establish financing requirements based on capital versus operational requirements resulting in project payback. They incorrectly assume that the FEI has already, or inevitably will, produce a value-added, differentiated product whose costs and revenues can be reasonably estimated. For comfort, they typically draw on previous projects to sanction their calculations. Marketing on the other hand seeks to understand the value proposition and how the product will be differentiated in the marketplace. In both cases, when they can't get a comfort level with the state of the product-market match, they inevitably request more "customer validation" before they can proceed.

Although many more issues impact the converging process, these are the essential ones. Thus, what are the options for the management of this part of the process? There are two classic approaches – one *quantitative* and the other *qualitative* which I will discuss in the next section. However, philosophically both involve examining the transition from diverging to converging through an iterative approach. I liken this to solving a mathematical equation with two unknowns. To put it in a modern context, I'll liken it to an algorithm with two inputs and one output. When solving such a problem, you need to hold one input steady while you adjust the other, then measure the output against a target value. Since algorithms are a complex set of parameters within a "black box," changing one input and measuring the output results in a discrepancy. You can then adjust one or the other input and rerun the algorithm. This continues until the output reaches a near-optimum solution. Bringing this back to concept development, at some point teams need to freeze their concept, test it against user feedback and then decide if they want to adjust the concept or adjust the profile of the user. This iterative approach continues until a "near" product-market match is reached.

Thus, no matter what the level of uncertainty, at some point the team needs to temporarily freeze their concept to begin the converging process. To resolve these dilemmas, both qualitative and quantitative approaches have been developed.

Quantitative Approach

There is a school of thought that quantifying criteria for each concept based on an aggregate score is the objective way to select concepts (Ulrich & Eppinger, 2012). This approach creates a list of requirements developed throughout the fact-finding activities. They are often categorized based on "must have," "should have" and "nice to have" criteria. Each requirement is ranked on a scale (normally low=0 to high=5). Team members vote individually on each concept with the top-scoring concept sanctioned by the team. There is often some give and take where concepts may be merged or adjusted before final designs are voted upon. Since there can be concepts whose scores can be very close, adjustments can involve creating a run-off where the lowest concept is dropped and a revote occurs. Another method is to create a weighted system, where certain criteria carry more weight than others (e.g., "must have" criteria would be weighted higher than "nice to have"). At first glance, this type of process would appear to be the most rational, unbiased and objective approach to converging on concepts. This might be true if it were not for human behavior. So, what is wrong with this method?

First, at this stage of the process requirements are by default incomplete. Thus, voting on incomplete information already adds a level of uncertainty. Second, the team needs to agree on the hierarchy of requirements. For instance, what are must-have, etc. This process is often ripe for "gaming" where Alpha individuals, or even worse – senior management, arrange criteria to favor the outcome of their choice. This is particularly acute when weighted criteria are introduced. This approach is hailed as removing the subjectivity inherent in team decision-making, when in fact it often ends up being a biased approach masquerading as an objective assessment. Third, no matter what checks and balances are used, this approach which appears to be quantitative is merely *quantifying the qualitative*. Thus, rather than executing an unbiased, objective and streamlined approach, this methodology often acts more like a coronation.

Qualitative Approach

To counter the inherent problems of seemingly quantitative approaches, many rely on more qualitative means. These approaches rely on the strength and collaborative nature of the team, where individuals are trusted to make consensus decisions in the best interest of the project. In the IDEO video, the interviewer asks the team leader why he is not responsible for making the final decision. He responds that it is unlikely that he (or any other individual for that matter) would have the experience and insights to make this judgment call. He defers to the team which he deeply believes will make the right decision. Individuals are asked to vote by suggesting improvements to core concepts, a technique that acts as both a vote of confidence and an enhancement process. This process is purely subjective and qualitative in nature. However, if we map it to the concept scoring system discussed previously, it intuitively makes more sense. First, it blatantly confesses that it is a subjective and qualitative approach, forcing management to reach a comfort level with qualitative information for decision making. Unlike scoring systems, it does not pretend to "quantify the qualitative," leading management into a false comfort level. Next, it is less susceptible to the alpha syndrome since it does not rely on a set of predetermined requirements that can be engineered to produce a desired outcome. Finally, it relies on the deep tacit knowledge developed by the team throughout the background research process leading up to concept development. This takes advantage of the nuances of each concept that do not necessarily translate through an arbitrary scoring system.

As with most systems, it is not without its problems. It still relies on human nature with all the subtle cultural, behavioral and psychological interactions that can influence the selection process. However, in my experience, it is vastly better than arbitrary scoring systems.

Concept Selection

Concept selection represents the end-result of each innovation cycle. It is not to be confused with concept evaluation, the focus of the next chapter. Concept selection is the result of a linear cycle of background research (secondary and benchmarking), primary research and concept development. It produces what the team believes has the qualities of a successful solution with characteristics of desirability, feasibility and viability. Since none of these aspects have been established, often these "fledgling concepts" are strong on desirability but weaker on feasibility and viability. Using the methods described in this chapter, the team selects one or two of these concepts they believe are worthy of evaluation. This begins the iterative transition from one innovation cycle to the next. For instance, the initial concept(s) emanating from the *discovery phase* will be evaluated and form the basis for the *adoption phase* and so on. A case example is presented in Fig. 10.

Case Study – Wakeup Light

Several years ago, I convinced a local company to work with my graduate innovation management class on a new concept which they termed a Wakeup Light. This type of light would use their proprietary lighting technology and know-how, to create a clinically valid treatment for people with seasonal affective disorder (SAD). New research from Columbia University indicated that this type of treatment had the potential to be as effective as bright light therapy. This could be a breakthrough in this type of treatment since it was much more convenient for users.

The initial problem statement was:

To provide a clinically relevant "wakeup" light for individuals with seasonal affective disorder – SAD.

The students were challenged to provide the background research (secondary and benchmarking), while the company undertook customer listening exercises. Once this was complete, students, company officials and even the key researcher from Columbia were brought together for an ideation exercise.

INPUTS

Secondary research (uncovered themes; convenience, clinical support, environment)

Benchmarking (included best practices in lighting technology)

Primary research (confirmed themes and uncovered convenience, accessories, alternate methods)

These inputs resulted in refining the *problem statement* which drove *divergent* and *convergent* activities. The problem statement is a dynamic activity where the problem is refined as more information becomes available. If done correctly, it results in increasing the effectiveness of the process by focusing on "doing the right thing right."

The refined problem statement was as follows:

To provide a clinically relevant "wakeup" light for individuals with seasonal affective disorder – SAD, that enhances their sleeping environment.

PROCESS

Diverging: The ideation process took the form of a brainstorming session
Converging: Voting (dot voting) with suggested improvements

OUTPUT
Three fledgling concepts resulted from ideation activities. These became the concepts that transitioned to the evaluation stage between phases.

In the figure, focused – analytical prototyping was used to evaluate aesthetics, lighting options and supporting technologies (e.g., clock radio, audio, wireless).

Fig. 10.   Wakeup Light Concepts.

NOTE: For more detailed information on the process, see Roach (2007).

Conclusion

Any ideation method will always be at the mercy of working on the *right problem*, the *skills of the team* and the *management* of the process. Problem definition is the result of proper background (fact-finding) research. As the old saying goes... luck comes to the prepared mind. So, it is with ideation...good results evolve from preparation. Ideation exercises like brainstorming are only as fruitful as the collective skill set of the team. A well-trained team will approach the ideation process from a strong position creating a much more effective process with stronger results. Managing the team to stay on topic and prompting them when necessary is as much art as it is skill and experience. However, when all these aspects come together, the results can be spectacular.

Chapter 8

Concept Evaluation and the MVP

Concept evaluation is a critical step in the innovation cycle, extending beyond initial concept selection to assess desirability, feasibility and viability. Evaluating the three most prominent approaches to concept evaluation the Stage Gate™ approach, Lean Startup (LS) and Design Thinking (DT) reveals several best practices. Each methodology offers unique perspectives and techniques with varying strengths and weaknesses. The Stage Gate™ method emphasizes predefined criteria and staged evaluations. The LS prioritizes hypothesis-driven experimentation to validate business models. DT focuses on human-centered design, emphasizing desirability. To be effective, concept evaluation should be performed between innovation cycles at the transitions between phases of the innovation approach. A more effective model for evaluation is then proposed, which simultaneously tests desirability, feasibility and viability. An approach to prototyping and testing hypotheses is recommended.

Introduction

Although concept selection was discussed in the previous chapter, concept evaluation is a more involved process. Concept selection is based primarily on the team choosing a solution that (i) best meets the criteria developed through the innovation cycle and (ii) best meets the current problem statement. It has more to do with the potential *desirability* of the concept rather than its feasibility or viability.

Concept evaluation dives deeper into these other aspects. *Feasibility* generally involves whether there are technical (i.e., design), operational (e.g., resource issues) or process-related (e.g., partner/supply chains) challenges. It requires the team to evaluate the uncertainty and risk profile of the fledgling concept. *Viability*, on the other hand, requires an evaluation of the economics of the concept. Initially, this should involve establishing a plausible business model, eventually leading to some form of business plan. Together, these form the basis for managing uncertainty and the foundation for hypothesis development and testing.

This chapter will first review various approaches to concept evaluation and conclude by proposing an approach to determining the desirability, feasibility and viability of concepts as they migrate through the phases of the innovation approach (i.e., the Innovation Helix).

The Innovation Approach:
Overcoming the Limitations of Design Thinking and the Lean Startup, 121–130
Copyright © 2025 by David C. Roach
Published under exclusive licence by Emerald Publishing Limited
doi:10.1108/978-1-83797-799-420241008

Evaluation Models

Three methodologies (or approaches) should be considered when approaching concept evaluation. First is the classic Stage Gate™ approach pioneered by Dr. Robert Cooper. The others are, unsurprisingly, Design Thinking (DT) and the Lean Startup (LS).

Stage Gate™ Approach

The Stage Gate™ approach uses several criteria as part of its assessment (Cooper, 1986). First and foremost is what it refers to as *market potential*, which speaks to the desirability of the concept. In the initial innovation phases, this is (i) based on alignment with customer needs and (ii) an evaluation of the competitive space. This first involves determining how well the concept addresses the identified needs and preferences of the potential target market. It next consists of an assessment of the position of the product or service relative to the competitive offerings. Of note, early in the process, market size and growth rates are generally disregarded since the target audience is still relatively imprecise. Next is *technical feasibility*. This assesses the level of uncertainty associated with implementing the technology and considers technical challenges, obstacles and availability of expertise. *Financial viability* involves an assessment of traditional cost accounting techniques. These include cost-benefit analyses and return on investment (ROI) calculations. The former is the overall cost of developing and implementing the concept compared to expected financial returns. The latter involves evaluating the projected economic gains in relation to invested resources. These calculations, however, are very subjective and often highly inaccurate at the front end of innovation (FEI), where the concept and target audience are moving targets. In Dr. Cooper's defense, these initial financial models are meant to begin the refinement process as more information becomes available. Lastly, the methodology stresses *strategic fit* with the organization. This is an assessment of how well the concept aligns with the overall goals and strategic direction of the enterprise. It aligns projects with the company's mission and objectives while assessing the fit with the organization's risk tolerance and portfolio requirements.

Each test grows progressively more detailed and involved as the innovation process unfolds. The Stage Gate™ approach conducts this evaluation between *stages* of the process, which they refer to as *gates*. Stages are where the action occurs, while the gates are where decisions are made. One of Cooper's nuggets of wisdom is that gate criteria should be agreed upon at the beginning of each stage. This sets the foundation for work targeting these gate criteria during the stage. It also minimizes "gaming" of criteria and/or dynamically establishing criteria as the stage evolves. One key criterion is the "kill" option, where teams must decide if the concept merits moving to the next stage. The ability to kill a poor-performing concept is not discussed in any depth with the other two approaches.

Lean Startup

The LS methodology encourages concept evaluation based on the development and testing of hypotheses (Ries, 2011). Although not as structured as the Stage Gate™ approach, it does approach this process from a business perspective. Its prime objective is to establish a viable business model, where the product's desirability and feasibility are seen as components of the model. As such, it is highly business model-centric, resulting in a lesser focus on the qualities of the innovation.

From a desirability perspective, the LS begins from the premise that the entrepreneurial team has a respectable idea that merely needs to be fine-tuned. Through customer validation exercises, the team attempts to validate whether there is a genuine need for the concept by engaging potential customers. This they argue will lead to perfecting the concept and will expose any product-market gaps. This spawns a series of hypothesis-driven experimentation exercises that lead to product improvements or adjustments. They contend that this build–measure–learn cycle will eventually resolve outstanding product–market fit issues. The result should produce a differentiated, value-added product or service.

From a feasibility perspective, the argument is much the same. Through hypothesis development, minimal viable product (MVP) prototypes are created, leading to the identification of technical obstacles that will be resolved as the process evolves. Pivots are used to adjust the concept as necessary until the concept is robust enough to "persevere" down the perceived path. Using this approach, they argue that this build–measure–learn cycle will eventually resolve any outstanding technical issues.

Their focus never strays very far from the business model, where many other aspects are tested through the same process. Value they assert will be created by listening to customers and incorporating their feedback. Technical feasibility will be resolved through MVP testing and prototype development. Building on these, viability can then be established through verifying customer acquisition costs, resource requirements, pricing and the cost model. The objective is to evolve a viable business model which is ready for scalable growth. This then activates the next phase, where customer acquisition cost, conversion rates and retention rates are monitored through key metrics. Other growth factors include human resource requirements, partnerships and promotional activities.

The methodology is generally sparse on details of how to execute these steps, relying on the capability of team members to (i) identify the correct hypothesis to test, (ii) execute a research methodology to confirm or refute the hypothesis and (iii) implement meaningful changes. The main flash of brilliance in the LS is its emphasis on hypothesis-driven gap resolution supported by MVP testing.

Design Thinking

DT is a human-centered approach to problem-solving and innovation that emphasizes empathy, ideation and prototyping (*Design Thinking Bootcamp Bootleg*, 2010). At its core, it is a concept development approach that purports to base evaluation on desirability, feasibility and viability. In contrast to the LS, DT is a desirability-centric approach that relies heavily on the user experience.

Desirability is determined through testing the interaction between the user and the product. It is based on evaluating how well the concept enhances the overall user experience and addresses challenges or frustrations they may face. They stress the need for testing with representatives of the personas that they have developed through the process. This they contend establishes the differentiated value proposition, which unlocks both the feasibility and viability aspects of the innovation. Many techniques are suggested to accomplish this goal. They include but are not limited to solution interviews, usability testing and/or A/B testing (Lewrick et al., 2020).

Feasibility is approached from the same perspective. Like the LS's emphasis on rapid and iterative prototyping, they acknowledge that any technical challenges or oversights will be uncovered and resolved as users are exposed to "hi-fi" (i.e., comprehensive) prototypes. This also implies that any resolutions can be implemented with available resources and technology. As a result, the evaluation of technical feasibility does not have the same profile as the needs-based desirability criteria. This can result in overestimating the feasibility aspects of concepts.

Viability relates to the concept's economic and business prospects. In DT this is weak since the methodology is not really designed to fully address this aspect. As stated in Chapter 3, one of the key components of the innovation definition is the concept of "success." Whether success is commercial or social is immaterial, since both must have a viable business model to be executable. DT purports to cover some aspects of viability, but in most cases, this merely involves establishing rough prices and costs. It does not delve into determining and evolving a business model.

DT's superpower is in its focus on value creation through satisfying unmet needs or improving existing solutions.

Evaluation Approach

In this book's proposed approach, evaluation occurs between innovation cycles, where fledgling concepts are recommended for evaluation prior to (or in conjunction with) the next cycle. Evaluation requires testing in three specific areas: namely, desirability, feasibility and viability.

Several best practices can be garnered from the previous section's analysis. The Stage Gate™ method is the broadest approach covering all three areas. Its strength is in its approach to setting criteria prior to the execution of the next stage. It effectively targets the areas of uncertainty in each of these three categories and generally establishes the testing framework by which the criterion will be assessed. Although it does not use the terminology of hypothesis testing, it works similarly. The LS's strength is in its business model focus and its emphasis on creating MVP tests to confirm or refute the hypothesis. Its weakness lies in its cavalier approach to desirability and feasibility. DT, on the other hand, is strong on desirability evaluation but weak on the other two aspects.

Consequently, an effective system of evaluation would ideally incorporate the best of each methodology while remaining effective, efficient and agile.

Viability

Following our proposed model, each innovation cycle results in a proposed fledgling model that must be evaluated. This evaluation must be assessed using three criteria: desirability, feasibility and viability. The evaluation must result in one of four outcomes. These include continuing to the next phase (i.e., a go decision), halting the project (i.e., a kill decision), conditional continuation (i.e., a pivot) or pause (i.e., a hold decision). The innovation approach is about the *FEI*, where the objective is to create a differentiated, value-added product or service ready for business development. This is normally considered a "up to a gate 3" under the Stage Gate™ system, the transition point to the development of a business case. This also roughly aligns with the LS methodology, where the transition point is a business model that is ready for early adopter testing. The fundamental difference between these two methods is the approach to assessing viability. The Stage Gate™ method emphasizes cost-benefit analysis and ROI calculations, while the LS emphasizes the business model. This is where I suggest that there are *hierarchy* and *timing* differences that come into play. For hierarchy, I refer to steps that build upon each other. For instance, ROI calculations really cannot be prepared appropriately divorced from the business model. Cost-benefit analysis however can be conducted prior to business modeling since its outcomes will impact the business model. This results in a *timing difference* since logically cost-benefit analysis must inform the business model. Thus, the cost-benefit analysis should be conducted after the first innovation cycle (i.e., discovery), the business model after the second innovation cycle (i.e., adoption), the ROI after the third innovation cycle (i.e., Lead User) and finally business planning following the fourth innovation cycle (i.e., sustainability).

One departure between these two methods is the ultimate test criteria. The Stage Gate™ method relies on an upfront contract with the team, where criteria are decided before the stage work begins. The LS, however, dynamically creates criteria based on their hypotheses. This is likely why no "kill" option is built into the LS since the process is fluid and decision-making dynamic. This is one of its shortcomings since the only remedy they provide for poor concepts is to *persevere* and *pivot*.

In any event, for viability testing I prefer hypotheses-driven criteria where the project scope can remain fluid until the four phases of the innovation approach are completed. At this point, viability testing should determine whether the concept should be a "go," "hold," "pivot" or "kill" decision. Business model development will be covered in detail in Chapter 14.

Desirability

Desirability is best modeled after the DT approach. Following concept development and selection, testing for perceived value, usability and differentiation are all necessary to establish the evolving desirability of the product or service. Many approaches, as described earlier, are employed by DT enthusiasts. However, I will argue that there are also *hierarchy* and *timing* differences that must be considered. For instance, there is not much benefit to performing usability test-ing when the concept is still in its infancy unless it is highly focused and narrow in scope. Thus, certain tests must precede others as the process unfolds. After the initial innovation (discovery) cycle, solution interviews are adequate since the objective is to confirm that the team has interpreted the information cor-rectly and that their fledgling concept addresses the main concerns of the target audience. After the second phase (i.e., the adoption cycle), when the concept is slightly more refined, deeper insights can be gained. This continues into the next cycle, where MVPs are more comprehensive and tangible, at which point full A/B testing may be appropriate. Specifically, this testing should be *relative to the customer's next best option* or benchmark. Finally, as the FEI concludes, usability testing is appropriate based on an MVP that has the characteristics of a comprehensive "Alpha" prototype. Prototyping will be discussed in greater detail at the end of this section.

Feasibility

Feasibility is fundamentally about assessing technical challenges and having the ability to bring the appropriate resources to the project. It must also be evaluated from a *hierarchical* and *timing* perspective. Thus, depending on the appropriateness and uncertainty profile of the technology, some level of feasi-bility assessment will be required. The hierarchy, in this case, refers to the level of challenge presented. A fledgling concept that integrates known technolo-gies into a new configuration presents little technical uncertainty. A concept that relies on complex or emerging technologies can present significant levels of uncertainty. Also, the availability of skills and experience must be considered. For instance, a concept that relies on artificial intelligence (AI) suffers from an extreme dearth of skills since human resources are scarce as demand outstrips supply. This poses two risks: lack of human resources and the generally poor quality of skills available.

One of the techniques I have successfully used over the decades is challenging the team to build concepts from scratch using only currently available solutions. This approach quickly highlights two fundamental aspects of feasibility. First, whatever aspects of the concept that cannot be obtained "off the shelf" swiftly underscores the major source of often "research-related" uncertainty[1]. Second, the interface interactions between "chunks" of architecture become visible, exposing the source of many "development" challenges. Uncertainty can then be candidly assessed (i.e., is it research versus development) which become the driv-ers for hypotheses development and testing.

---

[1]NOTE: this also quickly exposes gaps in resources, knowledge and skills of technical individuals on the team when they fail to deliver even basic functionality. They will often fall back on barriers of time limitations, lack of appropriate materials or other responsibilities. However, failure to provide workable off-the-shelf proof of concept is usually a red flag.

Prototyping and the MVP

Each testing level must correspond with both a *hypothesis* and a *testing* methodology. In my experience, the development of hypotheses, although involved, often comes down to the team's assessment of what is most important. There are always more questions than answers at the FEI, and the team must prioritize. Some questions are also *dependent* since they must be answered prior to determining which questions to ask for the next dependent task. For instance, a popular approach is to try to determine pricing or intent to buy. These are extremely difficult questions to answer at the best of times. However, they are *dependent* on the aggregate *value proposition* of the concept. In the early stages, both the value proposition and the target audience are moving targets thus creating a hypothesis and testing plan to answer such a question is normally an exercise in futility. A more appropriate approach would be to create a hypothesis about the relative value of the concept vis-à-vis some benchmark. A test can then be developed that most effectively answers this question. Suffice to say that hypothesis development is often a self-evident activity when managed by an informed team. As a result, it is more appropriate to focus on how to properly test hypotheses through prototyping (a.k.a. the MVP).

There are two aspects that must be considered when approaching the development of the MVP. The first is which phase of the process the concept inhabits. Is the concept the result of Phase A: Discovery or Phase D: Sustainability? The further downstream in the activity, the more fidelity is required of the prototype. At the discovery phase, only simple (directional) questions can typically be answered. Toward the end of the process, answers to much more detailed questions can be gathered. Second, is determining the type of prototype required to answer the question. There are many forms of prototypes, as highlighted in Fig. 11. The vectors of prototyping range on the *x*-axis from *focused* to *comprehensive* and on the *y*-axis from *analytical* to *physical* (Ulrich & Eppinger, 2012). Examining each axis individually, the earlier the concept, the more focused the prototype (or MVP) should be. Later stages of concept development should be more comprehensive in nature. Similarly, early stages lend themselves to more analytical prototypes rather than physical ones. These are general rules of thumb but should be kept in mind as the team decides how to approach their testing plans.

Fig. 11 highlights typical examples of prototyping in each quadrant. In the *focused–analytical* quadrant, typical prototypes cover the spectrum from CAD renderings to performance criteria or virtual A/B tests. In the *focused–physical* quadrant, prototypes include such things as ergonomic studies, 3D prints or graphical user interface (GUI) designs. In the *analytical–comprehensive* quadrant simulations, conjoint studies or advanced A/B testing are typical. The *physical–comprehensive* quadrant is best expressed as the classic "Alpha" prototype, which is a physical and functioning representation of the product. It comes with limited features but is considered to "look like" and "work like" a real product. Fig. 11 proposes the recommended sequence of activities, represented by the arrows. For a more comprehensive discussion, please refer to Ulrich and Eppinger (2012).

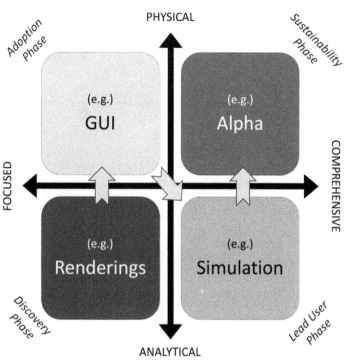

Fig. 11.   Types of Prototypes. *Source*: Adapted from Ulrich and Eppinger (2012).

Both DT and LS highly encourage building tangible artifacts as part of their system. These can range from wireframe mockups to 3D-printed representations of concepts. Often, there is an implied push to more comprehensive prototypes early in the exploration of concepts. The LS's drive for agility, speed, and efficiency often yields a comprehensive approach to prototyping. This can result in MVP tests suffering from confirmation bias[2] rather than input for concept improvement. Although this contravenes the spirit of MVP testing, in practice, this can significantly skew results. Conversely, in DT, confusion about the use of these more tangible artifacts can occur. The primary purpose of tangible artifacts early in the innovation process is internal communication. Using these for external feedback too early in the process is often detrimental to effective testing.

Prototyping Approach

A few decades ago, I was introduced to the concept of *vicarious prototyping* at an executive program at Harvard Business School. The faculty challenged us to use

---

[2]Confirmation bias, a phrase coined by English psychologist Peter Wason, is the tendency of people to favor information that confirms or strengthens their beliefs or values and is difficult to dislodge once affirmed (Plous, 1993).

this concept to expedite learning in the innovation process. First was the notion that small and more frequent prototyping was more effective than less frequent but more involved prototyping. Second, prototypes were not merely the purview of the R&D department, but focal points for learning for the whole organization and project. If teams are to go through the exercise of creating a prototype, why not have it answer multiple questions at the same time? This challenge necessitated a shift in attention from comprehensive prototyping to more focused approaches. One of the group exercises involved how to use this philosophy in practice to expedite learning and, therefore, decision-making.

When I returned from the MIT corridor, it occurred to me that for this approach to be successful, it required creativity in its implementation. Since then, I have regularly used Fig. 11 to challenge teams to come up with prototyping ideas. Using the themes of desirability, feasibility and viability, the challenge is to come up with prototyping ideas that cover all four quadrants of this prototyping framework. Once multiple ideas are generated, tradeoffs established and ideas combined, often a robust testing plan almost creates itself.

In Practice – Prototyping and the MVP

Prototyping and MVP testing are first driven by hypothesis development. Hypotheses by nature should be designed to be falsifiable[3], meaning that it must be refutable under testing. In practice, what is often considered a hypothesis in the LS system is merely a question clarifying an area of uncertainty. For instance, using our putter example, the statement that *all putters are made of metal* is refutable since some putters use alternate materials. However, for the purposes of MVP testing, this is not very helpful. Most MVP hypotheses, when reframed as uncertainty questions, would go something like this: *does [the target customer] see increased value in our solution relative to their next best option*? This is not falsifiable, but an MVP test can be developed to clarify the uncertainty surrounding value.

As a result, for the purposes of MVP testing, these so-called hypotheses must be framed as a *question* that addresses an area of *uncertainty* and must not be *vague*.

INPUTS

Completed innovation cycle (based on phase – e.g., discovery, adoption, lead user or sustainability)
   Fledgling concept

---

[3]A scientific hypothesis, according to the doctrine of falsifiability, is credible only if it is inherently falsifiable. This means that the hypothesis must be capable of being tested and proven wrong ("Falsifiability," 2024).

PROCESS

Establish the top three questions where *uncertainty* needs to be managed for the three themes: desirability, feasibility and viability. This results in nine primary areas of testing.

Then, within each theme area, push the team for MVP tests that cover each of the four quadrants of prototyping (see Fig. 11). This often resembles a brainstorming session, but it is focused on prototyping rather than concept development. This results in at least 36 possible MVP options.

Then, ask the team the following questions:

Can one MVP cover all three areas of desirability, feasibility and viability?

Which MVP is easiest to execute in (i) time and (ii) resources?

Is this MVP quantifiable in some fashion?

All things being equal, early in the front end of the innovation process, MVPs should trend toward *focused* prototypes. Late in the process, MVPs should trend toward *comprehensive* prototypes.

Develop and implement a test (i.e., MVP) plan.

OUTPUTS

This remarkably simple approach tends to expand the breadth of possibilities and generates the most *effective* MVPs.

Analyze and assess results. Reformulate the problem statement in preparation for the next innovation cycle.

Conclusion

Concept selection and concept evaluation are different approaches requiring distinctive techniques. Concept evaluation is the most difficult activity to execute in any innovation management system.

Since it is impossible to highlight every conceivable approach to evaluating viability, desirability and feasibility, this chapter proposes an approach that optimizes the likelihood of answering the major questions around uncertainty. It outlines an approach to concept evaluation that optimizes the effectiveness of this process over the various phases of the innovation approach.

Section III

Advanced Tools and Techniques

Chapter 9

Adoption Theory in Practice

For a solution to be considered an innovation – rather than merely an invention – it must be commercially or socially successful. Success is determined through adoption by the marketplace. Few innovation management systems however truly incorporate adoption theory into their practices, with even fewer blending this thinking into their final solutions. Further complicating matters is the fact that how innovations are perceived are often more important than the benefits they deliver. Highlighting adoption principles, prospect and behavioral economics, this chapter focuses on the barriers to adoption and how to craft final solutions that are more likely to be adopted. Adoption becomes focus of the second phase of the innovation approach.

Introduction

As discussed in Chapter 3, innovations that are not adopted are, in perpetuity, destined to remain as mere inventions or failed products. Rarely do products or services fail technically, since most organizations (even early-stage ventures) are reasonably good at technology development, testing and implementation. Products, however, frequently fail to meet customer expectations by not satisfying needs, providing no relative value vis-à-vis competitive products or having significant barriers to their use.

For a product or service to be considered successful, it must first be either commercially or socially adopted. Commercial adoption is measured not only by market share but also by the *rate* at which it is adopted. Social adoption, on the other hand, is commonly measured by the rate at which it is shared between individuals or organizations. For example, the use of emojis in digital communication has become a socially adopted norm.

Thus, any successful innovation management approach must consider the "adoptability" of the resulting product or service. However, few innovation management systems truly incorporate adoption principles into their practices, and even fewer blend this thinking into their final solutions. As a result, many innovation failures can be traced back to the team's disregard for basic adoption principles.

This chapter will explore what adoption is, examine classic successes and failures, and how to incorporate adoption into the innovation process. As a result,

The Innovation Approach:
Overcoming the Limitations of Design Thinking and the Lean Startup, 133–147
Copyright © 2025 by David C. Roach
Published under exclusive licence by Emerald Publishing Limited
doi:10.1108/978-1-83797-799-420241009

adoption becomes the theme for the *second innovation cycle following the discovery phase*. Fledgling concept(s) emanating from the discovery phase are subjected to an adoption assessment as they enter a fresh innovation cycle.

What Is Adoption?

Adoption is a complex phenomenon, but understanding this construct can significantly impact the success or failure of innovation activities. Adoption is often linked to innovation diffusion, a quasi-innovation theory advanced by Everett Rogers. A prolific social science academic in the field of communications, he is most remembered for categorizing populations into four categories: early adopters, early majority, later majority and laggards (Rogers, 2003). His work has been praised by both academics and practitioners and has become one of the most recognized models in the innovation literature. Interestingly, the origin of this work is often attributed to his upbringing as a farm boy in Iowa. His father, an early adopter of farm machinery, was otherwise reluctant to use new grain varieties even though they were known to significantly increase yields. Why would his father's behavior differ so much between these two innovations?

Roger's work has been enhanced and popularized over the years by such management consultants as Geoffrey Moore in his book *Crossing the Chasm* (Moore, 2003). Rogers highlights that innovators come before early adopters, while Moore advocates that firms need to understand that there is a chasm between early adopters and the early majority that must be "crossed" to access the mainstream market. Both approaches rely on describing customers based on a combination of demographic, psychographic and geographic profiles. Most managers now understand the importance of both positions and have adjusted their activities to reflect this. For instance, firms today understand that they must align their early innovations with what early adopter customers want. Methodologies such as Design Thinking (DT) have somewhat filled the void by advocating a more holistic way to develop innovations for superior value. On the other hand, the Lean Startup (LS) method advocates targeting early adopters to tap into emerging categories through customer listening. Although these approaches are valid, both fail to properly incorporate adoption principles into their methods.

A lesser-known part of Roger's work is the adoption behavior based on "product differences" (i.e., value proposition) rather than "people differences" (i.e., profiles). Some go as far as stating that "by almost any measure…this is a great oversight" (Gourville, 2005, p. 2). In his seminal book, Rogers examines up to 25 product attributes (or factors) that are known to have an impact on the rate of adoption. However, he suggests that there are five product factors that govern the capacity and rate at which products are adopted. He categorizes these into the product's *relative advantage, compatibility, complexity, trialability* and *observability*. He goes even further to highlight that all these factors need only be *perceived* to impact the rate of adoption.

At first glance, relative advantage seems deceptively simple. In Roger's model it merely refers to the *degree to which an innovation is perceived as being better than the idea it supersedes* (p. 212). This simple description is loaded with information pertinent to the success of innovations. First, it assumes that the team truly understands the customer's next best option. In practice, both DT and the LS frequently do not spend the time or effort to truly understand the customer's frame of reference. DT's emphasis on executing primary observational research (and less emphasis on current product features and benefits) limits the ability to conceptualize a product that meets the test of being *better than the product it replaces*. Similarly, the LS's enthusiasm for action over analysis often presents as a push for primary "customer discovery" before understanding what they are competing with, resulting in the same outcome. In addition, from the customer's perspective they need only to *perceive it to be better* in order to engage in subsequent adoption steps. A parallel approach from prospect theory adds to this principle by explaining how customers code outcomes as *losses* or *gains*. This is important because individuals weigh losses higher than gains by a factor of 2.25 (Soman, 2014). This results in gains needing to outweigh losses by a significant amount. Neither DT nor the LS are configured to address customers' perceived losses in this fashion.

Compatibility, in its most simplistic form, refers to the *degree to which an innovation is perceived as consistent with the existing values, past experiences and needs* (p. 224). Compatibility with the adopter's norms is perceived as less threatening, appears more familiar and fits with existing habits. This is often difficult to assess by nascent teams who are not culturally, educationally or practically aware of the values and experiences of their target audience. For instance, in medical devices it is hard for team members, no matter how well-trained, to understand the thought processes of highly educated medical practitioners. The DT community argues that this is exactly what their processes are designed to uncover through observation and probing interviews. Although I partially agree with this sentiment, I would argue that the value equation (particularly acute in medical fields) has more to do with perceived losses than any gains. With the Starting Lean approach – or even worse – medical hackathons, the ability to truly develop concepts that are compatible with norms of this category and industry is remote.

Complexity is roughly defined by Rogers as *the degree to which an innovation is perceived as relatively difficult to understand and use* (p. 242). There is an obvious inverse relationship between complexity and adoption, where the more complex the innovation is perceived, the less adoptable it is. All products fall on a complexity–simplicity continuum where ease of understanding and use tend to have higher adoption rates. For both DT and LS this again comes down to understanding the category space, since complexity is very often based on the customer's previous knowledge or their next best option. One way to think about complexity is Donald Norman's principle of "things in the world" and "things in your head" (Norman, 1998). Here he makes a distinction between knowledge that the general population understands; for instance, green, yellow and red acting as surrogates for "go," "caution" and "stop." On the other hand, depending on the target audience, they may have knowledge in their head that is as inherent as the traffic light example above. For instance, brain surgeons, I'm sure, have a general knowledge base that is essential to their profession (all brain surgeons have a similar baseline of knowledge in their head). Thus, complexity really is in the eye of the beholder. Since there are so many dimensions of what can make a product *perceived* as complex, this can be a difficult task at the FEI. Complexity, however, goes beyond easy-to-navigate graphical user interfaces (GUIs) or the layout of buttons on a remote control. Simple things like color, weight, size and even similarity to other products can have an effect. Thus, in practice, concept generation should start from a position *relative to competing products* and then be assessed for their perceived complexity relative to these benchmarks. I find that industrial designer's training gives them a strong grasp of this concept. For nascent DT or LS teams this is often an area of weakness.

Trialability is an interesting factor since it essentially relates to *the degree to which an innovation may be experimented with on a limited basis* (p. 243). Personal "try-outs" under one's own conditions provides context, meaning and dispels uncertainty. This has been successfully used by firms for decades, where trial periods allow the user to experience the product firsthand before making a commitment to the next level of the adoption process. For instance, car dealerships encourage potential customers to test-drive their products, while internet companies offer a freemium, limited time or feature-light versions of their products. These examples, however, are not product related but are more sales and marketing techniques. From Roger's perspective the question is *what we can do to our product to make it perceived as more trialable*. I often refer my students to Theodore Levitt's seminal article (Levitt, 1981) where he examines the use of surrogates when products cannot be trialed. He uses the example of buying a nuclear reactor. Since there is no opportunity to trial such a product, customers look for surrogates that make them *perceive* as if they have trialed the product. He uses the example of having a crisp proposal, supported by an A-level team, who show up for a presentation with scale models and leather-bound packages containing supporting technical details and referrals. Although the customer cannot trial the product, they feel as if they have. Perhaps a better example is that of luxury vehicles. The Infinity J-30 line of luxury automobiles ™ tested 90 leather smells before selecting one for the European and another for their North American customers (Leonard & Rayport, 1997). New car smell accounts for 11% of the purchasing decision for a new vehicle and people perceive that they have "trialed" the *value proposition* for luxury vehicles.

Finally, *observability* is in some ways my favorite. In effect, it refers to *the degree to which the results of an innovation are visible to others* (p. 244). I like to simplify this by restating it as *the degree to which a product's value is effortlessly visible*. This encompasses both its usage and impact. As an example, when Corona beer was first introduced to the US market, sales were mediocre. It had little taste (i.e., body), was light but not calorie-light and did not age well in its clear bottle. The company, at some point, either intuitively or unconsciously understood this adoption factor. They decided to require restaurants to serve it with a bright slice of lime stuck in the neck of the bottle. When customers would notice this from across the room, they would ask the waitress/waiter what this beer was. These employees were instructed to say that this was a "premium Mexican beer." This observably connected the brand's value proposition, and the remainder is history.

Corona, until recently, was still the largest-selling import beer in the US, boasting dollar sales of close to $3 billion in 2022 (*Best-Selling Imported Beer Brands U.S. 2022*, 2023).

There are many other insights provided by Rogers which include over-adoption, preventative innovations, fad innovations, the effects of incentives and the role of channels, to name a few. Although these are beyond the scope of this book, one particularly stands out in my mind as worth mentioning. Preventative innovations, which can include everything from wellness innovations to lifestyle changes, have particularly low levels of adoption. Although there are several reasons for this, it mostly comes down to the difficulty in perceiving the relative advantage, given that it mitigates a "non-event" (i.e., a potential future value). Without getting into too much detail, these types of innovations are high-risk innovations and as such should be addressed at the *project selection stage*. Should teams decide to pursue these types of projects, most of their process should be focused on strong benchmarks and lead users (i.e., firms or individuals who have solved these tricky adoption problems). The few medical hackathons that I have witnessed tend to heavily favor preventative innovations. Ideas are pitched devoid of even a fundamental understanding of the implications of adoption barriers. As a result, I am not a fan of these types of activities since their problem focus should concentrate on adoption issues rather than technical solutions.

There are also other factors to consider when examining the adoption of any innovation. There is still a perception that customers, in their own best interest, make rational decisions based on utility-maximizing choices, in a forward-looking and unemotional way. The growing field of behavioral economics and prospect theory, however, tends to view this paradigm as fundamentally flawed (Soman, 2014). As discussed earlier, individuals are inclined to process value relative to some neutral reference point and code any deviation as losses or gains. Unfortunately for innovators, losses are coded much higher than gains. Thus, merely finding areas where value can be improved may actually result in a *perceived net value loss* by the customer. Other related barriers to adoption include the *status quo bias* and *loss aversion*. The former asserts that individuals will tend to stick with current products or services even though better alternatives exist. The latter merely refers to the bird in the hand effect (i.e., what one possesses is perceived with greater value than what one does not possess). This inertia or cognitive laziness also seems to intensify over time. There are many other factors that can play a role in how customers make decisions that are beyond the scope of this book. However, innovators should be aware of some of these, which include the context of the decision, simplified heuristics, mental accounting and hyperbolic discounting. These can also impact the success or failure of innovations[1].

---

[1]For those interested I would highly recommend reading the article "The Innovator's Challenge: Understanding the Psychology of Adoption", *Rotman Management Magazine*, Fall 2014. It is concise and informative.

Case Example – Google Glass

Google Glass is a classic example of design and development devoid of understanding the basic principles of adoption.

In the late 1990s while working in the aerospace industry, we developed a technology that made micro displays more efficient. These micro displays had been used for years by digital video camera makers such as JVC, Canon and the like. They mostly used a micro display technology designed and developed by Kopin Corporation in Wellesley, Massachusetts. These displays paired with our technology and appropriate optics, provided high-resolution images. We had integrated this technology into our handheld GPS device which we began to showcase in the MIT corridor. At the time, several fledgling startups were working on various wearable glass-like devices and were quite interested in partnering with us on our technology. I spent some time investigating various applications and concluded that although our technology was effective, I could not find a compelling application that didn't have serious adoption issues. Except for one…

Fast forward to 2013, when Google, with much hype, started to promote its version of micro display technology known as Google Glass (Fig. 12). I was very excited since I assumed that with its infinite resources, Google had "cracked" the adoption code. As I began to follow the progress of this application, it became clear that this was not the case and that even Google was in for a hard road ahead. Using this as an example of adoption barriers in my graduate classes, I was met with a lot of skepticism. My assessment was that the application would find some traction in niche applications (as it had before), but the return on investment would be dismal. In retrospect, it was worse than I predicted.

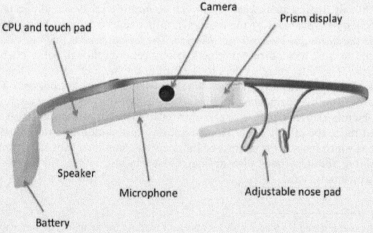

Fig. 12.   Google Glass

What was my assessment at the time of how well did Google Glass stacked up against adoption principles?

First, *Relative advantage*: what was the device replacing and did it have a relative advantage? This brings up two issues (i) what is the customer's frame of reference and (ii) what are the perceived *gains* and *losses* relative to the benchmark? Google, along with an army of partner startups, worked on a variety of applications ranging from surgery to lactation, but never really found an application where it was better than other wearables or simply a mobile phone. In addition, there were several "perceived" losses including the most prominent one – privacy.

Compatibility was also a problem. Google assumed that hands-free data was a "delight" need (see KANO Model) and based most of its conceptual thinking around this construct. Although hands-free data are compatible with some applications (e.g., surgeons, maintenance workers), it fails to be compatible with everyday norms which are better satisfied via a mobile phone, or in recent years, the Apple Watch™. (NOTE: customers have a long history of compatibility with watches)

Complexity was also another issue of concern. "How does this thing work" was the perception of the average customer we spoke to many years ago in the Boston area. How do I get my data to the micro screen, how do I change pages, can I use hyperlinks (or apps today), etc? Now at the time, mobile phones were not very sophisticated, and handheld computing devices were still evolving (e.g., Compaq iPaq). However, these were real concerns still relevant in 2013.

Trialability was also an issue, but in my assessment, this was not insurmountable. Google did give developers and startups access to this device and, as far as I know, were quite engaged with the user community. They also employed the time-tested marketing approach of enlisting celebrities to showcase the product at large sporting events and the like. This marketing approach works as a surrogate for trialability due to the audience's empathy with their sports and entertainment idols. They subconsciously feel as if they trialed the product.

Observability in some instances was done well…in other aspects, not so well. The design of Google Glass was very stylish, with smooth lines and accent colors. This made the value proposition of a "cool tech gadget" front and center. When asked "what is your first impression of Google Glass," most of my students would say that it is stylish, high-tech and aesthetically pleasing. I would then ask the question "how robust do you think it is"? The answer is invariably that it looks fragile. Thus, when examined based on the applications of the device (e.g., surgery or maintenance work), they were perceived as not very forgiving and fragile. The observable value was not Google's intended proposition (i.e., perceived gains), but that the product would not survive the application (i.e., perceived losses). The result was a *net value loss*.

Now as with all predictions, I was not exactly correct. It was worse than I predicted. What I didn't account for was the extreme negative publicity that supercharged the perception of privacy losses, which had a significant impact on the downfall of this product.

In any event, what are the learnings from an innovation management perspective? The first is a project selection issue. Even a cursory assessment of hand-free micro displays would have uncovered everything that is highlighted above. These devices had been around for almost two decades at the time. Second, is the problem statement. My best guess is that the problem statement went approximately like this: "develop a hands-free wearable computer interface which can communicate with the Internet using a head-up display for everyday use." This was probably adequate for the kickoff meeting; however early secondary research should have quickly highlighted a litany of adoption issues that needed to be addressed. This should have quickly refocused the problem statement to something like "how do we overcome the adoption issues to...." Third, primary research should have probed and learned about the adoption issues of all of the previous attempts at hand-free micro displays. If this approach resulted in fruitful avenues, then concept development could have addressed these critical issues with potential solutions which could then be tested. Alternately, as Dr. Robert Cooper emphasizes – every project needs a kill switch.

In summary, while Google Glass demonstrated innovation in technology and design, it lacked a strong product–market fit. The product had significant adoption issues and generally failed to align with user needs or value equation.

Adoption is considered by some as the "last mile of innovation problem," however, these issues have historically been managed as marketing "end of pipe" solutions. Instead of reconfiguring the product in the concept development phase to be more adoption-friendly, they rely on marketing activities such as advertising, education and promotion to resolve issues related to adoption uptake. These can produce mixed results as highlighted in the Google Glass example. Examining adoption in the FEI can often resolve the most pressing adoption issues. What remains then can be managed by traditional marketing techniques.

How and When to Mobilize Adoption

Given the importance of these adoption principles, it stands to reason that they should be incorporated into any robust innovation management system. Unfortunately, I am always surprised at the lack of knowledge or understanding of these basic principles. The LS method does not acknowledge their existence nor include them in any of its techniques. DT does acknowledge them in a roundabout way through its various techniques, but never fully makes it a focal point of its activities. As a result, adoption issues are often left to chance (i.e., picked up during customer testing) or more often, are eventually left to the marketing department to manage through their launch program.

Thus, if we believe there are product-related adoption principles, how and when do we bring these into the innovation management process? In my experience, the team should be introduced to the concepts early in the process, normally upfront during the secondary research phase. At this point, it should be presented more for awareness than a focus of the development process. If presented this way, it familiarizes the team to intelligence that they may uncover during their information-gathering activities. As the team progresses into their primary research activities, they tend to discover issues that may relate to adoption behavior. For instance, during probe and learn interviews, interviewees will often relate stories about products that confuse them, annoy them or are difficult to understand or use. An "attuned" team will tend to probe deeper if they discover what might be possible adoption barriers. Furthermore, it makes for much more robust discussions during team analysis of these interviews. Team members will challenge colleagues who performed the interviews because adoption forms part of the language developed by the team.

In this book's proposed innovation approach, adoption becomes the theme that guides the second innovation cycle. This is strategic, since it forces the team to examine the fledgling concept(s) emanating from the discovery round through an adoption filter.

Case Example – memsorb™

Several years ago, I was introduced to a German anesthesiologist, Professor Dr. med. Michael Schmidt, to whom this book is dedicated. Michael was an internationally respected researcher in medical ventilation and anesthesia and, as with most researchers, had many ideas. One of his concepts was to replace an archaic disposable component of an anesthesia machine known as a CO_2 absorber. This could have clinical, environmental and cost benefits. As with most researchers he had strong opinions about how this should be done, both clinically and technically. One of his concepts involved using amino acids to bind CO_2 rather than current granulates (e.g., soda lime).

The clinical problem (or initial problem statement) was how to extract CO_2 from an anesthetic circuit. However, by reversing the problem (a technique I have often successfully used) the problem became much clearer. The real problem was not extracting CO_2, but in fact, how to retain expensive and environmentally harmful anesthetic vapor within the anesthesia circuit. This changed the paradigm from "absorption" to "filtration." How could we design a long-lasting CO_2 filter?

After assessing the relative merits of this project (i.e., project selection), we decided to form a company to design, develop and commercialize what became known as *memsorb*™. Technically, there were many challenges - so many in fact, that as we conducted background research, we found that major Global competitors had failed and given up. To our surprise they never issued patents for any of their work (NOTE: in specialized technical fields scanning patents is part of the secondary research process). Thus, the field was open to innovation or in intellectual property terms – we should have freedom to operate.

The core of the technical challenge was how to use time-tested medical membranes in a new way while maintaining acceptable clinical outcomes. Among other things, our primary research involved benchmarking other medical products that used membrane technology (e.g., "blood-to-gas" separation for heart surgery). Again, to our surprise no one was working on gas-to-gas separation in medical applications. This eventually led to a beta prototype which entered a clinical study in what is known in the Medtech industry as "first-in-man" trials. After collecting data from approximately 20 patients, the data were analyzed and the device was found to be clinically safe and passed all requirements. With some minor adjustments it was ready for larger clinical trials on a path to regulatory approval.

This was the point where the solution was examined from an adoption perspective. One concern was that a key metric used in anesthesia was inspired CO_2 (the amount of CO_2 that is returned to the patient in the circuit). This is an artifact of absorption, since it indicates to the anesthesiologist that their absorber is nearing its end of life and should be replaced. In filtration, this metric is no longer meaningful since the clinically valid measure is end-tidal CO_2 (etCO_2 is the amount of CO_2 that the patient expires). The criteria is that etCO_2 must be stable and within a clinically acceptable range. Our device easily passed this test, however inspired CO_2 often exceeded the "legacy" inspired CO_2 criteria, indicating absorber replacement. This, I strongly suggested, would be a serious adoption issue.

Examining Roger's Five Factors, our concept looked something like this:

Relative advantage: In our case the customer's frame of reference was absorption. What were the *gains* and *losses* that these anesthesiologists would *perceive*? Perceived gains were generally strong. Anesthesiologist told us that they were never comfortable with daily disposal of absorbers (contaminated and hazardous medical waste). They also saw the clinical benefits which included elimination of toxic by-products and generally more stable machine operation. They also liked the ability to perform "low-flow" anesthesia, which saved money and more importantly saved exhausting aggressive ozone depleting vapors to the atmosphere. Many told us that they would walk or bike to work to reduce their carbon footprint, only to create CO_2 emissions equivalent of driving across North America during one shift of anesthesia! When examined based on perceived losses, most issues were minor and mainly revolved around clinical training (see compatibility section).

Compatibility: In our case, the customer's frame of reference was their medical training. They never considered, understood or were trained on the concept of filtration. Although anaesthesiologists had "knowledge in their head" (Norman, 1998) that told them $etCO_2$ was the only clinically relevant measure, their training made them feel otherwise. In my assessment, because of their training, they could be educated as part of a marketing plan, but that this *perceived* change in practice would be problematic. What could we do to the product to alleviate this concern?

Complexity was another issue of concern. There was initial skepticism around "how does this thing work" since our device required the inclusion of an additional air/oxygen blender attached to the machine. To keep it simple, this was used to maximize the performance of *memsorb*^{TM} by matching the air-to-oxygen ratio to the patient side. This had implications for both anesthesiologists and biomedical departments in charge of equipment. From the anesthesiologist's perspective, their main concern was how often would this need to be adjusted during surgery. When it became clear that this was normally a one-time step, this issue resolved itself. For the biomedical department however, there were numerous perceived problems. How does this impact the machine, will it void warranty and how much more work is it going to require for setup and maintenance?

Trialability was less of an issue since all hospital systems have standard procedures and processes to conduct purchase assessments (i.e., cost/benefit studies). Most hospitals have standard packages which they require, including peer reviewed articles and referrals. This could easily be handled as part of a marketing program.

Observability might also be an adoption issue since standard absorbers were buried underneath the machine, surrounded by tubes and wires – virtually sight unseen. To our credit, anesthesiologists told us after trialing the device that they noticed no difference in clinical practice. However, the objective from an adoption perspective is to be able to communicate the value proposition in an *observable* way. Since it had become clear that the most resounding aspect of our value proposition was the potential environmental impact, we decided to concentrate on this aspect of the value proposition.

How did we adjust our prototype (Fig. 13) based on this adoption assessment?

The most pressing matter was *compatibility* and thus the redesign process focused on ensuring that 95% of patients would be at, or below, the threshold for inspired CO_2. Although this was not clinically necessary and increased costs, it would alleviate any concerns based on training and speed up adoption. As I often stated to the team – this will alleviate anesthesiologists getting sweaty palms! For the 5% (or 1 in 20) patients where inspired CO_2 rose above absorber levels, we were quite confident that this could be handled this through education. Next, to resolve the *complexity* issue we

Fig. 13. memsorb™

simplified our air/oxygen blender arrangement by incorporating an exhaust component directly into the device. We also made the case that machine maintenance would be reduced since caustic absorber dust would be eliminated from the system. We further confirmed with the top two machine suppliers that they would not void the warranty if our device was used. (NOTE: they became very supportive of our efforts to solve an industry problem). Finally based on *observability* we changed the top and bottom caps of the device from standard clear medical plastic to bright environmental green. This made the device stand out in a crowded operating room (OR) setting and, as we hoped, made it the topic of conversation within the OR from surgeons, nurses and anesthesiologists.

Most other issues were deemed to be minor and would be resolved using standard marketing techniques.

Once adoption becomes a standard part of the team's vocabulary it tends to permeate throughout their activities. For instance, during the concept development phase, very often, creative ideas arise that address adoption problems and, as a result, increase the potential solution space. Furthermore, it often increases the robustness of concepts making this activity more *effective* than standard brainstorming processes.

After the initial innovation cycle (i.e., discovery phase) the team converges on a few concepts they feel passionate about. This is when the use of an adoption exercise is quite helpful to break groupthink. The exercise involves having each team member individually assess each concept based on the five principles. This avoids any potential Alpha (i.e., dominant) bias that may have developed within the team. This is followed by a group presentation and discussion about how the concepts could be *perceived* through an adoption lens. The information generated becomes the kick-off for the next cycle of innovation where an informed team conducts additional secondary research, updates benchmarking, conducts "adoption-focused" primary research and finally uses this new knowledge in a "re-ideation" process to improve upon previous concepts.

I also sometimes include a challenge part way through this phase and have the team conduct a brainstorming session on how they would redesign the product to *reduce its adoptability…yes…reduce*! This *problem reversal* is a great way to stress test preferred concepts and frequently leads to new insights (see lateral thinking techniques). This approach creates a scenario where the team is forced to examine their work from a completely different angle, often resulting in radically new approaches to the problem. These sessions can also be a lot of fun, since many silly concepts or personas can emerge. Depending on the project, the team dynamics, and the category chosen, I sometimes save this exercise until after incorporation of lead user input, which we will cover in the next chapter.

In Practice – Adoption

As emphasized throughout this chapter, the innovation management process can benefit significantly from an understanding and deployment of adoption principles.

In brief, the process should look like the following:

INPUTS

One full innovation cycle (i.e., Discovery phase) which includes:
Secondary research
Benchmarking
Primary research
Concept development
Concept selection

PROCESS

This works well as a "kick-off" for the second innovation cycle (i.e., adoption) where fledgling concepts are examined through an adoption lens.

As a warmup activity prior to secondary research, conduct a group learning exercise with the team. I find this sequence tends to work well:

Give a brief take-home exercise such as a reading (for instance, the description section of this chapter or suggested references) or online videos describing the concept and principles of adoption. Ask team members to think about examples of good and bad implementation of adoption principles.

Conduct a brief introductory presentation on the concept and examples of good and bad practice. Have a group discussion and reinforce these principles.

Conduct a challenge exercise to "stress test" fledgling concepts by exposing them to the five principles of adoption. Summarize issues into a document highlighting potential adoption areas of improvements. These become inputs for a new innovation cycle.

Have the team conduct a condensed round of secondary research focusing on highlighting adoption issues. This information should result in a reexamination of benchmarking with a specific focus on how competing products have incorporated adoption principles into their attributes and features. This background research informs a new round of primary research based on a revised discussion guide, guided by adoption impediments.

Revise the problem statement before ideation activities begin.

This new body of knowledge sets the stage for revised ideation activities leading to improved (or new) concepts.

OUTPUTS

Revised concepts featuring aspects of adoption ready to be prototyped for user feedback.

NOTE: For reference I would highly encourage readers to read the following sources prior to undertaking this approach:

Gourville (2005) *Note on Innovation Diffusion: Rogers' Five Factors*, Harvard Business School Publishing, 2005, 505075-PDF-ENG

Soman (2014) *The Innovator's Challenge: Understanding the Psychology of Adoption*, Rotman Management Magazine, Fall 2014

Conclusion

This chapter highlights the critical role of adoption in the success or failure of innovations. Many innovations fail not due to technical shortcomings but because they do not meet customer expectations often due to significant adoption barriers. Unfortunately, adoption principles tend to be overlooked in many innovation management systems, including popular methodologies such as DT and the LS.

The concept of adoption is inextricably linked to Everett Rogers' innovation diffusion theory through his lesser-known work on *product attributes* rather than his *behavioral classification* of adopters. His five product factors, namely relative advantage, compatibility, complexity, trialability and observability are strongly linked to the rate of adoption. When aligned with behavioral economics and prospect theory, it highlights that customers' decisions are very often influenced by factors beyond rational utility maximization. This is perhaps why all of Roger's factors need only be *perceived* to be of concern.

This chapter provides a broad exploration of adoption principles, highlighting their significance and why relying solely on "end of pipe" marketing solutions is an ineffective approach. Considered the "last mile of innovation," adoption is best incorporated early in the process for more effective outcomes.

Chapter 10

Learning from Lead Users

Dr. Eric von Hippel famously stated that "imagining the future is difficult – understanding it by living there is easy". There is a class of consumers known as lead users, who demonstrate needs ahead of the mainstream marketplace. These users have complex needs which cannot be satisfied by existing solutions and are thus forced to innovate to satisfy their requirements. Although in most cases their solutions are not viable for mainstream consumers, their requirements can often foresight latent needs in the marketplace, which may become differential features and benefits in the future. Often confused with early adopters or extreme customers, they are fundamentally different in several ways. Extreme customers have a-typical needs in the target application however fail to innovate in any meaningful way. Early adopters are merely the first to embrace new products introduced to the market. As a result, neither foresight solutions. This chapter focuses on the three types of lead users and how their knowledge can be incorporated into successful solutions. Aspects of lead user research form the third phase of the innovation approach.

Introduction

I first became aware of lead user research (LUR) in 1996 at a conference in Boston, Massachusetts. The presenter, Mary Sonnak, had been seconded from 3M Corporation to work with Dr. Eric von Hippel at MIT to find a way to operationalize his research on lead users. Dr. von Hippel (who coined the term) made a very compelling case that most breakthrough innovations come from users, not R&D departments in organizations. His proposition was that if companies were willing to spend the time and resources to find these unique individuals, understand their problems and examine their solutions, this knowledge could then be used to develop breakthrough products and services. After Mary Sonnak's presentation, I approached her and had a brief conversation. I told her that not only was this an approach to developing breakthrough products, but it was a breakthrough in thinking! We communicated again in the following months, and I still have a copy of her initial manuscript in my office.

What I found most compelling about LUR was that it incorporated many of the cornerstones of good innovation management, although executed with a twist.

The Innovation Approach:
Overcoming the Limitations of Design Thinking and the Lean Startup, 149–165
Copyright © 2025 by David C. Roach
Published under exclusive licence by Emerald Publishing Limited
doi:10.1108/978-1-83797-799-420241010

The twist was finding individuals or organizations at the edge of the markets or technologies, fundamentally understanding why they were playing at the fringes and what solutions they had discovered to resolve their problems. What I also found intriguing was that the approach was not directly focused on the market. It relied on finding lead users, not only in the market but in parallel markets (which they called analogs) and, even more interestingly, in key attributes. Although we will discuss this in more detail throughout this chapter, it was a radical departure from traditional innovation management thinking. As I watched her presentation, it occurred to me that this process was fundamentally about identifying the *correct problem to solve*. The methodology she had developed, along with her colleagues at 3M and MIT, began like most processes with a problem statement, but was forced to continually adjust as new information came to light. What really intrigued me was that the method was robust enough to even eliminate (if necessary) the initial problem statement in favor of a more sophisticated one. This, along with gathering lead users together in a workshop environment, seemed to make a lot of sense. The lead user approach is now generally considered an early form of open innovation, a term popularized years later by Henry Chesbrough (Chesbrough, 2003).

So, who are lead users, what is LUR and how can these principles be applied to the innovation management process?

Who Are Lead Users?

Lead users, by Dr. von Hippel's definition, are users who present strong needs that may become general in a marketplace months or years in the future. Since they are familiar with conditions that lie in the future, they can serve as a need-forecasting laboratory for marketing research (von Hippel, 1986). Moreover, these users have extreme needs in the marketplace that cannot be satisfied by existing products or services and are thus forced to innovate. An easy test or rule of thumb for identifying lead users is that they must display strong or *extreme needs* and have *created their own solution*. Lead users are not only individuals but can be groups of people or organizations that display these two fundamental characteristics.

Unlike traditional market research that collects information from the center of the target market, the lead user approach collects this information from the fringes. The fringes of the market tend to be populated by users with atypical needs (i.e., extreme customers) who are inclined to use existing products in offbeat ways. In addition, they have invented novel solutions to solve their perceived problem. This allows innovation teams to simultaneously collect information about both *needs* and *solutions*. Also, lead users are not only found at the leading edges of the target market but in markets facing similar problems in a more extreme form (*Innovation at 3M Corporation (A)*, 2002). As a result, lead users can be broken down into three fundamental types, each of which bring a unique perspective to needs assessment. These include:

Lead users in the *target market or application*: While traditional market research investigates either the mainstream market or well-defined (and attractive) segments, these users are at the fringes and are often in unattractive or uncompetitive segments. As a result, they are often ignored by traditional market research or innovation management teams. An example of lead users in the market can be observed in 3M's development of cost-effective surgical bandages, where they engaged with surgeons in third-world markets to understand how they controlled infection (von Hippel et al., 1999). These surgeons had an important problem they needed to solve and could not access or afford existing solutions, so they developed innovative techniques because they had no other choice.

Next are lead users in *analog* markets: These users are found in adjacent markets who experience similar limitations with existing products, albeit in a different market application. They exhibit extreme needs in their market and have developed their own workaround solutions to their unique problems. Using the same 3M example, the innovation team engaged veterinary surgeons who had developed infection control techniques for their customers (and I paraphrase) who "don't bathe, are hairy and don't have any money" (*3M Lead User Research*, 2012). A good rule of thumb when thinking about analogs is to identify products or services that are either used for the *same purpose* or in the *same environment*. As an example, a microwave could be an analog to a kettle. Both can be used for a similar purpose (i.e., boiling water) and/or are used in the same environment (i.e., the kitchen). Many decades ago, I did an in-class exercise for executives on establishing analogs. My challenge to them was to redesign a men's razor. When the class was floundering, I asked "What is the most common item found in the same environment"? The answer was easy – a toothbrush. I then asked what we could learn from this analog that would help in shaving? Eventually, one person spoke up and suggested the vibrating motor from the electric toothbrush. Years later, as I predicted, Gillette came up with a vibrating razor (although I don't believe it was very successful). The point is that a lot can be learned from understanding analogs, which I still consider the most underutilized concept in the innovation management toolbox.

Finally, lead users in key *attributes*: In my experience, this is the most interesting of the lead user categories since it examines users outside of the application itself. Attributes are generally related to the product or technology but in my experience can also be related to the user. Attributes of a product could be things like styling, weight or processing speed (see benchmarking). Attributes of users could include the need for status, conspicuous consumption or adoption behavior. Using another 3M example in medical diagnostic imaging, it became apparent that pattern recognition was a key attribute of the technology. As a result, they searched for experts in pattern recognition and even ballistic experts for ultra-high-speed image processing. This led to industry leading pattern recognition in medical diagnostics. In another surgical bandage example, the team identified that adhesion to the skin was a key attribute of infection control (i.e., sealing the wound was paramount to infection control). As a result, the team worked with Hollywood makeup artists who were experts at adhering silicone and other materials to the skin (von Hippel et al., 1999).

Lead User Misconceptions

True lead users are rare and often difficult to locate. As a result, the concept is frequently misunderstood and often poorly applied. There are several reasons for this, but fundamentally it comes down to a few key issues. First and foremost, there is confusion between the concept of early adopters and lead users. Early adopters are individuals or firms that are predisposed to be the first users of new products or services in the marketplace. They quickly embrace new products, services or technologies and are among the first to try and adopt innovations. They pride themselves with keeping up with the latest and greatest in the market, tend to be tolerant of limitations of new technologies and are comfortable with some level of uncertainty. Early adopters see value in new features and are often not very price-sensitive. This is why they are often touted as the target audience in methods such as the Lean Startup (LS). Lead users, on the other hand, precede early adopters since they perceive needs ahead of the general population and are thus forced to create their own (often impractical) solutions. They foresight latent (unspoken) needs in the general marketplace, which eventually enter the mainstream market as delight features that attract early adopters. One of the failures, in my opinion, of the LS approach is that it promotes attracting early adopters, but their approach to the innovation process does not understand where the next innovations come from.

Next is a general misunderstanding of criteria. As discussed, lead users demonstrate extreme needs in the marketplace, and since they cannot find products or services to satisfy these needs, they are forced to come up with their own solutions (i.e., inventions). This leads to confusion with the "do it yourself" (DIY) community and/or extreme customers. DIYers are motivated by the challenge of solving problems themselves and their solutions are often based on cost-saving measures (i.e., their solution avoids purchasing an existing product). They are motivated by the joy of hands-on creation and see their results as a personal expression of who they are. Extreme customers, on the other hand, are outliers who use products or services in unconventional ways and tend to stretch the boundaries of what these products can do. They often use products to the extreme limits of their capabilities, revealing potential weaknesses or opportunities for improvement. Consequently, although their needs may be interesting, neither meet the criteria of lead users.

Another area of confusion is between lead users and lead use experts. Lead use experts abound and are often found in research labs, academia and/or think tanks. These individuals are experts in their field and, in some cases, may even have added significantly to the body of knowledge in the category of interest. They tend to focus on very narrow aspects of research since their motivation is not commercially focused. They are rewarded by publishing research papers and applying for grants. This process is poorly aligned with developing product and services for users. As a result, they are rarely lead users, since they do not demonstrate strong or extreme "customer" needs and have not created matching solutions. They are, however, key to the LUR process, since they often provide links to lead users in their network.

Next is the inventor community. There is a large community of individuals that invent for the sake of invention. A huge and profitable industry has built up around them, offering everything from evaluation of their idea, assistance with patents, to licensing deals (*What's the BIG Idea?*, 2001). There are very few "professional" inventors (i.e., individuals that make a living as inventors), but most inventors think they are merely one break away from reaching this status. Inventors are not lead users since, in most cases, their process focuses on solving their perceived problem which is typically not perceived by the market. As a result, their solutions are most often impractical since they are not based on a true market need. Thus, inventors should generally be used with extreme caution because if perceived as lead users, they can pull an innovation project in an unrecoverable direction.

Finally is the process of finding and engaging lead users. In my undergraduate and graduate classes, I am always amazed by students' general lack of investigative research skills. When asked to engage in finding lead users, they begin by typing the term "lead user" into a search engine, AI model or crowd-sourcing site, and are disappointed when this results in poor outcomes. They then double down and perform what they coin a "deep Google search" which generally results in the same outcome. There is an approach to uncovering lead users since they tend to hide in corners and are not that easily found. Once they understand that the process is more akin to investigative journalism, their fortunes often improve. This will be discussed this in more depth later in this chapter.

Initially conceived as a market research technique, the lead user approach is one of the most fruitful techniques to uncovering latent *delight* needs for the innovation management process (see KANO model). This is based on its unique methodology of simultaneously collecting information about both *needs* and *solutions* from the leading edges of the target market, from analog markets and markets facing similar problems. The concept of engaging lead users in the front end of innovation (FEI) has been developed into a system known as Lead User Research (Churchill et al., 2009) championed by 3M Corporation. As a system, it has many benefits, although from my understanding is no longer used as extensively as it was. It can, however, provide many insights into the FEI.

Next, we will examine LUR as a system and then discuss how it can be successfully used in practice.

Lead User Research

LUR is a method used to identify innovative solutions to emerging problems by involving users who face similar challenges but are ahead of the curve in addressing them. Its fundamental premise is that "lead users" experience needs or problems before the mainstream market. Not only do they experience needs ahead of the market, but they have a unique drive and ability to develop solutions that go beyond current market offerings. This unique combination of (i) early recognition of emerging trends and (ii) innovative problem-solving approaches can make them invaluable in the early stages of the innovation process.

The ultimate focus of LUR is opportunity discovery leading to concept generation. It is a methodology that provides key insights while the concepts are still fluid at the FEI. It goes beyond merely brainstorming concepts based on information gathered from the marketplace. It extracts information from the fringes through individuals who live there. As with most methodologies, it relies on a multifunctional team to prepare the study, conduct the steps and analyze results. A typical time frame for conducting these phases is roughly four months, if team members can devote at least 25% of their time on the project. According to Churchill et al. (2009), in their thorough practitioner's guide, there are four distinct steps in an LUR study.

The first step is *project selection and scope*. This classic corporate step is where management decides the product category of focus based on competitive threats and/ or market opportunity. These decisions are multifaceted, complex and often political. Similarly, in entrepreneurial settings, these are often driven by opportunity recognition and/or attractive market dynamics (e.g., large and fast-growing markets). In this phase management must select and empower a team, often cutting across departmental or functional lines. One of the criticisms of the success of LUR is that cherry-picking the top talent with a mandate to report to the team rather than their functional silos, may have as much to do with its success as the method itself. Once the project has been determined and the team selected, the core of the process can begin.

Next is the *identification of trends and needs*. As with all successful innovation management systems, LUR relies on deep and thorough secondary research focusing on identifying emerging market *trends* and *needs*. As these requirements begin to be uncovered, the team looks for individuals at the cutting edge of these activities. At this point, the purpose is not necessarily to identify lead users, but to begin understanding where they might live. Often this part of the process tends to identify *lead use experts* who can be the first point of contact in identifying lead users for the next part of the process.

Collection of *needs and solutions from lead users* follows. In this phase, the team begins to identify potential lead users through a networking (or investigative journalism) approach. The team focuses on the three types of lead users, namely, market, analogs and attributes. This process refines the trends and needs identified in the previous secondary research phase, creating a deeper understanding and new insights into the problem at hand. This phase concludes with a *refined problem statement* followed by the team conducting internal ideation activities to generate preliminary concepts.

Concept development with selected lead users is at the heart of this methodology. This phase takes the form of a two to three-day workshop retreat, where selected lead users are invited to join the team as they refine initial concepts. In essence it is a form of open innovation. These sessions are often extended to team members who may provide additional insights into the project at hand (e.g., manufacturing, sales). These sessions frequently involve a combination of ideation exercises (e.g., brainstorming) and business case development (i.e., business modeling). The results of this phase are proposed product or service concepts for management's consideration.

At first glance, this process does not look that dissimilar to most corporate product development processes. However, there are both synergies and differences that make this a powerful approach to the FEI. Similarities include its focus on strong, early, and thorough secondary research focused not on market size and growth, but on *trends* and *needs*. This aligns it with all successful innovation management systems that understand innovation is a separate activity from project selection. The LUR method includes a project selection component at the beginning of the process, however, this activity is highly business unit focused and frankly does not differ much from most corporate business unit decision making processes. Other similarities include its emphasis on primary research activities (informed by secondary research) focusing on probe and learn, semi-structured open-ended interviewing activities. Likewise, the concept generation activities do not differ from the ubiquitous brainstorming norms.

Where they differ, however, is the important differentiator of this methodology. First, the direction of activities in the secondary research phase is not merely confined to trend and need-finding. Focus is also placed on examining the bleeding edges of these activities, concentrating on identifying networks that are ahead of general trends. The objective of primary research then shifts direction since key informants are selected based on their role as leading edge users rather than the requirements of typical customers. As Dr. von Hippel states, *"Imaging the future is difficult – Understanding it by living there is easy"* (Churchill et al., 2009). This leads to the concept generation activities that are much more narrowly focused on emerging "delight" needs rather than expected needs in the category. Also, in the latter phases, the methodology employs aspects of open innovation where individuals with demonstrated needs and solutions are engaged with the team to collaborate on concept generation. The last, and in my opinion, the most powerful aspect of LUR is that it breaks the chain of myopically looking within the market for needs and solutions. By looking at what they refer to as "advanced analog" markets, the team is forced to look further afield, resulting in two outcomes. First, it helps refine the "need" since individuals outside of the market space often see the problem from a different angle. This helps the team truly understand the various aspects of the *need requirements*, which often cannot be fully understood within the target market. Second, their approach to solutions invariably differs from what even advanced users in the target market might envision. This has to do with the unique context or environment and the difference in the actual tasks performed (see usability model). Similarly, is the focus on "key attributes" of the product or service. When the team is required to clarify what they believe are key attributes of the product or service, it opens an entire new area of inquiry.[1] No longer are they delving deeper into the needs of mainstream market but are forced to think in other dimensions (i.e., lateral thinking) where problems and solutions are fresh. Together these are the most powerful aspects of LUR.

The result is an FEI process that focuses on solutions to latent or dormant needs that are outside of the mainstream market. By focusing on these emerging needs, there is a much higher probability of identifying latent requirements and developing solutions that address these issues in a customer-friendly way.

---

[1] This closes the loop on the benchmarking exercise where "attributes" of products have been identified. These key attributes should be used to jump start the lead user phase.

Case Example – Lead User in Market

Returning to the Handheld GPS example; Our various probe and learn activities had confirmed both trends and needs along with a subgroup of customers with more intense needs. These customers were what we referred to as "outdoor professionals" who not only loved the outdoors but chose careers where much of their work was conducted in these environments. These included forestry firefighters, park rangers, armed forces personnel and the like. Although many constructs such as safety, dependability and context arose, one prominent problem identified was the loss of GPS signal in dense forest cover. When asked how they overcame this problem, most told us that they did "workarounds" such as living with poor (or no) reception, or charting a path based on lower density cover. Given the prominence of this problem, I suggested that we look for lead users in GPS tracking under dense forest cover.

After reviewing articles, websites and talking with lead use experts, I found an individual who had solved this problem. This person was a surveyor whose primary work was to set survey lines in the deep woods for forestry companies planning to log new areas. His specialty was doing a preliminary survey of these extremely remote locations. His job was to tag trees that needed to be cut down for the surveyors to have a clear "line of sight" when conducting full surveys of the area. Since he was usually dropped by helicopter on his own, he required only gear that he could carry to perform this task. He was paid handsomely for this work; thus, he had an urgent need to solve his problem. As a result, he developed an ingenious solution at the time, which involved using a Compaq iPaq (the only sunlight readable handheld display at the time) with specialty mapping software that used USGS Topographical maps. Although there was a GPS antenna that could be attached directly to the iPaq, he chose to use an antenna with a 5-foot cable that he could attach to the top of his baseball cap. He then lined his cap with tin foil to create an electrical "ground plane" that could amplify the signal to noise ratio of his antenna. This allowed him to use an "off the shelf" antenna (albeit the best on the market at the time) and amplify the signal several fold. He could then georeference the position of trees that needed cutting thus saving significant time and effort of full survey teams later in the process.

What we learned from this individual was invaluable. At the time, all of the large consumer GPS companies were reducing the size of their handheld GPS devices. Their consumer research told them that their mainstream customers wanted these devices to match the size of mobile phones, which were becoming smaller and smaller as shown in Fig. 14. Their solution was to develop smaller GPS antennas, while trying to match (but not exceed) their current performance. What we learned from *lead use experts* was that this was an important unsatisfied need. What we learned from this *lead user* was that there was a solution to this problem, namely a larger ground plane. As a result, we designed our device to have a wider area where the GPS antenna was located. We added $0.90 worth of metal behind the antenna which gave us the best GPS reception in the industry, allowing us to double our selling price.

Fig. 14.   Handheld GPS.

Downside of LUR

LUR, when used by 3M Corporation, was found to be significantly better than the company's baseline development process. There are likely many reasons for this, including selection of top team talent, mandate to use open innovation and general senior management support. However, it appears to have waned as a full-blown method over the past decade, in favor of more agile methodologies. As a method, it never really succeeded in breaking through into SMEs or early-stage entrepreneurial firms, mostly due to its complexity, time and resource commitments. It was also displaced in these environments by the popularity of Design Thinking (DT) and the Lean Startup (LS) which offered a less vigorous and agile approach to innovation management.

One of the key criticisms of LUR was that it was too focused on future market needs at the expense of the current needs of the mainstream market. The methodology pushes for the discovery of breakthrough innovations in some cases going beyond what the market would ever want. Since it relies on the extreme needs of fringe users, these needs could be isolated to a small group of users rather than emerging delight needs of the market as a whole. In fairness to the methodology, they highlight that care must be taken to confirm with customers that the collective need requirements have been met through downstream, back end of innovation (BEI) processes.

Including lead users in the concept development process also has some downside, since many lead users consider themselves "designers," despite their solutions rarely being close to market-ready. These individuals can have considerable egos, dominant personalities and narrow views. As with all group activities, care must be taken to avoid the entrenched positions of these types of actors. This is a group management problem which, in my experience, is always problematic at some level. Lead users can tend to be dominant (i.e., disruptive) in a workshop environment, and without mindful management of the process, activities can drift off target. In some cases, this can have significant implications for the original business unit requirements which drove the project in the first place.

Lastly, conducting a workshop with lead users sponsored by a marquee company such as 3M Corporation is radically different than with SMEs or early-stage ventures. According to Churchill et al. (2009), getting lead users to participate in innovation workshops is relatively easy since they are eager to share their knowledge and expertise. In my experience, getting them to participate with an unknown firm, with unknown outcomes is a different story. Patent ownership and how they will be compensated in the long term for their brilliance becomes a significant issue. Consequently, getting the best lead users to participate is quite difficult and often results in picking the "second best" participants, which somewhat negates the power of bringing them into an open innovation workshop.

Case Example – Lead User Attributes

In the mid-1990s I was engaged by a manufacturer of giftware to examine streamlining their product development process. The company would release products twice per year to align with traditional corporate buying cycles (e.g., Christmas). Among other things, management wanted to explore continual product releases rather than staged releases. The internet was also relatively new and untested as a sales channel, and senior management wanted to explore what the possibilities might be. One aspect of interest was the ability for on-line customers to configure their own products which would require the support of a synchronous manufacturing process.

I recruited a new graduate, and we went to work on this challenge. E-commerce at the time was in its infancy, but we quickly established workable solutions. Next was developing the ability for the customer to configure a product such as a picture frame online. This required building a database of three-dimensional models and the software code to render and display the final solution over the internet. Building the database was achievable using a combination of various computer-aided design (CAD) software products. Rendering and three-dimensional display was a challenge, but there were solutions available that seemed to be steadily improving as were internet speeds. This left the ability to physically produce these products, which required a "master" that could be cast into a final product using rapid (silicone-based) tooling. Having been quite familiar with rapid prototyping (i.e., 3D printing) since the early 1990s, we tested various combinations of systems until we arrived at a solution. There was only one problem…file size. At the time all rapid prototype machines could only handle file sizes (.STL) up to a maximum of 10 Mb. The complexity of our files meant that our file sizes would be in the hundreds of Megabytes or even greater than a Gigabyte! It was time to find lead users…

After exhausting the prospect of finding lead users in the market, we undertook trying to find lead users in the attribute of "file compression." It became clear that file compression for CAD (or STL files for rapid pro-totyping machines) was radically different than compressing files such as word documents or images. This we learned through discussions with lead use experts in the field. Armed with this knowledge and a few leads we began to look further afield. We eventually found an individual who would attend machine tool tradeshows to display his expertise with a unique selling proposition. He would come to tradeshows and over a weekend would machine a three-foot tall stainless-steel eagle, using a five-axis CNC machine (rare at the time) using jewelry tools. He seemed to clearly fit the criteria of a lead user and would likely have had to solve the same attribute problem we discovered. As with all lead users, I just wanted to know "why" this solution. I contacted him and we had a pleasant and frank discussion. He was showcasing his abilities in this emerging space and had become a highly paid consultant in his field (i.e., he had an extreme need to stay at the bleeding edge). When I eventually asked him if he had solved our problem, he took a long pause and said "yes, but I won't tell you how I did it." I asked a few more questions and he said that he would be happy to work with us on a consulting basis.

This is where a proper team structure pays dividends. Gathering a small cross-functional team, we laid out the facts that we knew. We knew that someone had solved it, thus the problem was solvable. We had additional information that he had shared that provided an opaque map of where to find the solution. Armed with this information and a bit more sleuthing, we found a post on a discussion board from an individual that had created a piece of software to scrub animation software files to reduce their size. It was a piece of DOS (disk operating system) software that effectively loos-ened conditions at the intersection of planes in animation and, as it turned out, CAD files. This allowed us to reduce our files sizes 20-fold (20X) and solved our problem.

Here, I learned two things. First, that there are always lead users some-where for any problem that can be conceived. Second, conducting a full-blown lead user research workshop is rarely necessary with the right team.

We tested our solution using a prototype of the most difficult problem I could envision – a three-dimensional interlocking sphere (Fig. 15). This would test all the technologies (e.g., rapid prototyping, rapid tooling, 3D rendering and casting) as a system. For fun…I made it into a golf ball which we cast and eventually made about one hundred for sale. I still retain the rights for this puzzle and still have inquiries decades later…

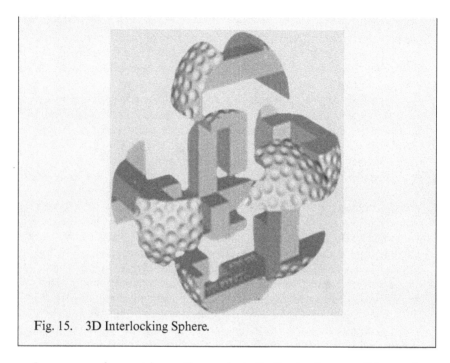

Fig. 15.   3D Interlocking Sphere.

In summary, for most innovation projects, finding lead users, talking to them and getting their input into "why, what and how" is highly beneficial to any innovation project. I no longer see the incremental benefit of bringing these individuals into an open innovation workshop. I prefer to rely on an innovation team that is multidisciplinary, balanced and properly managed to take findings from lead users into the concept development phase.

How and When to Use Lead Users

In my experience conducting a full-blown lead user research study is not the best approach for most innovation projects. There are many reasons for this, as outlined throughout this chapter, but it invariably comes down to the allocation of time and resources. In a corporate setting, with clearly defined strategic objectives and supportive senior management, many of the benefits of using this system can be achieved.

In an entrepreneurial setting, early-stage companies, or small- to medium-sized enterprises (SMEs), the overhead, coordination and general ability to operationalize such a study makes this method too burdensome. Furthermore, in an SME environment, lead users are reluctant to participate and have an overblown sense of their value to the process. They perceive that they are being brought in as "expert inventors" when, in fact, their solutions are very often unrealistic. They believe they should be compensated through equity, royalties or stock options, especially in today's startup-crazed environment. However, I did learn the power of including lead user input into the innovation management process, at the right time, in the right amount and with the right scope.

One of my main learnings was the importance of timing. Bringing in lead users too early can often drag the entire project in an irreversible direction. Too late it becomes an exercise in validation since the team has already locked themselves into a course of action with preferred concepts. The appropriate time, in most instances is following the adoption phase of the innovation approach, before concept refinement. Following this approach, the discovery and adoption phases should have produced fledgling concepts grounded on the problems, needs and trends of the mainstream market. Often this results in novel solutions to existing problems, with creative aspects that "might" delight the customer. Many times, these delighters stem from observations (the preferred method of DT proponents) made during primary research. Although, as discussed, observation is a good approach, but does not magically translate itself to delight features conceived through a brainstorming session. Lead users, however, can bridge this gap.

Similarly, the right scope and right amount are also key to the success of this method. After the concept generation phase, the team should be in a strong position to answer the question of "what attributes are the key to success in this category" (see benchmarking). This may seem like a simplistic question; however, in practice, it can have a significant impact. First, the exercise of conducting secondary research, benchmarking, primary research and concept development should ground the team in the category to a point where they can subjectively determine what the key attributes of the product should be. The mere fact that the team has created concepts from this background work often highlights what attributes the team *believes* are important. These can range from esthetics (e.g., for products like golf putters) to cooperation (e.g., for products like boardgames). What I find useful is to conduct a review of the concepts with a keen eye on what attributes each concept highlights. Often, two to three attributes are dominant and easily agreed upon by the team. This attribute exercise can also unlock the team's thinking about analogs. For instance, if esthetics is a key attribute of a product category, what are other categories where esthetics are dominant? These could include categories such as perfume, watches, etc. This scoping activity I find to be most productive after the discovery phase. It redirects the team into digging deeper and has the additional benefit of moving them off their "preferred" concept (à la groupthink) at this part of the process.

Once the scope and timing are correct, all that remains is how much time should be spent on this activity. In my experience, as we say in academia...it depends... The reality is that it forces the team to go back and engage in a new innovation cycle, albeit from a different perspective. No longer is the team looking for mainstream problems and trends but are looking at extreme problems and offbeat solutions. I normally task the team to spend a half day (four hours) looking for lead users or lead use experts *in each of the three categories* (i.e., market, attributes and analogs). They then report back and spend another two to three hours presenting and digesting this information. I then find it good to take a break for a few days and let it sit. In most cases, team members can't help themselves and continue to poke away at this exercise in their downtime. When we reconvene, we agree on a list of potential areas of investigation and send the team members off for another half day and repeat the process. This normally results in a handful of interesting lines of inquiry, often involving additional follow-up from both the secondary and primary research perspective. The team is then dispatched to conduct whatever research is agreed upon (normally over the next working week) followed by a full team meeting to share the knowledge gained from this exercise. Baring the team wanting to gather additional information, this is the time to ask "what problem do we need to solve next, and how does it relate to our initial concepts?" This is the point where I deviate from the full-blown lead user research approach. I find that once the problem has been redefined from a different perspective, the fledgling solutions become apparent to a well-rounded team. The team can then enter a new round of brainstorming where these fledgling concepts can be expanded and built upon. This results in revised concept(s) with added features and benefits that have the potential to delight the user.

Example – Lead User Analog

Revisiting the handheld GPS category, it became clear that one of the challenges was to increase perceived value in a stagnant category. At the time Garmin™ was the dominant player in the handheld GPS market with prices ranging from USD$99 to USD$299. The top end of the market was controlled by a few specialty companies such as Brunton™ (an outdoor company) with a GPS that retailed for USD$399. The objective was how to pierce through the ceiling of the market into the ultra-premium price range. The challenge was to find a lead user in an analog market, who had successfully repositioned a product from commodity to premium within a category.

After several hours of searching, a few potential lead users were located and examined. The most interesting one was a Scandinavian industrial design firm that was hired to take commodity cookware products and upgrade them to a premium offering in the category. The interesting approach that they took was not so much to upgrade the cookware itself, but to upgrade its status in the kitchen. They had conducted research into working professionals who had a need for convenience, simplicity and status. Their solution was to create an aesthetically attractive storage center for these pots and pans, so that they were no longer hidden in cupboards, but were elegantly displayed as a center piece of condominium kitchens. This simplistic design created pride of ownership of the cookware while making it convenient to use, clean and store. This analog became the kernel of a solution for how to instill a sense of pride of ownership in the handheld GPS category.

Instead of executing a full-blown lead user workshop, the team was entrusted to come up with concepts that would satisfy this requirement. First, they revisited notes and interviews from primary research and did further probe and learn activities with end-users. The specific probe and learn question was "what is the most precious item you normally take into the wilderness?" Since many of these outdoor professionals were also hunters and fishers, many of them said their riflescope. These precision instruments, many costing thousands of dollars, were so precious that they carried them in a Pelican™ case (Fig. 16) to protect them. Remembering our cognitive mapping associations, we knew that ruggedness unlocked pride and status so the team felt that the rugged Pelican™ case would be associated with pride of ownership and hence value. The team ordered several Pelican™ cases for an upcoming tradeshow and the cognitive link was instantaneous. Like the cookware example, the consumer perceived that this GPS was so "precious" that it should be carried in a Pelican™ case, effectively positioning it in the same category as thousand-dollar riflescopes. Our volume cost for these cases at the time was roughly USD$10 per unit, which allowed us to increase our retail price for our GPS by USD$250.

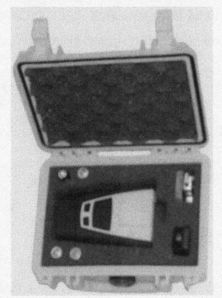

Fig. 16. Pelican™ case

Conclusion

Lead user research is a very powerful innovation management technique. In my opinion, it is the best technique available to discover unspoken (latent) delight needs from which best-of-class solutions can be developed. Like all best-of-class innovation management techniques, it relies on a strong foundation of secondary and primary research, albeit with a focus on the edges of markets and technologies, rather than the mainstream.

The success (or failure) of lead user research rests on the team's fundamental understanding of what a lead user actually is. They are *individuals, organizations or groups who have an extreme need in the marketplace that cannot be satisfied with existing products or services and are thus compelled to innovate.* They are not early adopters, nor are they inventors, extreme customers or do-it-yourselfers (DYIers). They live not only in the peripheries of *markets* but at the edges of parallel (i.e., *analog*) markets or on the fringes of technical *attributes*. As a result they are difficult to find. Teams must employ more of an investigative journalist role rather than that of a market researcher. Once teams understand this approach, the rewards can be immense, since these unique individuals provide a clear foresight into future market requirements and a bridge to unique and differentiated solutions.

In Practice – Lead User Research

As highlighted throughout this chapter, the innovation management process can benefit significantly from lead user input. It is not necessary to conduct a full lead user research study, including open innovation workshops with lead users. For most innovation projects, conducting secondary and primary research to discover lead users, understand their motivations and examine their solutions is all that is required. If the team is truly structured in a multidisciplinary and collaborative fashion, I've rarely witnessed a project where the team cannot develop superior solutions once they understand the fundamental problems discovered through lead users.

In brief, the process should look like the following:

INPUTS

Completed "Adoption" innovation cycle.

PROCESS

Coming out of the concept development phase, pose the following questions to the team "what other markets might be experiencing the same problems" (i.e., *analogs*)? "What are the key *attributes* of our product or service concepts"?

Conduct secondary research with a focus on identifying lead use experts initially in *market, analogs* and *attributes*. Disseminate findings within the team and continue to conduct secondary research until lead users have been identified.

Conduct primary research (i.e., probe and learn interviews) with lead users focusing mostly on "why" they were compelled to innovate, more than on "how" they solved the problem. The latter is normally apparent.

Conduct revised concept development activities (e.g., ideation) with a focus on solutions to the "why" (i.e., problems) revealed from the lead users.

OUTPUTS

Revised concepts with potential delight features, ready to be prototyped for user feedback.

NOTE: For reference I would highly encourage readers to read the following sources prior to undertaking this approach:

Creating Breakthroughs at 3M (von Hippel et al., 1999)

Lead user project handbook: A practical guide for lead user project teams (Churchill et al., 2009)

I can say without a doubt that this approach consistently delivers fruitful avenues of inquiry in any product category or industry. When harnessed by a well-managed multifunctional team, rarely has this approach failed to deliver delight features.

Chapter 11

Sustainability

Sustainability is a broad concept that has applications for both the front end (FEI) and back end of innovation (BEI). It involves aspects of environment and social responsibility that cut across products, projects and enterprises. For the purposes of the innovation approach, sustainability is focused on the environmental aspects of the product itself, while social aspects are relegated to the BEI. This chapter examines the link between eco-development and environmental customer behavior; what is possible from a design perspective and what is adoptable from a user perspective. Various approaches are examined including life cycle analysis (LCA) and principles of eco-design. The chapter concludes with proposing a Cradle-to-Cradle (C2C) approach for refining concepts as the final phase of the innovation approach.

Introduction

This chapter focuses on the final phase of the innovation approach, which I describe as *sustainability*. Sustainability is a broad concept that has applications at both the FEI and BEI. It is part of a larger framework known as the environmental, social and governance (ESG), which focuses on the governance of organizations' impact on the planet and their constituents (i.e., people, staff, customers and community).

For the purposes of the innovation approach, sustainability relates to planet impact since these are decisions that are made during the FEI and are predominantly irreversible. Social aspects, on the other hand, transcend the organization and are only tangentially related to the product or service design itself. These are considered BEI decisions, made at the organizational level that cut across operations, projects and other aspects of the firm.

Nowadays, it is unthinkable that environmental and sustainability aspects of new products should evade the innovation process. Consequently, this chapter focuses on the integration of environmental attributes into the innovation process while balancing social and economic requirements.

The Innovation Approach:
Overcoming the Limitations of Design Thinking and the Lean Startup, 167–183
Copyright © 2025 by David C. Roach
Published under exclusive licence by Emerald Publishing Limited
doi:10.1108/978-1-83797-799-420241011

Eco-development

I choose to use eco-development as an umbrella term for assessing innovations through an eco-friendly prism. However, there are many descriptions associated with this umbrella construct.

Eco-design refers to the integration of environmental characteristics into the product development process, by balancing ecological and economic requirements. It considers environmental aspects at all stages of the product development process, striving for products that make the lowest possible environmental impact throughout the product life cycle[1]. Eco-design is one of many terms that describes an approach to sustainable design. Other well-established terms include Design for Environment (DfE) and Design for Sustainability (D4S).

DfE is a broader framework that incorporates environmental strategies from cradle to grave. Eco-design is a specific approach within DfE that focuses on integrating environmental considerations into the design process, while DfE goes a step further by focusing on the entire product life cycle. As a result, it further examines waste reduction, energy consumption and logistical impacts.

D4S, in addition to environmental principles, also advocates for the integration of sustainability into the design process. It is an approach that not only advocates for environmentally friendly products, services and systems, but adds a focus on social responsibility. It emphasizes the importance of considering sustainability from various perspectives in the early stages of design. This requires the examination of inputs (e.g., supply chains), processes and disposal through both an ecological and social lens. Overall, it challenges designers to contribute positively to both environmental and social aspects through their work.

For the purposes of the innovation approach, the emphasis is mostly focused on DfE since it is more aligned with the FEI. Other aspects of sustainability are generally relegated to the BEI since they are often related to supply chains, outsourcing and inclusivity issues. For instance, developing, managing and auditing supply chains are important corporate responsibilities but are activities that must be managed post-development. Similarly, inclusivity both inside and outside the organization is often a strategic priority supported by corporate processes. These are system-wide strategies that transcend individual innovation projects.

It is estimated that over 80% of all product-related environmental impacts are determined during the design phase of a product[2]. Businesses that design environmentally friendly products should be able to successfully differentiate themselves in the eyes of consumers. This should result in an improved environmental footprint, less waste and better outcomes for the planet. However, for this to occur, eco-friendly products must be adoptable by the target audience they intend to serve. This is where design and consumer behavior intersect with respect to environmentally friendly products.

---

[1] https://www.eea.europa.eu/help/glossary/eea-glossary/eco-design
[2] European Commission, Eco–design for Energy Using Products, 2009. Directive 2009/125/EC of the European Parliament and of the Council establishing a framework for the setting of eco-design requirements.

Eco-development and Consumer Behavior

What can be provided to the customer and what the customer is willing to adopt are at the core of the innovation process. Customers need to perceive an *aggregate value proposition* that satisfies their needs better than their next best option. Understanding this complexity requires knowledge of the growing body of research on consumer behavior, psychology and related methodologies. Despite efforts to link demographics, attitudes or knowledge to ecological behavior, challenges persist. Thus, before developing eco-friendly concepts, it is imperative to understand consumer behavior with respect to environmental features and benefits.

Eco-behavior

Environmentally meaningful consumer behavior is dauntingly complex in both its variety and its understanding of causal relationships (Stren, 2000). Ecological consumer behavior remains a challenging field with little consensus among scholars, methodologists and applied researchers. This complexity stems from various interdisciplinary influences and methodological approaches within consumer behavior research. As a result, understanding and predicting pro-environmental behavior has proven to be remarkably difficult to assess (McCarty & Shrum, 2001).

In cognitive consumer research, a product is understood as a collection of tangible and intangible attributes. It is viewed as a bundle of information cues (e.g., price, package, brand) which consumers selectively use when evaluating products to make purchase decisions (Wagner, 1997). This raises questions about the interpretation of product attributes, the subjective nature of consumer cognition and the potential application of eco/social marketing to bridge the gap.

The Elusive Green Consumer

Green consumers are environmentally conscious individuals who purchase (i.e., display green buying) and consume products (i.e., exhibit environmental consumerism) (Mainieri et al., 1997). They are a subset of a larger construct known as the socially conscious consumer, who considers the public consequences of their private consumption. They attempt to use their purchasing power to bring about social/environmental change. While most standard models of purchase intent assume that benefits accrue to the individual, pro-environmental benefits accrue to society over the long term. Since the results are future-oriented and don't benefit the individual directly, this behavior relies on their willingness to move from *eco-intent* to *eco-behavior*. However, this is not characteristic of mainstream customers who display limitations between intent and action.

The two most studied attitudes in the ecological literature are "importance" and "inconvenience" (Laroche et al., 2001). Amyx et al. (1994) defined environmental importance as the degree to which one expresses concern about ecological issues (i.e., is it important to them). Inconvenience refers to the *perception* of how inconvenient it is for individuals to behave in an ecologically friendly manner.

As an example, if municipalities make composting convenient through such services as supplying bins, weekly pick up, and perhaps periodic cleaning of bins, most people (i.e., mainstream customers) will adopt. They perceive both importance and convenience and move from intent to action. On the other hand, if municipalities also offer plastic recycling without clear guidelines and require drop-off at a central location without a rebate program, most people will not adopt. The importance is roughly the same, but it is highly inconvenient.

This highlights the difference between consumer *attitude* and consumer *behavior*. Many studies focus merely on consumer attitudes toward eco-friendly solutions, with few examining the messy link to behavior. The reasons for this are many but include weak research methods, use of convenience samples and ease of attitude surveys versus behavioral research. However, the studies that have examined this relationship have invariably found either inconclusive or weak links between eco-attitude and eco-behavior. As I've stated many times to my graduate students, "never believe what people say, only trust how they behave." The question is why?

Diekmann and Preisendörfer (2003) examined self-reported (rather the observed behavior) and found that it was biased toward ecological correctness. They concluded that it was especially strong because respondents knew that they were participating in an environmental survey. In another example, Laroche et al. (2001), relying on self-reported answers to consumers' willingness to pay more for eco-friendly products, found that willingness to spend more did not match their behavior. The reasons for this vary but may come down to the so-called halo effect (Webb & Mohr, 1998) or the alibi. The halo effect refers to consumers who claim to prefer goods on an ethical basis, but when making purchasing decisions, defer to other factors, such as the relative price of the product. The alibi is substituting highly visible and convenient eco-behavior to avoid cognitive dissonance. Cognitive dissonance is the discomfort people feel when their behaviors do not align with their values or beliefs. It is a psychological phenomenon that occurs when a person holds two contradictory beliefs at the same time. As an example, an individual may compulsively shop online, purchasing fast fashion or tech gadgets, both highly wasteful, and carrying a high carbon footprint. However, every Monday morning, they will diligently roll their compost bins to the curb while greeting the neighbors in an effort to rationalize their behaviors.

Consumers also make decisions based on heuristics. When they perceive a complex decision, they rely on rules of thumb and tend to simplify their decision by focusing on a narrow range of criteria. This is the phenomenon that leads consumers to make large purchase decisions such as vehicles based on coffee cup holders or heated seats. These decisions appear illogical to the uninitiated but are, in fact, real. To put it in an environmental context, consumers often rely on narrow product attributes that they can easily understand when making decisions. For instance, they may consider products made from recycled paper as the same as those made from postconsumer waste. This can make them susceptible to greenwashing since savvy marketers understand this phenomenon and are incented to exploit it.

In any event, there are a myriad of reasons why customers may or may not adopt eco-friendly products. There is no effective profile of the green consumer; thus, to be successful, innovators must consider both what is possible through design and what is adoptable in practice. This should not, however, discourage innovators, but understanding eco-consumer behavior is foundational to the development of more environmentally sustainable products.

Eco-development and LCA

According to Wagner (1997), a *product* is conceptualized as the promise of a bundle of value expectations from which the customer derives need and value satisfaction when he (she) buys. The bundle of value described is an aggregation of the product attributes, which include such things as size, color, brand or in our case eco-friendliness.

Many environmentalists approach eco-development from the position that all that ails the product should first be determined, followed by a radical redesign based on its environmental footprint. They rely on the rigor of LCA studies to pinpoint the deficits of existing products that must be remedied. They assume that radical change is necessary and scoff at incremental stepwise approaches to the innovation process. This approach has significant limitations since (i) it does not consider consumer behavior and (ii) business is not very good at "all or nothing" development (Hopkins, 2010).

What Is LCA?

LCA is a systematic and comprehensive method used to evaluate the environmental impacts of products and processes throughout the entire life cycle. It examines these from extraction of raw materials through to production, distribution, use and disposal. LCA is also commonly referred to as life cycle assessment.

Typically, the process of conducting an LCA involves four main stages.

Scope Definition. This initial stage involves defining the objectives of the analysis and determining the boundaries of the study. It includes identifying the product or system to be analyzed, specifying the functional unit (e.g., per kilogram of product, per unit of energy produced) and setting the boundaries of the life cycle stages to be included.

Conducting a *Life Cycle Inventory*. In this stage, data are collected on all inputs (e.g., raw materials, energy, water) and outputs (e.g., emissions, waste) associated with each stage of the product's life cycle. This involves compiling detailed inventories of resource consumption and emissions using proprietary databases and other sources of information.

Next is the core of the process *Life Cycle Impact Assessment (LCIA)*. This step evaluates the potential environmental impacts associated with the inputs and outputs identified in the previous stage. LCIA involves assessing the environmental consequences of resource use and emissions.

The final and most crucial stage is *Interpretation*. In this stage, the results of the LCA are analyzed and interpreted. This includes aligning the findings with the original scope, identifying opportunities for improvement and providing recommendations for reducing environmental impacts.

An LCA must start from a known position (i.e., an existing product) and build its audit from there. As a result, it is a *forensic audit* rather than a *development activity*. This highlights the stark difference between the analyst and the innovator.

What Are the Limitations of LCA?

LCA is a valuable tool for assessing environmental impacts, but it has several limitations.

Although improving, data quality and availability continue to be a challenge in conducting LCAs. Complex supply chains and processes can produce data gaps that impact accuracy, potentially leading to inaccurate conclusions. Defining the boundaries of the life cycle stages (i.e., what to include or exclude) can also significantly impact results. Different boundary conditions can lead to varying conclusions, which may not capture the full environmental impact (Heijungs & Suh, 2002). The choice of methodology can also affect results where certain environmental impacts may be prioritized over others (International Standards Association, 2006). Finally, interpreting results and translating them into actionable decisions can be challenging, particularly when trade-offs between environmental impacts exist. For instance, decision-makers often struggle to prioritize competing objectives between the impact of materials and their carbon footprint.

This ex post facto process is also resource-intensive, time-consuming and costly. It assesses what has already taken place, rather than providing inputs in real time for decision-making. It often can only lay out the evidence and rarely provides a definitive answer as to the best solution. Like academic research, they often invoke the rationale that "it depends." This usually refers to the boundary conditions that frame the study, which can be arbitrary, inconsistent, and in rare cases, manipulated. It can also prioritize environmental metrics over other important aspects, such as social, economic and ethical considerations (Guinée et al., 2011).

Case Example – Nappies

In 2005, the Environment Agency released an LCA outlining the environmental impact of using disposable and reusable nappies (i.e., diapers) in the UK. The study was conducted over a one-year period at an estimated cost of over £1M and aimed to assess the environmental impacts of using disposable nappies versus reusable nappies in the UK for the years 2001–2002. Three different nappy types were assessed: disposable nappies, home-laundered flat cloth nappies and commercially laundered pre-folded cloth nappies delivered to the home. The study was conducted by an independent environmental consultancy, Environmental Resources Management Limited (ERM), and complied with international standards for LCA.

The study found that there was *no significant difference in the over-all environmental impacts* between the three nappy systems. Their conclusion was that there was no clear winner in terms of environmental performance. However, the life cycle stages that contributed to these impacts differed for each system. The most significant environmental impacts for all three systems were on resource depletion, acidification and global warming. These impacts were roughly comparable to driving a car between 1300 and 2200 miles over a period of two and a half years for one child.

The study, however, excluded impacts such as noise, biodiversity and land use, focusing instead on resource depletion, climate change, ozone depletion, human toxicity, acidification, fresh-water aquatic toxicity, terrestrial toxicity, photochemical oxidant formation and nutrification of fresh water. However, depending on where the boundaries of the study were drawn, some options could be considered as performing better than others. Although the study was inconclusive with respect to the best option, they concluded that it provides a framework for assessing the environmental impacts of reusable and disposable nappies and *should be used to guide future efforts in reducing these impacts.*

This study has not resulted in any appreciable changes in nappies.

As a result, approaching an innovation project *primarily* from an LCA perspective is ineffective. LCAs should be considered inputs into the secondary research portion of the innovation cycle, used to expose issues, while informing the innovation team. LCAs are nonetheless influential decision-support tools for comparing different design inputs (Klöpffer, 2006) and should be used as support instruments rather than drivers of decisions.

McDonough & Braungart (2002) refer to the "lock-in" effect to describe the limitations of the LCA method and its focus on eco-efficiency (Bakker et al., 2010). LCAs, they contend, tend to lock designers into a mindset of improving the efficiency of existing systems rather than seeking more effective and sustainable solutions. This occurs because LCAs analyze a product's environmental impacts within predetermined system boundaries and functional units. Once these boundaries are established, designers are limited to making improvements only within those boundaries. This can lead to a narrow focus on optimization of existing processes rather than questioning the fundamental design and purpose of the product.

As a result, it does not challenge the underlying assumptions and paradigms of the current industrial system. Instead, McDonough and Braungart advocate for a shift toward *eco-effectiveness*, which involves rethinking and redesigning products and systems to mimic the regenerative cycles found in nature. By embracing eco-effectiveness, designers can break free from the "lock-in" effect and explore more innovative and sustainable solutions.

Eco-development and Innovation Management

Many nascent entrepreneurs believe that consumers will beat a path to their door if they create an eco-friendlier version of a product. They tend to approach eco-development from a solution-centric approach (i.e., their concept drives the process) rather than the process driving a value-creation approach.

Ecologically friendly aspects of products are rarely "delight" features (see KANO Model Chapter 4, Fig. 6). However, they are often considered such by innovators who begin from an eco-centric perspective rather than a value-based approach. This mimics the solution-based approach, where the driving force emanates from a well-meaning but altruistic vision of the process outcome. Much like technocrats who approach innovation based on the seduction of their technology, eco-projects often begin from the premise that customers will adopt products merely based on their ecological attributes. Both approaches tend to be seduced by their own vision, resulting in selection bias which severely restricts the solution space. This unfortunately often results in a "net negative" value proposition for most customers. While the intentions are commendable, the innovations are often not adopted or adopted by a small niche of customers, resulting in little positive eco-impact.

Academic researchers and eco-innovators tend to focus on designing products that are more ecologically friendly, isolated from the realities of consumer behavior. The bulk of the literature seems to be focused on "building-in" green features under the assumption that this eco-knowledge will be readily understood (and acted upon) by the consumer. This flies in the face of the bulk of consumer behavior research that predicts that "knowledge" does not consistently affect "attitude" and that it certainly does not significantly impact behavior. Thus, relying on educating the customer on eco-benefits is mostly an ineffective approach. However, creating a solid value proposition with "value-add" eco-benefits can be a winning formula.

It's a Material Problem

In an MIT SLOAN interview, Dr. Steven Eppinger emphasized in no uncertain terms that sustainable design is fundamentally a materials problem. He criticizes taking a "black and white" approach to eco-innovation and the push to complete LCA studies before "ever lifting a tool" (Hopkins, 2010). He strongly advocates for an incremental approach since all toxins and waste are designed-in at the front end. When approaching eco-design there are two principal aspects that must be considered. First is that the problem invariably comes down to a materials selection problem. Second is the greenhouse gas (GHG) emissions created over the production, distribution and disposal of the product.

He contends that materials are generally considered bad. We see images of landfills filled with garbage and beaches littered with plastic waste. Even more concerning is the breakdown of these materials into the human food chain. As bad as this may seem, materials are unfortunately a necessary part of our daily lives, from packaging our food to life-saving medical devices. The reason plastics (the main culprit) have proliferated is not merely based on capitalistic greed, but because they are tremendous engineered materials. They can be designed to fulfill almost any function required of a material even options that are not currently available any other way. These materials have given us applications we could only dream of as a society half a century ago. Although I dearly wish that we could get rid of them altogether, the reality is that they are here to stay. Since over 80% of material decisions are irreversible once the concept is finalized, our only practical solution is to *eliminate them at source*, which means innovators must lead the way.

There are two schools of thought. One is elimination, the other is the classic 3R approach, namely reduce, reuse, recycle. Complete elimination is extremely difficult, mostly involves regulation, and is impractical in most situations (often due to the material characteristics themselves). Low-hanging elimination activities are finally beginning to be implemented. Banning of single use plastics is now being regulated in many Western countries and includes such products as plastic bags, bottles and cutlery. Conversely, the 3R approach begins with "reduce" which is mainly based on consumption reduction, rather than source reduction. Reuse models still rely on consumption, but often take the form of new business models where entrepreneurs develop clever ways to reuse otherwise disposable materials. For instance, the reuse of takeout containers through rental, cleaning and restocking (*Reusable Takeout Options Are Popping Up Across Canada | CBC News*, 2021). Finally, "recycle" is the last resort for materials that reach the disposal cycle. Since this is highly jurisdictionally regulated, recycling rates are still quite low globally.

There is, however, a third way…

Cradle to Cradle (C2C)

In their 2002 seminal book, William McDonough and Michael Braungart challenged the traditional concept of waste and proposed a paradigm shift in the way innovators design and manufacture products. They advocate a vision of a sustainable future where materials could be continuously reused and regenerated, mimicking natural systems.

The authors introduced the concept of the "cradle-to-cradle" (C2C) design framework, which contrasts with the conventional "cradle-to-grave" linear model of production and consumption. In the cradle-to-grave approach, products are manufactured, used and then discarded as waste, contributing to environmental degradation and resource depletion. In contrast, the C2C model advocates for the creation of products that can be perpetually recycled or returned safely to the environment as nutrients, without generating harmful byproducts.

Central to the C2C philosophy is the idea that "waste equals food," where all materials used in production are designed to be either biodegradable and safe for the environment or endlessly recyclable without loss of quality. They illustrate their principles with numerous examples, ranging from architecture to consumer products and textiles. Their book itself is a C2C creation, made from reusable plastic and biodegradable inks. Once the book reaches its end of life, the ink can be removed in boiling in water and discarded into the biodegradable stream, while the plastic pages can be reused in a new form through the technical stream.

One of the key propositions of the C2C methodology is the differentiation between "eco-effectiveness" and "eco-efficiency." While eco-efficiency focuses on reducing resource consumption and minimizing environmental impact, eco-effectiveness aims to optimize ecological benefits and create value for both humans and the environment. This shift in mindset encourages designers and businesses to prioritize innovation by considering the entire life cycle of products and their impact on ecosystems. As such, the book critiques traditional environmentalism, arguing that merely minimizing harm or reducing pollution is insufficient for achieving true sustainability. Instead, the authors advocate for a proactive approach that seeks to create positive ecological footprints through regenerative design and responsible stewardship of natural resources.

How Does It Work?

The C2C approach shown in Fig. 17 has two primary layers, namely stream separation and reuse.

Stream separation is at the core of the C2C methodology. The first concept is the distinction between biological nutrients and technical nutrients. Biological nutrients are represented by materials, for example, natural fibers such as wood, plant-based materials or iron which will biodegrade to iron oxide. The technical stream involves everything from plastics to metals, glass and chemicals. These will not biodegrade, but unadulterated can be reused in a technical fashion to produce new products. In essence, it is a form of recycling. However, these nutrient streams are only made possible if the streams can be *easily separated* into their constituents. If they cannot, these *fused streams* become what C2C refers to as *monstrous hybrids* (see Fig. 17).

Monstrous hybrids create the need for design for disassembly (DfD), a common practice in eco-design. These not only refer to physical items but can also involve chemicals. For instance, a biodegradable vegetable oil, if mixed with a chemical surfactant, would be considered a hybrid. Similarly, a biodegradable wood laminated with a plastic covering would also create a monstrous hybrid.

Once the biological stream is isolated from the technical stream, the latter can be investigated in more depth. The technical stream can then be further segregated into up-cyclable and recyclable materials. Up-cyclability refers to materials that do not degrade when reused. For instance, most metals and glass can be reused virtually in perpetuity, since their material properties do not degrade. Plastics, on the other hand, degrade as they are repurposed and thus enter a downgrade cycle. As they are reused their performance degrades until such a point as they are no longer reusable and thus must be disposed of. Chemicals based on their nature can be either up-cyclable or recyclable depending on their properties.

As a result, designers should always approach any innovation project from a C2C perspective before locking in their design.

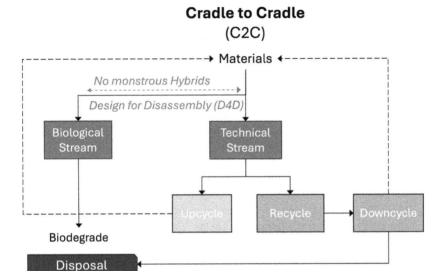

Fig. 17. Cradle to Cradle (C2C) Approach.

Case Example – Mirra™ Chair

The most prominent example of the use of C2C methodology is the Mirra™ office chair. The office furniture company, Herman Miller, had a long history of environmental stewardship in their operations and was at the cutting edge of eco-efficiency in the late 1990s. At the time, they had eliminated virtually all their production waste, minimized their energy requirements and implemented waste stream management into all of their operations. Their waste became so minimal that employees claimed they would not want to be the ones who created any garbage, even in the cafeteria (Lee & Boni, 2009). At this point, it became apparent that any further improvements could only come through examining the product itself to eliminate its environmental impact at the source. This led them to collaborate with William McDonough to create a system for designing C2C products.

Using the C2C methodology, their goal was to reduce their footprint by designing a chair that *appealed to the market* with the *lowest possible environmental footprint*. This required rethinking their long-held designs to incorporate DfD, increased use of recycled materials and improved material selection. None of these activities came easy. For instance, DfD, although conceptually simple, posed some engineering challenges. How should a chair be designed to be easily disassembled without the risk of it falling apart during use? Recycled materials are nice in theory, but they must continue to adhere to their requirements, both structurally and aesthetically. Material chemistry was also a challenge since many suppliers were reluctant to share their trade secrets. This would require the creation of a simple materials selection system based on green, yellow and red characteristics of materials (Rossi et al., 2006). However, through perseverance and strong management support, they were able to produce a chair with an 80% rating on their DfE product assessment instrument, developed in collaboration with McDonough.

The most significant challenge rested (no pun intended) on the armrests of the chair (Fig. 18). These were traditionally made with polyvinyl chloride (PVC). PVC was considered ecologically unsuitable due to its organochlorine content, generation of enduring toxins in manufacturing and production of dioxins and furans when burned. It was considered a "red" material from an eco-design perspective. This industry standard, however, provided for long-term wear, scratch resistance and structural integrity. Marketing information highlighted that scratches were a significant cause of customer complaints and returns. Although the company had been working for some time on a replacement material (i.e., vinyl), it was difficult to mold and suffered from surface imperfections. The company decided to employ the same technique as Toyota where they parallel processed these two materials until such a time as the project dictated that a decision needed to be made. When the time came, the company was still unsure whether the vinyl technology was ready for commercial use, but management took the bold step to proceed. Their rationale was that if we commit to this technology, the organization will be forced to step up and solve the remaining issues. They hoped the gamble would be worth it from a strategic perspective as well as for company culture. This enlightened management approach overcame

Fig. 18.   Mirra™ Chair.

the uncertainty and risk associated with this new technology. It resulted in an industry leading capability and drove a significant portion of the chair's DfE rating.

The Mirra™ office chair appealed to the target market based on its overall value proposition, which included its eco-friendly design.

There are however critics of this approach who focus on its limitations. These include the incomplete data on materials composition, knowledge of new materials, lack of closed-loop material flows and associated energy consumption. Energy consumption is becoming understood as a gap in the C2C methodology, given the heightened emphasis on reducing CO_2 emissions, which requires a thorough understanding of energy flows. They also cite a lack of methodological rigor (i.e., the approach can be ad hoc) and that it may not be applicable to all design situations (Bakker et al., 2010). All of these critiques are valid.

These limitations, however, should not discourage innovation teams from this approach. There will never be enough knowledge about existing or new materials. Closing the materials loop is an ongoing process and energy consumption (a direct driver of CO_2 emissions) is source dependent. However, all these issues can be generally estimated to a point where informed decisions can be made. For instance, any chemical with an "ene" at the end of its name (i.e., benzene, xylene, toluene, etc.) are likely "red" materials. A quick internet search can suggest alternatives. Energy estimates for alternatives can be used for comparison regardless of the energy source.

A few years ago, I attended an executive course at the University of Chicago. In the class were many senior executives from multinational corporations, including McDonald's. At the time, McDonald's was basking in their strategic move into coffee, a remarkably profitable offering for them. In my discussions with them, using simple principles of C2C, I highlighted five aspects of their coffee offering that contravened C2C thinking, none of which would affect their cost base. They confessed that they didn't know why this had not been part of their design criteria. The takeaway is that it is the responsibility of all commercial entities to consider the impact of their decisions. Using simple C2C guidelines, any product can be improved to reduce its long-term impact. Years later, I see some changes for the better, including a move away from single use offerings. They still have a way to go...

How Is It Used in the Innovation Approach?

The C2C methodology becomes the foundation for the final phase of the innovation approach. It repeats the *innovation cycle* through a prism of sustainability beginning with secondary research. The focus of this research is to establish best practices and garner relevant information, specifically on materials. For instance, a scan of LCA studies related to the category or general material science can be a very powerful input to the process. LCA studies can highlight critical environmental gaps where the innovation team may want to focus their eco-design activities. Often these LCA studies provide a rich amount of information on the GHG footprints of the category, along with commentary on their drivers. Since many of these studies are commissioned by governments or research institutes, they are largely freely available to the public. Another focus of secondary research is the properties of the materials themselves. Understanding the footprint of various chemical and plastic options for design can be invaluable to the team. These help the process of determining the inevitable material tradeoffs throughout the design process. One good approach is to follow Herman Miller's example and rate chemicals and plastics using a three-tiered coding system (i.e., green, yellow, red). This avoids getting caught up in the minutiae of material science and simplifies decision making for the team (Rossi et al., 2006).

Benchmarking continues to play a role, although a nominal one. Taking a fresh look at the product category is always helpful. When examined through a materials lens, the team can assess alternate approaches to material selection. Often, it becomes a forum for discussion of alternatives to existing category-specific materials rather than a revelation of a novel material selection. The culmination of this background research (secondary and benchmarking) then becomes the focal point for the development of a discussion guide for primary research.

Primary research can then be centered around material *characteristics* rather than the materials themselves. This can provide an increased understanding of critical material properties integral to the design. Another suggested approach is to use a technique called *barrier busting* used in environmental psychology to modify behavior. It comes out of research on environmental change, where it criticizes the "information intensive" education campaigns that attempt to affect attitudes, to modify behavior through slick marketing "awareness" campaigns (McKenzie-Mohr, 2000). Instead, it approaches issues from spoken and unspoken *barriers to adoption*. When developing a discussion guide and conducting probe and learn interviews, a focus on *barriers* can be an effective approach to understanding approaches to design changes.

Armed with this renewed body of knowledge, the team is then ready to enter a refined ideation stage, where material characteristics, tradeoffs and design criteria can be developed.

What About the Other Aspects of Sustainability?

Other sustainability aspects should also be considered but do not necessarily impact the design process. Sustainability goes beyond the ecological footprint to encompass social and economic dimensions, including considerations of equity, well-being and economic prosperity. Impacts on employment, community and resources can be essential for achieving holistic sustainability outcomes. For example, promoting packaging solutions that support local economies, creating job opportunities and enhancing community resilience can contribute to broader sustainability goals.

Although related to the design process, these considerations are generally relegated to the BEI, where supply chain and societal decisions are made. These are more often business model decisions rather than design decisions. Thus, these should be examined and dealt with during the BEI processes.

Case Example – ETEE™

etee™ is a Canadian company founded based on the vision to eliminate plastic waste. The company's singular purpose is to *develop genuine solutions to plastic pollution, so that (customers) can live more simply, sustainably and in greater harmony with (the) planet.*

Although the vision was based on developing eco-friendly products, the co-founder Steve Reble was astute enough to understand that customers buy based on value. For his company to be successful, it needed to make *"it easy for (the consumer) to make a change."* He understood the fundamentals of consumer behavior, namely the relationship between *importance* and *inconvenience*.

Their inaugural product was a food wrap and associated bags made from organic cotton impregnated with beeswax and other natural ingredients. These products replaced single-use plastic wraps and plastic sandwich bags with an eco-friendly solution. These types of products had been available from small craft suppliers, but the quality was poor, they were limited to wraps and were less appealing to a mass market. As a result, they had very little consumer uptake and limited positive ecological impact. Steve reformulated the product to improve the quality using a variety of natural ingredients that improved the seal of the wraps. Then using eco-friendly dyes, he created a rainbow of colors and packaged them into attractive recycled packaging. He also examined the customer journey and included videos on the proper care and washing of these products. The result was a highly successful and attractive product line that eliminated plastic. When the product eventually reached the end of its useful life, customers could merely compost it since all materials were aligned with the biological stream[3].

It then occurred to Steve that sourcing eco-friendly washing solutions – to clean the reusable wraps – suffered from the same problem. Generally, the quality was inconsistent; some of the adoption requirements (e.g., grease removal, suds and aroma) were missing and shipping mostly water was not very eco-friendly. With an understanding of the C2C approach and adoption theory, he began by reformulating dishwashing liquid to

---

[3]Dr. Andrew Clark of East Tennessee State University was commissioned to conduct a compost study which confirmed the company's claims.

eliminate water while improving grease removal, aroma and bubbles. His initial approach was to create either compressed powder or "hand soap-like" tablets, however, this was inconvenient for customers – a classic adoption *compatibility* issue. Pivoting from solid options he was able to reformulate a liquid–gel option that reduced more than 70% of the water content. Satisfied by the consumer's positive reaction, he then tackled the packaging by examining material options. Initially, selling the product in a glass bottle (an up-cyclable material) appeared to be the only option. This would solve the plastic problem but shipping heavy single-use glass seemed counterproductive to the company's mission. He wondered if there might be a biological stream solution. After brainstorming and experimenting with several solutions, he was able to develop a wax-based, "backyard compostable pod" (Fig. 19), using similar materials from the food wraps, that could be easily shipped and reconstituted by the customer into a multiple use glass bottle. The packaging could then be disposed of in a home or municipal compost bin.

The result was a low carbon footprint, eco-friendly, value-added solution that delighted his customers using C2C thinking. It also won a prestigious national packaging award and he is considering licensing the technology to larger organizations.

He continues to push the boundaries, most recently with skin care products*.

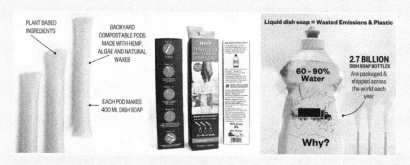

Fig. 19.   Compostable Pod.

Conclusion

Designing sustainable products is challenging. These challenges include how to approach these projects, what methodologies to use and how to create value in a sustainable way. There are also common misconceptions among entrepreneurs that consumers will prioritize sustainability over other product attributes. Since

---

*For more information visit https://www.shopetee.com

innovations must be *successfully adopted*, sustainability must be approached from a value-based perspective.

Sustainability is a broad construct. It spans from the development of eco-friendly products, services and systems, to the social responsibilities of the enterprise. Developing eco-friendly products is primarily an FEI activity, while social, ethical and inclusivity activities are mostly relegated to the BEI. The former is project based, while the latter is enterprise based. Since this book is about the innovation approach, the focus of this chapter is primarily focused on eco-development.

Eco-development requires a blending of eco-behavior (i.e., what customers will adopt) and design (i.e., what the possibilities might be). This combination does not lend itself very well to radical innovations but is based on an incremental innovation approach. Radical eco-innovations are exceptionally rare, and accounting for their high failure rate makes this approach mostly ineffective. Incremental innovations have higher success potential and are more likely to be adopted, resulting in increased impact.

Central to the discussion is the C2C design framework, proposed by William McDonough and Michael Braungart, advocating for products that can be continuously reused or recycled without generating harmful byproducts. The C2C approach involves stream separation and reuse, categorizing materials into biological and technical nutrients and designing products for easy disassembly and recycling. This approach provides a framework for *making the inevitable tradeoffs* required for eco-development. Even given its limitations, the C2C approach is considered by most as the most *effective* approach to eco-development.

Approaching the *sustainability phase* of the innovation approach from a C2C perspective can take fledgling concepts from *value add* to *value plus*.

Section IV

System Level Capabilities

Chapter 12

Team Selection, Structure and Governance

Much has been written about team diversity and its impact on the innovation process. Although there are several factors that should be taken into consideration when selecting teams, diversity within the team should at its core be capability-based. For team selection in a post-disciplinary world, such factors as personas, problem-solving propensities and psychological profiles can all provide inputs into the process. Although broadness of team capabilities is an asset, the proper role of management can make or break any team advantages. Many multidisciplinary teams have been usurped by silo-based management structures. Team structure also cannot be divorced from the innovation project they are undertaking. The more complex the project, the greater the reliance on functional skills. This chapter discusses team structure, dynamics and management influence over the process.

Introduction

In my mid-20s, while working as an automotive engineer, I was asked whether I'd be interested in joining a multifunctional team for the development of a new engine. It would involve acting as our plant's liaison on issues related to the design, development and manufacturing of a limited-edition, high-performance engine. The corporate objective was to streamline the traditional concept-to-launch timeframe from five years to four years. It would be a significant departure from the conventional functional model of development, the first in the corporation's history. New techniques and tools would be employed to reduce time to market, increase quality and reduce costs. To put it in perspective, our plant had just ordered a revolutionary three-dimensional computer-aided design (CAD) system from Lockheed Martin for one million dollars per station! This was going to be a great opportunity and I was excited to take on the challenge and join the team.

Over the next few years, I was able to participate and interact with many individuals from different backgrounds and experiences and learned a great deal about the integration of multifunctional teams. I also observed several consultants who seemed to do nothing more than act as translators between the technical

The Innovation Approach:
Overcoming the Limitations of Design Thinking and the Lean Startup, 187–198
Copyright © 2025 by David C. Roach
Published under exclusive licence by Emerald Publishing Limited
doi:10.1108/978-1-83797-799-420241013

and business factions of the organization. What I learned throughout the process was that these individuals were crucial to the smooth operation of this large project and diverse team. Their ability to understand, communicate and unite the team were crucial to the execution of project goals. This inspired me to follow a passion for product design and development, which has taken me all over the world as a practitioner, academic and entrepreneur.

Almost a decade later, in the mid-1990s, I was asked to spearhead a set of courses that would bring together business students, engineering students and art students into a multifunctional program to design, develop and commercialize products. Along with two other faculty members from engineering and the art college, we began an experiment in what is today known as Design Thinking (DT). At the time, there were fledgling multifunctional programs at the Rhode Island School of Design (RISD), Delft University, Carnegie Mellon and, of course, Stanford. Our little experiment resulted in some interesting work and a much keener understanding of cross-disciplinary dynamics. One of my key learnings was that "constructs" could have radically different meanings between disciplines. They could easily be misinterpreted due to differences in language, thought processes and cultures. For instance, even the simple word "design" can mean something completely different between engineers, businesspeople and artists. As a result, even commonplace constructs must be communicated in a fashion that creates a team-based language. Much of what is now used in both DT and the Lean Startup (LS) is for team communication rather than user feedback.

This chapter will examine why the team approach is necessary, how to approach team selection and how to manage teams in an effective way to optimize the power of this gathering of minds. As an entrepreneur who I respect once told me, "The team will always make the best decision if you give them the opportunity."

Why a Team Approach?

Since the mid-1980s, a shift occurred in the understanding of innovation team structures and formation. Gone were the days when innovation was left up to the technical departments of firms such as Procter and Gamble, General Electric or in my case, General Motors. Robert Cooper wrote extensively about this in the early eighties and has often been credited with this seismic shift in the approach to innovation and new product development. In his seminal book, *Winning at New Products* (Cooper, 1986), he highlighted not only the attributes that separated winning approaches but put management on notice that innovation should not be the sole responsibility of the R&D department. He likened most innovation processes to throwing projects over functional walls from R&D to design, design to manufacturing, manufacturing to marketing and so on. He likened this waterfall approach to a relay race rather than a rugby scrum. One of his key findings was that successful innovation approaches had one thing in common – cross-functional teams throughout the life of the project.

So why are cross-functional or multidisciplinary teams needed? There are several factors too numerous to mention in this chapter, however there are a few that require special mention. First and foremost is the distinction that must be made between the terms *cross-functional* and *multidisciplinary*. Cross-functional is an organizational term that refers to classic departmental structures such as finance, engineering, marketing, quality, etc. Multidisciplinary, on the other hand, refers to the disciplinary expertise of individuals such as legal, medical, anthropological and such. For clarity, cross-functional teams may not necessarily be considered multidisciplinary. Multidisciplinary teams bring a different set of skills, knowledge and diversity, which yield a more comprehensive approach to problem-solving. Systems such as DT (and to some extent the LS) endorse multidisciplinary team structures, in many cases divorced from functional roles. Thus, for the purposes of team structure, I will use the term multidisciplinary.

Next is the team's involvement in all aspects of the process, from secondary research through concept development to product launch. Multidisciplinary teams see aspects of the process from different perspectives. This holistic view of the innovation process allows for combining diverse disciplinary perspectives. They not only perceive aspects differently but, in many cases, use a different language. They also often bring cultural differences to the process. For instance, trained artists think and talk visually, often in a nonlinear fashion, while engineers think linearly in terms of technical requirements and specifications. When one speaks a different language, it is often difficult to communicate thoughts accurately. One of the bedrocks of DT and, to a lesser extent, the LS is the advent of communication tools ranging from personas to tactile representations of constructs (i.e., prototypes). These act as focal points for the team to accurately share information and solve problems.

The third factor is continuity of thought, or put more simply, the reduction in handoff errors. Although all projects have roles that weave in and out over the course of development, a baseline of continuity should be sustained throughout the project. For instance, in the transition from the front end of innovation (FEI) to the more detailed back-end activities, continuity is key. This is why Cooper stresses that marketing involvement should begin at the front end and continue through the launch of the product. For instance, it can be easy to leave engineers and computer programmers alone during the heavy design phase, however, this can lead to misinterpretation of requirements, scope creep and groupthink.

There are many other benefits including faster decision-making, increased creativity, improved risk mitigation, customer-centricity, adaptability to change and employee engagement to name a few. Suffice to say that the synergy created by bringing together individuals with diverse skills and perspectives contributes to more *effective* and *efficient* innovation outcomes.

Team Selection Approaches

I have worked for several companies that all took different approaches to team selection. However, there appear to be two common approaches.

The traditional way is to select team members for their product knowledge, technical expertise, project management abilities and general knowledge of the subject area at hand. Consultants and specialists are brought in as required for specific activities or expertise. For instance, it is not unusual to have an organization bring in a DT consultant to "help with ideation." As anyone with even a cursory knowledge of DT will tell you, this type of cherry-picking of activities is not very productive. These firms see this process as augmenting their already solid team since they consider their industry "special," requiring deep tacit knowledge. Other times they go a step further and hire such a consultant to train in-house project managers on the DT process. I recently visited one such large medical device company. One year onward, what remained were cool workspaces, many intriguing bubble diagrams and siloed technical departments desperately trying to get innovations to market despite this new approach.

Other more progressive organizations understand that the team is the focal point of the innovation process and that diversity of thought, functional capability and tacit knowledge are the foundations of a broadly based innovation team. The corporate challenge, however, is how to configure such a team. I've worked with some organizations that rely at least partially on individual profiles. Their logic is that no matter the background of individuals, there are other factors, such as their personal tendencies and problem-solving abilities that should be considered. Issues such as general communication styles, decision-making processes and interpersonal dynamics can all impact the dynamics of the team. For instance, an engineering firm could build a team around all the functional engineering disciplines along with business development and marketing personnel (often with engineering backgrounds), only to find that they all have the same philosophical approach to problem-solving. Instructing such individuals that they must have a "beginner's mind," as espoused by DT consultants, is not very effective.

Thus, the objective should be to first generally understand which functional backgrounds would be helpful to the project since all projects bring different challenges. Next, some industry knowledge is helpful, while too much can be counterproductive. Too little and the project can get drastically off track from the beginning, too much and only risk-free, incremental solutions will come out of the process. Once this framework is drafted, all potential individual profiles should be established.

Profiling Tools and Techniques

There are many personality assessment tools, all purporting to categorize individuals based on various characteristics. Some are more targeted to certain aspects, while others may have more scientific validation. Some are proprietary and costly, while others are open source. I've worked with companies that have incurred significant profiling costs, while others rely on inexpensive alternatives. In my experience, I've observed no difference in team dynamics or innovation outputs. As one senior executive once told me, "...We've profiled ourselves into oblivion, to a point where we can no longer make decisions." Suffice it to say that the effectiveness of personality tests depends on the specific context and purpose and that no assessment tool is perfect. Interpretation should be done with caution.

As a result, I personally have relied on combining three approaches over the years: the Myers-Briggs Type Indicator (MBTI), the IDEO Ten Faces of Innovation and the Basadur problem-solving index. I have found that these three approaches tend to produce rounded profiles and balance how teams interact, solve problems and ideate.

Myers-Briggs

The MBTI is a psychological tool designed to measure personality preferences and categorize individuals into one of sixteen personality types. Developed by Katharine Cook Briggs and her daughter Isabel Briggs Myers, the MBTI is based on Carl Jung's theory of psychological types.

The test assesses individual preferences in four dichotomies which they represent with a capital letter. The first is whether an individual displays characteristics of extraversion (E) versus introversion (I). This represents each person's comfort level and where they choose to direct their energy. Next is how individuals acquire and process information. In their model, people either rely on their sensing abilities (S) or intuition abilities (N). The next is their decision-making predisposition, where they categorize individuals as either thinking (T) or feeling (F). Finally, is whether people are judging (J) versus perceiving (P), which reflects an individual's preference when dealing with the outside world. This results in 16 distinct personality types, described by their four-letter acronym. For instance, I am considered an ENTP.

The MBTI has been used in various contexts, including personal development, team building and career counseling. The tool was first released in 1944, with the current version dating back to 1962 and, as a result, is often considered the grandfather of personality testing. Although popular, critics argue that it oversimplifies personality and lacks scientific validity. However, it has stood the test of time and is frequently used by many for team formation. Its relevance lies in fostering better communication and collaboration, but it should be utilized with an awareness of its limitations.

Although a proprietary tool, nowadays, the MBTI can be accessed in various forms all over the internet. I tend to use a high-level description of the sixteen personality types and have team members merely self-report their best fit. Although today there are many better-validated tools, I find this simple method to be surprisingly helpful in characterizing individuals for the purpose of balancing teams.

IDEO Ten Faces of Innovation

Tom Kelly of IDEO fame (the brother of David Kelly) released a book two decades ago that revealed IDEO's experience with individual personas and their contribution to fostering innovation. It highlights the combination of diverse perspectives required to drive creativity in the innovation process. His categorization has, to my knowledge, never been validated but is based on years of observation and practice across industries. Although I've read the book, I often refer students and colleagues to his 2006 summary article in the Rotman magazine (Kelly, 2006).

Briefly, the 10 personas presented in his book are as follows:

(1) An *Anthropologist* is a persona who observes human behavior within its cultural context to gain insights as inputs to the innovation process.
(2) The *Experimenter* embraces a mindset of experimentation through prototyping, taking calculated risks and learning from failures.
(3) The *Cross-Pollinator* draws inspiration from diverse fields and disciplines, seeking to bring fresh ideas and perspectives by connecting seemingly unrelated concepts.

(4)   The *Hurdler* is a master of overcoming obstacles and challenges by finding novel ways to navigate and move forward despite difficulties.
(5)   The *Collaborator* is focused on building effective teams and fostering a collaborative environment through open communication and idea-sharing.
(6)   The *Director* enjoys the leadership role and likes to provide vision and direction to the innovation process, guiding the team toward a common goal.
(7)   The *Experience Architect* is concerned with creating compelling and meaningful experiences for users, customers or stakeholders.
(8)   The *Set Designer* enjoys shaping the physical and virtual environments to enhance creativity and innovation.
(9)   The *Caregiver* fosters a supportive and nurturing environment for innovation by attending to the needs and well-being of others.
(10) The *Storyteller* enjoys communicating the vision and ideas in a compelling and engaging way, helping to build a narrative that inspires others to participate in the innovation process.

Again, these categories have been given names by IDEO that reflect individuals' propensities. Like many personality profiles, they are neither complete, accurate, nor validated, but based on deep practitioner experience. I find their approach useful since, for example, one would not want a team made up of all "Directors."

In practice, I use these personas in a self-reporting way, where I ask team members which persona best and least describes them. This tends to create an interesting picture of potential team members since knowing "who they are not" often says more about them than who they are. For instance, individuals who self-identify as Directors often list the Caregiver as the persona they least identify with. In my case, I associate with the Hurdler and am least like the Caregiver. This can foreshadow leadership style. In any event, this is always a fun exercise and leads to much discussion about team dynamics.

Basadur Problem-Solving Index

The Basadur Creative Problem-Solving Profile is a tool developed by Min Basadur, a Canadian creativity researcher and consultant who began his career at Proctor and Gamble. His approach to creative problem-solving (the Simplex™ process) is based on the idea that individuals have different preferences for how they approach problems and generate ideas. His profiling tool is designed to identify these preferences and help individuals understand their natural problem-solving styles. It assesses an individual's preferences across four thinking styles.

(1)   *Generators* are individuals who excel at generating ideas and thinking broadly during the idea generation stage.
(2)   *Conceptualizers* are individuals who prefer to clarify and define the problem during the problem definition stage.
(3)   *Optimizers* are individuals who excel at evaluating and refining ideas during the solution stage.
(4)   *Implementers* are individuals who are focused on implementing solutions and taking practical actions.

He uses these profiles to understand everyone's natural problem-solving style to establish their effectiveness in group problem-solving settings. It provides a practical framework for teams to navigate the complexities of problem-solving by recognizing and leveraging diverse thinking styles.

The Basadur problem-solving index is a proprietary cloud-based profiling tool that I have used in the past[1]. I find it insightful since it profiles how individuals approach problem-solving rather than their general characteristics. This becomes particularly important as the team prepares for ideation activities. For instance, a team dominated by Generators would likely never go much further than the concept stage. Thus, I find that this profiling tool, when combined with the Briggs Myers and IDEO Ten Faces of Innovation, produces a rounded profile of potential team members.

Other

There are as many profiling tools as there are self-styled innovation systems, all with slightly different nuances and claims. I cannot do justice to all of these; however, from a team profiling perspective, they all have their strengths and weaknesses. Some are scientifically validated, while others purport to be based on practical experience. There are too many to list in this chapter, thus I will let the readers determine which ones are best for them.

In my experience, I find that a combination of (i) personality profiling, (ii) innovation-specific practitioner profiles and (iii) problem framing and/or solving styles provides a rounded approach to team building. The examples above are the ones I continue to use and find quite suitable for the task. Regardless of which tools are used, none can guarantee how individuals will react within a team, but they *can* avoid creating lopsided teams resulting in costly missteps in the innovation process.

Beyond these three types of assessments, others have added aspects such as behavioral interviews, cultural fit, collaboration/communication skills and role-specific evaluations (e.g., technical skills, project management abilities or domain expertise). These are all valid and should be considered on a project-by-project basis.

Another interesting caveat to consider is the role of creative abrasion. Creative abrasion is the clash of intellectual, cultural and societal factors, which can create friction within a team (Roach, 2012). A certain amount of constructive friction is helpful for innovation teams. Research shows that innovation productivity decreases with repeat collaborations since familiar individuals refrain from disagreeing with their peers (Skilton & Dooley, 2010). Productivity can also be affected by disputes becoming personal, leading to the breakdown of the innovation process (Leonard & Straus, 1997). Since many organizations are conflict-averse, the propensity to pick team members based on group harmony is frequently unbeneficial to the innovation process. In early-stage companies, this is reflected in founding teams, which are often of similar mind, culture and training.

---

[1]See https://basadurprofile.com where individuals or teams can purchase the profiling tool.

Ultimately, profiling can only act as a guide which must be supported by proper management involvement and solid team leadership.

Structure, Leadership and Management Support

Management support is always key and goes beyond providing a vision for the project. Senior management plays a crucial role in shaping the innovation environment and provides the necessary support for effective team guidance. Their role should be creating a culture that supports innovation (and accepts failure), allocates appropriate resources and rewards performance. They also direct the overall structure of projects and the selection of team leadership.

Project Structure

There are various structural issues that can affect team formation. I always refer to Steven Wheelwright's work on team structures, which categorizes different team structures based on the strategic outcomes required. Updating my research for this book, I was pleased to see that it is still the recommended framework from the Product Development Management Association (PDMA) in the Body of Knowledge (BOK) (Anderson & Jurgens-Kowal, 2020). Although written for large corporate entities, there are some lessons that apply to Startups, early-stage companies and SMEs.

Wheelwright breaks down teams into four categories, which he calls functional, lightweight, heavyweight and autonomous. Functional teams are "as described" and are most often used for incremental innovations that rely on operational expertise, both technical and market. Lightweight teams are where cross-functional skills are allocated to a project but report to functional managers rather than team leadership. These types of project teams are useful for minor upgrades to products or what he refers to as hybrids and derivatives. Heavyweight teams are recommended where technical and market development is complex and require dedicated skills that report directly to the team, rather than functional areas. Autonomous teams are independent and self-reporting and should be used for new platform development or radical/disruptive innovations. Finally, he refers to another category which he calls research. Research, by its nature, is uncertain (and thus unpredictable), resulting in time, scope and cost risks. He strongly advises that any innovation project whose ultimate outcome is to deliver a product or service *must never include a fundamental research component* inside the project. This is one of the shortcomings of the LS since it often conjoins research with the development process.

So how can this knowledge be aligned with SMEs, early-stage companies or Startups? First, all these entities have (at best) loose functional structures and, in the case of Startups, often functions in name only. Thus, their technical and market expertise is limited. Second, as highlighted above, they frequently mistake *research* for *development*. Research involves risk, where technical success cannot be guaranteed, market acceptance is untested and complexities of integration with supporting technologies are unproven. Development, on the other hand, mostly involves the integration of proven technologies into a unique configuration that produces distinctive value. Development is predictable and thus manageable; research is an unpredictable/dependent activity and results in continuous reshuffling of time, costs and scope. Third, budding companies often mistake what type of project they are working on. For instance, many early-stage companies have told me that they are working on a radical or disruptive (i.e., breakthrough) innovation when in fact they are working on a derivative. This is often due to a lack of proper background research (secondary and benchmarking), combined with a technology push strategy.

As a result, management (or founders) must be clear about what type of project they are undertaking. Once background research reveals that the target product is an enhancement, derivative, hybrid or platform (in excess of 98% of all projects), the team can then be structured accordingly. As you can see by Fig. 20, as the complexity of the product increases, the degree of change (i.e., personnel, processes and risk) also increases. This significantly impacts team structure since the team must include key functions as part of its core team. As discussed above, management must also be clear that research is tangential to the project, not the project itself. If research is, in fact, required, it *must be parallel processed along with existing best-of-class technology until such a time as it is stable, scalable and outperforms the incumbent technology* (Kennedy, 2003). This necessitates that the team understand the customer's next best option, which typically comes out of a proper benchmarking exercise. One of the significant limitations of the LS is the palpable disregard for incumbent products or services in the pursuit of breakthrough innovations.

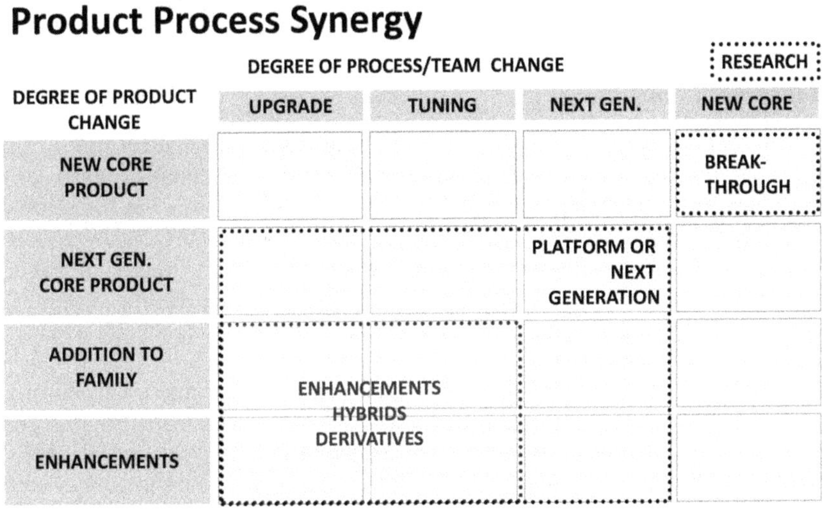

Product Process Synergy

DEGREE OF PRODUCT CHANGE	DEGREE OF PROCESS/TEAM CHANGE			RESEARCH
	UPGRADE	TUNING	NEXT GEN.	NEW CORE
NEW CORE PRODUCT				BREAK-THROUGH
NEXT GEN. CORE PRODUCT			PLATFORM OR NEXT GENERATION	
ADDITION TO FAMILY	ENHANCEMENTS HYBRIDS DERIVATIVES			
ENHANCEMENTS				

Fig. 20.   Product/Process Synergy. *Source*: Adapted from Wheelwright and Clark (1992).

Leadership

I profess that I am not a leadership researcher, nor do I purport to be an expert on the subject. A quick internet search reveals that effective team leadership in the innovation process involves a combination of vision, open communication, empowerment, adaptability, collaboration, risk-taking and resilience. Although I agree with all the above, from my experience, I would add the following (in no order):

Task focused. A leader must put the task at hand ahead of personal gain or credit. When you observe any high-caliber athlete, they tend to focus on group objectives, downplay their accomplishments and give credit to the team.

Humble. Those who need to talk excessively about their accomplishments have typically not accomplished much; they are merely skilled at self-promotion. Leaders let their accomplishments speak for themselves.

Trustworthy. Team members must have faith that the leader has their back, no matter what the situation.

Integrity. Leaders can be trusted to do the right thing even when no one is looking. They are guided by strong moral principles and honesty.

Sets high standards. Leaders set a standard by which the team must aspire. They are demanding but fair. They expect excellence but not perfection.

Respectful. Leaders treat everyone equally. They treat people as they would want to be treated.

Able to make tough decisions. When called upon, leaders have the ability and courage to make tough decisions even if they are perceived as unpopular. Team members appreciate leaders who are forthright when managing difficult situations.

In my experience, leaders emerge throughout projects when team members allow those with leadership abilities to take the reins. For the FEI projects, I prefer to let the team decide whom they would like to appoint to "represent them to management" (rather than calling them a leader). This eliminates stigma and sends a message to the team that they are acting as a unit, with no hierarchy.

Management Support

For most of my career, my role has involved acting as senior management on innovation projects. This is more about setting direction and making critical decisions than team leadership. I often joke that I have veto power but have rarely had to use it. If you observe the IDEO shopping cart video (*IDEO the Deep Dive*, 1997), you can observe David Kelly's role where he defers to the team leader, except when the direction of the project seems to be drifting. He then convenes a group of "grownups" to provide direction and works with the team leader to disseminate the information.

For the FEI projects, excessive senior management involvement beyond providing direction is not very productive. In fact, it can take away from the approach I've outlined throughout this book. In Startups, early-stage ventures, or SMEs, management/founders often want to direct every aspect of the project. They tend to hand-pick their team based on allegiance, cultural similarity and followership (effectively "yes" people) rather than their necessary skill set for the team. As a result, I have regularly found poorly constructed teams in both DT and LS situations. As David Kelly says in the video (and I paraphrase) "If you want to be successful at innovation, sometimes you need to hire people that disagree with you." He understands the concept of creative abrasion.

Other

Other potential factors can affect team structure. The ones that frequently come up are the role of gender, culture and/or racial diversity.

As a test with students and executives, I have routinely created "blinded" profiles of individuals on the three aspects of (i) personality, (ii) practitioner role and (iii) problem-solving abilities. On occasion, I have added to the profile the terms "male" or "female" on a binary basis and on other occasions, not. I then asked the class to select their teams based on only the information provided, followed by a debrief about how teams were selected. When I have shared gender information, invariably, the classes have voted for a gender balance. When I haven't shared it, it inevitably comes up as an aspect that they believe should be considered for team building. Now, I know that a binary approach to gender is not an accurate reflection of the class population, but for privacy reasons, I am not allowed to ask (or access) any other information. However, there tends to be a strong propensity to create such balance within teams. This also goes for cultural or racial diversity.

Having begun my career in a binary worldview, in a highly male-dominated profession (i.e., engineering), locked into functional structures, I can say without a doubt that the more diverse the team, the better the results that can be achieved. It is not without its challenges, but in the end, it always proves to be worth it.

Conclusion

Team structure and governance is dependent on many factors. These include the skill set required, the type of project and the support systems surrounding it.

First and foremost is understanding the difference between cross-functional and multidisciplinary skill sets. The former refers to the individual's functional role within the enterprise, while the latter refers to the skill set and propensity of the individual. As a result, cross-functional teams may or may not be multidisciplinary. Multidisciplinary teams may or may not cover the functional specialties of the project at hand. A mix of functional and disciplinary skills is required for all innovation projects, and part of the art of management is to assess these requirements. There are many tools available to assist management in profiling team members to better understand their role within the team. The objective should always be to structure the team as broadly as possible.

Next is understanding the type of project that is to be undertaken. As projects increase in complexity, the greater the impact on team structure. Breakthrough projects require a different balance of experience, functional expertise and disciplines than incremental innovation projects. Neither should begin from (nor include) a research component – defined as untested science or technology that is unproven in applications. This approach is plagued with uncertainty and renders many projects unmanageable even with the best team with the best intentions. Research must be parallel-processed to be effective.

The third is management's relationship to the project and team. Management's responsibility is to provide guidance to the innovation team rather than directing their activities. They are responsible for team selection and should avoid the classical traps of building teams around harmony, functional specialties and rewards. Founders of Startups are also cautioned not to pick teams of "true believers" and seek diverse talent from inside and outside the organization.

Chapter 13

Project Management Essentials

Project management (PM) capability has become an essential skill set for any innovation project. As with other popular methodologies it comes with limitations, which when applied to innovation projects can create complications. One of the key activities of PM in the innovation process is how to deal with uncertainty. Innovation projects by design are inherently uncertain endeavors, however PM systems, training and tools are generally ill-equipped to deal with uncertainty within this process. This chapter discusses the role of uncertainty in innovation projects and practical approaches to managing innovation projects. The chapter concludes with practical guidelines for the self-management of team members, including managing thrashing, procrastination, open-end transactions and responding to false senses of urgency.

Introduction

Over the decades, I've managed multiple projects across numerous industries, from small strategic projects to large, complex projects with multi-million dollar budgets. I've taught PM to graduate students and have managed business, engineering and science-based projects. Although I'm quite familiar with both academic and practitioner approaches to PM, I've never gone so far as to obtain my Project Management Professional (PMP) certification (offered by the Project Management Institute – PMI).

In any project, there can be many twists and turns, but every successful project manager understands that planning is key and that there is no substitute for informed experience. I was very lucky to begin my career with a large automotive manufacturer where I worked with mid-career and senior engineers who took me under their wing and taught me practical approaches to PM. Today I try my best to pay it forward with young colleagues.

I once asked a colleague who, early in his career, won a top Canadian PM award, how he described PM. His response was simple; PM is about "seeing around corners accurately." These few words really captured the essence of PM.

The Innovation Approach:
Overcoming the Limitations of Design Thinking and the Lean Startup, 199–214
Copyright © 2025 by David C. Roach
Published under exclusive licence by Emerald Publishing Limited
doi:10.1108/978-1-83797-799-420241014

It crystalized all the key aspects of managing scope, team dynamics, risks, time frames, etc. It was also practical since what he was really saying was that you need to think through all the obvious scenarios to avoid being caught flatfooted when things deviate from plan. In effect, always have well-thought-out plans B, C, D, etc. More recently, I was having lunch with another colleague who is now a successful entrepreneur and senior manager. Like myself, he now spends time mentoring younger people on managing business, technology and production projects. He enjoys the challenge of helping these folks move from "textbooks to reality." He was relaying a story about a new hire who came with a good resume and a PMP designation. He gave her a small project to manage as a way for her to get familiar with the organization, the industry and the team. After a few project updates it became clear that the project was behind schedule, drifting off scope and the team was losing faith. After some prodding, it became clear how things had progressed. Using PM software, she had broken every menial task down to the work package level, had then worked it up to a project level, minimized every possible activity and virtually eliminated all slack in the project. Although she had done exactly what her training had taught her, the project was unmanageable. This put a lot of stress on the team, who quickly lost faith in the project as a whole.

In this chapter, I will cover PM essentials. I will then discuss how this relates specifically to innovation projects, where uncertainty and risk prevail. I will then conclude with general tips and tricks that can assist in managing innovation projects.

What Is PM?

According to the PMI, PM is *the practice of using knowledge, skills, tools and techniques to complete a series of tasks to deliver value and achieve a desired outcome* (*What Is Project Management*, 2024). They go on the say that a project is a *series of structured tasks, activities and deliverables that are carefully executed to achieve a desired outcome.*

Building on this definition, this chapter examines the knowledge, skills, tools and techniques that are required to properly manage an innovation project rather than other types of projects, such as infrastructure or enterprise software.

Knowledge

The first critical piece of knowledge is the interrelationship between scope, time and budget (Larson & Gray, 2021).

In PM, the term *scope* refers to the defined boundaries of a project. It normally encompasses the objectives, deliverables and major tasks at the beginning of the project. It also creates the framework around which costs and timelines are established. For effective PM, project scope must clearly define what is included and, more importantly, what is *excluded*. This is crucial to providing a clear understanding of what needs to be accomplished. Operationally, it helps prevent progressive scope creep; the tendency for the project to gradually expand beyond its original goals.

Costs refer to the financial resources required to complete a project successfully. It includes all expenses associated with planning, executing and closing a project. The PMI defines cost as "the cost of the resources needed to complete project activities, (such as) as labor, materials, and equipment (including) overhead, general and administrative expenses..." (*PMBOK Guide*, 2021). Understanding and managing costs is crucial for effective project budgeting, monitoring and control. Project managers must estimate costs during the project planning phase and continuously monitor and control costs throughout the project's life cycle. Accurate cost estimation helps in budgeting, resource allocation and decision-making, ensuring that the project stays within financial constraints while delivering the desired outcomes.

Time refers to the duration and sequence of events required to complete a project. The PMI defines time as "the amount of time that a scheduled activity can be delayed without delaying the project finish date or violating a schedule constraint." This definition is important since it introduces the concept of time as a *relationship between activities*. Activities refer to tasks or work packages that contribute to the overall project. Each set of activities has an estimated time frame; however, some may be independent while others are dependent. An *independent* activity is one that has no precursors and is not a prerequisite for another task. From a time perspective, *dependent* activities are ones that must wait for another activity to complete before they can begin.

Although scope, time and cost must be understood and managed independently over the duration of the project, the critical piece of knowledge concerns their relationship.

Fig. 21 emphasizes that the overall quality of the project is based on the relationship between scope, time and costs. Any changes in these variables affect the others. For instance, if the project requires a scope change (rather than scope

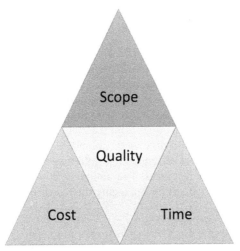

Fig. 21. Project Management Trade-offs.

creep), it will influence time and cost. If management needs to speed up a project, it will affect cost and scope. The rule of thumb is that management can change scope, costs or time...but not all three.

This was driven home to me early in my career as an automotive engineer. I oversaw a partial factory teardown and rebuild scheduled for twelve weeks. This was a very tight schedule, and as such, we had two shifts working ten hours per day each, seven days per week (i.e., 20 hours per day). It became clear midway through the project that we were behind schedule and in jeopardy of missing our planned start date. Management's solution was to increase our shifts to 12 hours per day, 7 days per week (i.e., going to 24–7). I interjected and suggested that we should do a proper analysis since there was a significant amount of literature indicating that productivity is reduced based on repetitive shift length. Digging out old industrial engineering reference books, I was able to make the necessary calculations. This analysis showed that increasing our shift loading to 12 hours would *not* improve our schedule, but in fact would make it worse! The losses outweighed the gains by approximately fifty percent. The result was that we kept our shift loading the same, and I learned another important PM lesson. As my supervisor told me, "This is the automotive business; we can marshal whatever money is required to meet the schedule." She intuitively knew that the scope of the project was fixed, so the solution had to be to adjust time and/or costs. The solution was to do a "spot buy" of components from another factory to gain another week on our schedule. Thus, the scope remained, the time was extended and the costs increased.

Skills

Effectively managing a project requires a diverse set of skills that encompass various aspects of leadership, communication, organization and technical understanding. In this section, I will only touch on a few that have a significant impact on managing innovation projects.[1]

Collaboration and Communication

First and foremost is *collaboration* and *communication*. I often refer my students to the IDEO shopping cart video where the announcer describes the group leader, not as the higher-ranking employee, but as the best at managing groups. The key skills required are the ability to foster an environment of trust, inclusivity and collaboration. This cannot be separated from the ability to communicate effectively with individuals, the team and other stakeholders. Somewhat related is the skill of *adaptability*. Every project will encounter unforeseen situations, whether based on people, technology or resources. The ability to be open to change must be embraced as a key requirement for managing the front end of innovation (FEI).

---

[1]For a more comprehensive list of skills, please refer to Larson, E., & Gray, C. (2021). *Project Management: The Managerial Process*, 8th Edition, McGraw Hill. ISBN 9781260238860.

The ability to effectively address and resolve issues that arise during the project life cycle is the sign of a successful team.

Leadership

Of course, this is dependent on *leadership*. Leadership is a complex area and involves many facets. At our university, we have concentrations in leadership throughout our undergraduate, graduate and executive programs. I cannot hope to do justice to such a body of knowledge but simply revert to my late colleague's words of wisdom. Dr. Sunny Marche was a seasoned management consultant, academic and administrator. He taught PM at every level, bringing his wealth of experience along with his keen sense of humor. He once told me that leadership can be defined in one word: "followership." My current academic colleagues would cringle at this thought, but what he meant was that some individuals are given leadership roles because people *trust* them based on their vision, competence, communication skills and decision-making. In my and Dr. Marche's estimation, these individuals are rare, and no amount of training can replace these innate skills. However, we both agreed that training can soften the rough edges and that individuals willing to continually improve their skills can overcome many of their leadership deficiencies. We also agreed as practitioners that for many projects, bellicose individuals who seek leadership roles are often very poor project managers. These are individuals who aggressively seek to join high-profile projects and have a knack for jumping to the next project about midway through their current assignment. All PM deficiencies show their ugly face in the second half of the project, while all the glory comes at the front end. I often joke to students that if they seek to climb the corporate ladder, they should never stick around for the second half of a project. This was never my strength; I always took pride in finishing the job. True leaders can make or break any project.

Managing Uncertainty and Risk

Management of *uncertainty* and *risk* is probably the most important aptitude and skill for managing FEI projects. Uncertainty and risk are related concepts, but it is important to distinguish between the two. Uncertainty refers to a lack of knowledge or predictability about future events. It implies a situation where the outcome is not known or cannot be accurately determined. It is most recently associated with the term VUCA, which stands for volatile, uncertain, complex or ambiguous conditions. Uncertainty can arise from states of incomplete information based on any of these other conditions. Risk, on the other hand, involves the likelihood of an adverse outcome or loss. It involves assessing the likelihood of different outcomes (probability) along with their potential consequences (impact). It typically results in the quantification of probabilistic estimates, where uncertainty is the precursor to risk. In the FEI, when many characteristics are fluid, the objective is to uncover and understand where the uncertainty lies while putting in place activities designed to reduce it to a point where risk can be assessed. Many of the undertakings related to Design Thinking and the Lean Startup (LS) are, in fact, uncertainty reducing activities. These activities revolve around establishing a product–market match, where the target audience is established along with their requirements. The LS approaches it from a different perspective. It is more concerned with business model uncertainty, which goes beyond product–market match activities to establish business risk as a whole. Thus, at the FEI, project managers need to focus on *uncertainty reduction* rather than trying to establish risk through analysis.

There are other noteworthy skills that separate good project managers. These include their ability to think strategically, their technical competence, their negotiation and conflict resolution skills and financial management, to name a few. However, for the FEI, I believe the critical skills are leadership, management of uncertainty, strong communication, adaptability and collaboration.

Tools and Techniques

There are many tools and techniques associated with PM. Any PM textbook or training course will highlight the breadth of these options. These range from project strategy development to network management. Most of these are beyond the scope of this book but are nonetheless important in the realm of PM. One of my critiques of many university PM courses is that they spend an enormous amount of time on the intricacies of developing PERT charts or critical path diagrams, often at the expense of soft skills. This level of detail *may* be appropriate for the back end of innovation (BEI), but only confounds the FEI. For the BEI, even these activities must be "right sized" to the project. My criteria for right sizing has always been whether accurate and topical variance reports can be generated in order to keep scope, time and costs under control.

What Is Necessary to Manage the FEI?

How does the above knowledge impact the management of the FEI, as a project? The short answer is that it, in many ways, it simplifies it. The FEI is about project selection, information gathering, concept generation and concept refinement. Once concepts are deemed to be robust enough to enter the entrepreneurial or business planning process, they essentially enter the next stage where a fully detailed project plan *must* be developed. If we look at Dr. Robert Cooper's Stage Gate™ model, this is the point where the organization develops the business case for the new product or service. This requires a detailed PM plan from which timelines and budgets are generated.

In the FEI, there should be an attrition of potential projects as they go from the ideation to concept phase. This process involves killing questionable opportunities, allowing resources to be redirected to higher potential prospects. This breaks innovation projects into two sections (i) the FEI and the (ii) the BEI. The front end is where projects are conceptualized and where value is established. The back end involves much of the traditional heavy lifting, including engineering, testing, market planning and launch activities. This is where much of the conventional PM activities, including developing a critical path, are required for success.

For the purposes of this book, we are concentrating on managing the FEI, specifically from inspiration to final concept selection resulting in an Alpha prototype. This is because 80% of the innovation's features are locked in by this point. The next section will discuss some PM priorities and techniques for approaching uncertainty and adaptability, two characteristics of the FEI.

Uncertainty

First and foremost is the *management of uncertainty*. Unlike shipbuilding or developing enterprise software, where uncertainty does exist but is mostly controllable, innovation management begins and ends with uncertainty. There is uncertainty in project selection, uncertainty in requirements and uncertainty in information gathering and interpretation. Thus, the objective of PM activities should be a process of systematically reducing uncertainty. When uncertainty can be reduced to a point where risk can be assessed, this is the point where innovation management activities transition into entrepreneurial activities.

For instance, in project selection, entrepreneurs and their supporters very often jump directly to risk mitigation by selecting projects where the market is known, large and growing rapidly (i.e., double-digit, Compound Annual Growth Rate – CAGR). As an investment strategy, this makes perfect sense, since large and growing markets are very forgiving to mistakes. Also, in growing markets, new entrants can attract customers merely based on increased market size, rather than having to entice customers away from incumbents. Also, as fast-growing markets eventually slow, the industry consolidates around a few dominant players. This provides entrepreneurial exit possibilities since there are ample opportunities for mergers and acquisitions. This is why methodologies such as the LS look for opportunities in these types of markets. From an innovation management perspective, however, picking an attractive market is helpful but does not in itself lead to the creation of uniquely better, highly differentiated and profitable products or services. Thus, picking which project to select should be more than examining attractive market characteristics, but should take into consideration other factors. Looking back at our Google Glass example (see Chapter 9 Case Example), I'm sure that the projected CAGR of the wearables market looked attractive. However, a cursory look at the two decades of failed attempts would have uncovered significant areas of uncertainty that should have been considered. From an innovation management perspective, project selection must include an assessment of the challenges of creating a superior product or service within the category. As always, "pick an A-team with a B-idea" since the team will always find a way (Spinelli & Adams, 2016). I would echo this logic by stating "always pick an A-category with a B-CARG," since superior products always win.

Perhaps the most difficult aspect of the FEI is the uncertainty of requirements. Unlike projects like shipbuilding, where the customer establishes a set of requirements that must be met (usually through a detailed tender process), most innovation projects have no such guidelines. Requirements must be established through a process that is designed to reduce uncertainty of both "who" the customer is and "what" this type of customer really wants. As stated previously, it is akin to an equation with two unknowns, where one impacts the result of the other. This can only be solved through an iterative process where one factor must be held steady while the other is assessed. For instance, the team should have an initial idea of who their customer might be, often established during the secondary research phase. Then, during primary research, the team probes to understand what this customer's requirements might be. Often, this leads to a rethinking of who the customer really is, reducing uncertainty and the cycle repeats. In our handheld GPS example (see Chapter 6, Case Example), our initial target audience was "outdoor enthusiasts" who were weekend hikers and nature lovers. As we probed to understand their requirements, we identified a sub-group of "outdoor professionals" who had more intense requirements. Refocusing on these individuals allowed us to adjust our requirements, which became the basis for our unique value proposition. This target group was much smaller but more profitable since they were willing to pay almost 10 times the retail price of outdoor enthusiasts.

There is also much uncertainty in information gathering activities since the information collected tends to be *qualitative* and the analysis *subjective*. Many years ago, I was a board member of a company that made home healthcare products. Other board members were from financial backgrounds and were used to relying on quantitative information to make decisions. Under their paradigm, surely requirements (i.e., what customers wanted) could be assessed through questionnaires that could be quantified. They were approaching these innovation activities from an investor perspective, where they could then calculate such things as ROI, break-even and payback. I eventually convinced them that any "hard data" would merely be "quantifying the qualitative." We were then able to separate the innovation management process from the entrepreneurial process. This led to an understanding that the best that could be accomplished was to reduce the *product–market match* uncertainty by following best practices in innovation management. Quantifying risk, developing the business case and conducting confirmation testing would follow in sequence in the BEI.

Team Resource Management

The team is the backbone of any innovation project. In an earlier chapter, team structure, skill sets and functional backgrounds were discussed, so need no to be repeated here. From a PM perspective, there are certain traps that can occur no matter how well intentioned and structured the team.

The first is *thrashing*. Thrashing is a PM term that refers to the amount of unproductive activity between tasks. One of the best descriptions was provided to me during a week-long executive program at Harvard Business School. Professor Steven Wheelwright was conducting sessions based on his most recent book *Revolutionizing Product Development* (Wheelwright & Clark, 1992). Although there were many learnings, two things particularly stuck with me over the years. The first was thrashing, where he explained that all individuals on a team must have unproductive time between project tasks. These can range from personal time to "task switching." Task switching often occurs when team members have more than one project or task. People will work on a task until they reach an impasse, for instance, when they require information from a teammate or merely reach the end of their working day. At some point, they reengage in the task and must spend some unproductive time regrouping and reorientating themselves. This is *necessary* unproductive time, but it can add up if task switching is excessive. This occurs when an individual has too many responsibilities. What Wheelwright's research found was that if individuals were working on two projects, they were slightly underused, while if they were working on three projects, they were slightly overused. To clarify, the amount of thrashing did not impact individuals working on two projects because they had some slack in their schedules, but it ate into productive time when working on three projects. His conclusion was that all things being equal, the optimum project load was three projects per individual, since the overall productivity was optimized. The second "ah ha" moment for me was that his research into large organizations revealed a significant problem. Using his metric of three projects (or responsibilities) per person, organizations, on average, had more than *three times the projects per person* than it could support. After much class discussion, he hit us with the punch line. Under these conditions, thrashing would take up more than eighty percent of the productive time of any innovation team. His conclusion was that organizations were *systematically under resourcing their innovation activities* (i.e., they had created systems that largely ensured failure of their most important projects). Now there were many reasons for why organizations behaved this way, including politics and adversity to killing projects, but it was frightening, nonetheless. His remedy was to right size project loads to the available resources and if a project had to be added...another must be finished or killed.

I carried this knowledge into all my future innovation projects. Since most of my work is with SMEs and early-stage startups, other aspects of his research became more evident over the years. One of the exercises he had the class conduct was a project-resource inventory (my term, not his). The exercise involved listing all projects as columns and all the people resources as rows, then globally allocating resources to projects. For smaller companies, I also include a person's day-to-day functional responsibilities as a project. In this simplified form, I would work with clients to allocate resources based on a binary format. If the person was working on a project, they were coded as a "1," if not a "0." Clients would often try to justify "0s" saying that certain individuals really were not spending very much time on a certain project. I would simply rephrase the question as no time as a "0," some time as a "1," with the caveat that this would all resolve itself in the end. This simple exercise was always eye-opening. It very often revealed what Dr. Wheelwright had predicted...too many projects, not enough resources. But it was his other insight that became clear to me when working with smaller companies, namely that some individuals were spread very thin, while others are underutilized. It was not unusual to find individuals who were carrying loads of 8–10 projects. These individuals would effectively spend their entire existence thrashing! Even more concerning was that these individuals became the *bottleneck for all projects* and thus governing the entire output of the innovation process. The real question then was "who" and "why"? Almost invariably, it was either the founder or the Chief Technology Officer (CTO). These individuals felt the need to make every, even the most insignificant decisions, and almost single-handedly created a cascade of thrashing throughout the teams, projects and organization. When confronted with this knowledge, a few modified their ways, while others acknowledged this as a concern but failed to adjust.

So, what are the learnings of thrashing as it applies to PM of FEI projects? These learnings apply at the firm level, project level and individual level. At the firm level the learning is simple. If the firm fails to right size its resources to its projects and responsibilities, the organization will continue to allocate excessive resources to thrashing. The only cure is to manage projects using a "one in – one out" system combined with a process where projects are killed to let better projects live. At the project level, it is important to make sure the team is populated with individuals that have both the time and management support to devote to the project. Also, individuals involved in decision making bottlenecks should be uncoupled from the process. Lastly, individuals must avoid other distractions that can add to their thrashing load. In an era of social media and limited attention spans, it is easy for individuals to create the equivalent of an additional project just by their behavior. I will discuss techniques to manage the latter in the IN PRACTICE summary at the end of this chapter.

PM Software

For the FEI, unduly complex PM software is unhelpful. As discussed, there is a time and a place for highly detailed PM work breakdown structures, critical path charts, work packages and resource leveling, but not at the front end. The FEI should be treated as *one activity* drawing from *one resource pool* with a *general timeline and budget*. Unfortunately, I often see elaborate Microsoft Project plans complete with work assignments, linked to all manners of resources, intricately tied to budgets. These are often created by individuals who are trained as project managers, frequently with credentials such as PMP. They regularly over manage the FEI projects in the belief that this will result in better scope adherence along with time and budget supervision. This creates undue "overhead" on the project which often leads to losing flexibility and, in my experience, tends to alienate the team.

I wondered whether others had the same experience, so for fun, I asked Chat-GPT to outline criticisms of project managers' behavior using these software tools. It responded that project managers can develop micromanagement tendencies, leading to unwarranted scrutiny of tasks and timelines, causing stress for team members. This disproportionate focus can lead to prioritizing deadlines over team collaboration and creativity. The tool's structure discourages flexibility, making it challenging to adapt to unexpected changes or dynamic project environments. There is a tendency toward overreliance on the tool as a communication mechanism to avoid direct team communication. Excessive dependency on software-generated status reports can create a disconnect with team activities, hindering actual progress.

I can say that this accurately reflects my experience with these tools at the FEI. Since the power of the FEI is the team's ability to navigate an uncertain set of activities with flexibility, adaptability and shifting requirements, overly complex PM overhead is ineffectual.

My approach is to keep it simple. I've never been involved with an FEI project that could not be managed with a simple Gantt Chart. This type of chart can highlight the timelines, budget and simple dependencies and can be created using any spreadsheet software. I combine it with a running list of activities where responsibilities are assigned, and target completion dates established. I provide an example at the end of the chapter in the IN PRACTICE section.

Other Project-Related Issues

Scope creep and *scope changes* are often cited as major problems with most projects, and rightfully so. However, it is important to distinguish between the two. Scope changes are a necessary part of any project. It is impossible to fully predict the scope of activities that must be performed over the length of a project. As such, all project managers understand that there must be mechanisms to accommodate inevitable changes in the direction or deliverables of even the most rudimentary projects. The process is normally executed using a *scope change request*, formally signed off by management and the team. Within this document, the change is described, implications are assessed and adjustments recommended (e.g., implications on both time and budget). Once the changes are agreed upon, the project plan is revised, and the team continues.

Scope creep is another matter altogether. It refers to incremental changes that are deemed insignificant at the time, but as these small changes add up, they can become highly problematic. A good example would be the boiling frog analogy, where the temperature of the water incrementally increases until the frog perishes. There is a second type of scope creep which is even more insidious, which is often driven by hidden agendas. This is where individuals will concoct creeps in the scope until such a time that their impacts become irreversible. This results in forcing management to revise the entire project involving significant increases in time and specifically budgets. Whenever I see large projects go drastically over budget, this is often at the root of the problem.

In any event, for the FEI, project scope changes and creep are not as important. This is because the initial scope of the project is set by the *product statement*, which by design is a fluid artifact since its purpose is to be a "touchstone" for team direction. It is meant to be reviewed, discussed and adjusted as more information becomes available throughout the process. As a matter of fact, if the product statement does not change extensively over the iterations of the project, there are deeper concerns about the process. That is why at the end of every group session the last thing on the agenda should be a review of this statement. As stated repeatedly throughout this book, once the correct problem has been identified, solutions invariably become apparent. This makes all activities more effective. As far as scope creep, it is always a concern but tends to be minor if the team is following an iterative pattern of reviewing the product statement. In my experience, it only raises its ugly head if there are larger internal political agendas at play.

Self-management

Finally, is individual self-management. No project can run efficiently if the primary resource inputs (i.e., people) are themselves inefficient. I am always amazed at the general lack of productivity of individuals, not only in the workplace but in daily living. Over the decades, as "time saving" technologies proliferated (e.g., email, text messaging), individual productivity has gone down. This is not necessarily reflected in the overall statistics, since these technologies have also increased overall productivity, but I can say without a doubt that individuals are less productive than they were a few decades ago. Consequently, what are the issues and what are the solutions?

I've talked extensively about *thrashing*, which is essentially unproductive time while switching from one task to another. There is nothing wrong with this unproductive time since it is a basic requirement one must go through to "get back up to speed." For instance, every morning when writing this book, it takes me approximately thirty minutes to remember where I left off, perhaps read the last page that I wrote and generally plot the direction of my writing. I then sit down for three or four hours of dedicated writing. Thus, my thrashing time is approximately 20–25% of my time meaning that my efficiency rate is roughly 75%. This is about optimal. I then typically duplicate this for my afternoon's work, resulting in an overall daily productivity rate of 75% or greater.[2] However, this takes planning and resolve. What if I just let the day take its course? I would likely be forced to switch tasks at least four times, resulting in a productivity rate of 50% or less. This would equate to one full working day per week. Consequently, my recommendations to students, colleagues and employees are to take a mental inventory of a typical working week with an eye on how much time is spent thrashing versus being productive. This is often eye-opening for individuals willing to slowly adjust their behavior to get back to 75% productivity. Once implemented, it is surprising how much this can improve someone's day-to-day life. Adherence to this standard over the years results in someone who is perceived as effortlessly getting things done on time, with quality and on budget.

The next self-management issue is *procrastination*. Procrastination is an innate behavior where individuals delay or postpone something that they know they should attend to. Experts define procrastination as a self-defeating behavioral pattern marked by short-term benefits and long-term costs. Individuals are also gifted with another inherent ability to fully rationalize this behavior. There are many reasons for this, but since I am not a psychologist I will not delve into its origins or causes. Suffice it to say that procrastination exists, it affects all individuals and is as constant as gravity. From a productivity perspective, it can have a disastrous impact. My solution, which I've advocated for years, is what I've termed "tasks and treats." Begin everyday with one item that you've been procrastinating on.

---

[2] A 75% productivity rate is generally considered a target rate for industrial workers. This considers several factors including breaks, workflow interruptions and other unproductive activities.

Force yourself to take at least the first step toward the task and reward yourself with a treat. There is a twist however, since the treat is not necessarily grabbing a latte or a pastry. Take a self-inventory and ask yourself what you were inclined to do to postpone this unpleasant task. It could be checking your social media account or flicking through emails. *Make that your treat* (along with a latte if necessary), and you'll be shocked at how this will improve your days and weeks. Also, the satisfaction of completing something that you've been pushing off is infectious and inspires your entire day!

The next is the classic *open-ended transaction*. When I observe highly effective people, I often find that they are masters of transactional tasks. They tend not to leave loose ends and, as a result, seem to manage everything that they touch effortlessly. I have often asked colleagues and business partners how do you know when you have good management? The answer is simple…"It's when you don't see it." Good managers have developed skills in closing open-ended transactions. Thus, what is an open-ended transaction? In PM terms it is a "dependent" task. These transactions must be completed before the next transaction can occur and often need to be fulfilled by arm's length parties. This can range from critical information required for decision-making, to the status of resources. During status updates when a task is not complete, I often hear that an email was sent but there has been no reply. When I ask what the content of the email was, I find that it was a simple request, with no deadline or other transactional details. This is a classic open-ended transaction that the recipient can ignore, delay or procrastinate on at their leisure. A better approach is to be clear, create a sense of importance, impose a time frame and hint at repercussions. If an email is the best way to reach the individual (which is debatable), explain concisely what you require (clarity), why you need it (importance), when you require the information (deadline) and when you would like to set up a call to discuss (repercussion). This way you *engineer the transaction* in advance for the outcome you require. The recipient understands what they need to do, why they need to do it, when it is required and the forum in which they will be held accountable. They may counter with a different scenario, but now you have forced them to commit to the transaction, or as they say in sales training – they've committed to an upfront contract.

The last self-management issue I will cover is the *false sense of urgency* problem. I think we have all worked with individuals who seem to always be in a constant mild panic about their "to do" list. These are the folks who come to you at the last minute and need something usually relatively minor as a favor. You oblige them because they are pleasant colleagues, and what goes around comes around. But in many cases small tasks continue to come and they are conveniently absent when you need a favor (often their excuse is that they'd love to help, but they have their own deadline that can't wait). What they are actually displaying is a management style, albeit a poor one. They tend to (often unconsciously) create false senses of urgency to obtain assistance to accomplish their tasks. However, when you observe their day-to-day behavior, you often find that they are constant thrashers, procrastinators and are easily distracted. Thus, they tend to work late hours because of their inefficiency and are frequently perceived by management as hard workers. Over time, they surround themselves with colleagues that enable this behavior to the detriment of their own productivity. If one is conscious about self-management, this type of relationship must be disentangled. The solution is quite simple. When asked repeatedly for small last-minute tasks, engineer delays of usually 48 hours. This is outside their window of urgency, and they'll inevitably say something to the effect of "never mind…I think I can get (insert name) to do it." Quickly they realize that you won't enable their management style and refrain from distracting you with their self-created urgencies. Now, if this person is in a supervisory role, it can be difficult to say no. If this is the case my initial advice is to find another job or department. If this is not possible, then strategically play the "hit and miss" game, where you are sometimes available and other times not. They eventually realize that you are not available to reliably bail them out and tend to move on to the "lighter touches." Another variation of the false sense of urgency problem is the perception that time is of the essence to make an important decision. These often come up in projects where individuals under time pressure (mostly of their making), create a scenario where they put pressure on others to make time-bound decisions based on *their urgency* not the recipient's. Suffice to say that responding to someone else's crisis is a slippery slope that rarely ends in successful outcomes. Always avoid making critical decisions based on someone else's manufactured crisis.

On a closing note, whenever I hear how much time individuals are spending on evenings and weekends conducting company work, this is a classic sign of someone who cannot manage themselves. There are many other distractions, small-p political issues and gaming that can impact self-productivity, but in my four decades of experience, these are the critical ones. Anyone can increase their productivity significantly by paying attention to these simple behaviors. It is also a constant work in progress since the best of us tend to let things slip here and there. The objective should be continual improvement over time.

In Practice

Every FEI project begins with what is sometimes referred to as the inspiration (Liedtka, 2018). This vision should encompass the proposed value proposition, for whom the value is perceived and the why this the opportunity exists.

In brief, the process should look like the following:

INPUTS

Prior to *Discovery* phase:

Team selection and leadership
Assessment of individual project loading
Self-management awareness and training

PROCESS

The inspiration needs to be refined into a consolidated *product statement*. This statement should include the *problem*, for *whom* and *relative* to what. This initial statement becomes the scope of the FEI project.

In parallel, the team must establish baseline time frames for activities and a reasonable budget for resources (labor, materials, other expenses). This can then be rolled up into a Gantt Chart and task list using a simple spreadsheet.

Following our proposed approach, the project plan should outline the following:

> *Secondary research*
> *Benchmarking*
> *Primary research*
> *Concept development*
> *Concept selection*
> *Concept refinement and testing*
> *Business proposition*

Below is a typical Gantt Chart of the FEI process for a standard product. In my experience, four to six months is required for the team to become fully immersed in the project and have the ability to conduct the necessary iterations to produce a uniquely better solution. Planning for less invariably leads to rushing through steps, resulting in erosion of the process and its outputs. This project plan includes necessary slack time between activities, giving the team the indispensable time to integrate learnings. As with all projects, twist and turns will result in some deviations from these estimates. Significant deviations in scope, time or budget should result in a reassessment of project plan through formal change requests.

Activity per week	MONTH A				MONTH B				MONTH C				MONTH D				MONTH E				MONTH F			
	1	2	3	4	5	6	7	8	9	10	11	12	13	14	15	16	17	18	19	20	21	22	23	24
Phase	Discovery				Adoption				Lead User				Sustainability				Alpha							
Secondary research																	Denotes dedicated time							
Benchmarking																	Denotes slack time							
Primary research																								
Concept development																								
Concept selection																								
Concept refinement & testing																					on-going			
Business proposition																					on-going			

Budgeting should be broken down into three categories, namely labor, materials and other. For most projects, labor is a sunk cost since it is often a reallocation of resources from other departments or budgets. Nonetheless, it should be accounted for. Materials are consumables that are required for the project (e.g., 3D printing). The other category refers to "out of pocket" expenses and can include such things as consultants or project-specific resources not covered by the other categories (e.g., testing requirements). I normally estimate these costs on a week-to-week basis, which I then total over the length of the project. The project plan should be reviewed once per week with the team for scope, time and budget variances and appropriate adjustments made.

OUTPUTS

An easy plan to communicate, execute and follow.

Conclusion

All innovation projects should include a project plan. All project plans begin with a scope that is refined by estimating resource requirements (i.e., projected as costs) over a period of time. This is reflected in the consolidated product statement. As the old saying goes, "no plan survives contact with the enemy."[3] All plans require monitoring and adjustments as necessary as more information is gathered for refinement of estimates and predictions of future events. In the FEI, excessive planning and complex project plans are detrimental to the fundamental goal of creating superior, value-added product or service concepts. The FEI is characterized by techniques that progressively reduce the uncertainty inherent in new concept development. The objective is to systematically refine requirements and develop concepts that satisfy and delight the end-user.

To accomplish this, the PM focus should emphasize uncertainty management flexibility and collaboration. These are the project characteristics necessary for effective FEI management. No project, however, can be divorced from the quality of the individuals involved in the process. As a result, every team member needs to be familiar with common project inefficiencies, including thrashing, scope creep and self-management issues. Awareness of these issues can turn a good team into a great team.

Although PM as a vocation has gained prominence over the past several decades, most of this training should be reserved for the BEI. Once concepts are reasonably robust the detailed design, engineering, testing and business-related activities can begin. At this juncture, traditional PM planning is not only appropriate but necessary.

---

[3]I'm an avid reader of First World War history. The origin of this saying is attributed to the "Elder" Helmut von Moltke who was a Prussian field marshal prior to the First World War. His exact saying was "No plan of operations extends with certainty beyond the first encounter with the enemy's main strength." It was later shortened by multiple historical characters.

Chapter 14

Heuristic Business Modeling

Determining a viable business model requires an understanding of the drivers of business model innovation. Business models are the synergistic relationship between value creation and value capture. The former is an innovation management activity, while the latter is an entrepreneurial (or intrapreneurial) activity. Neither Design Thinking nor the Lean Startup methodology fully integrate these two somewhat disparate activities into a cohesive system. In this chapter, business model innovation will be examined in its most simplistic form; as a revenue model supported by a cost model. It proposes approaching business modeling using standard rules of thumb – or heuristics. Once a viable business model is established, creativity can then be applied to the drivers where innovation can have the most impact. These business drivers become the genesis for hypotheses development and minimum viable product (MVP) testing, making business model development more effective.

What Is a Business Model?

Introduction: A Brief History

The history of business modeling dates to the sixteenth century and can be traced back to the mercantilism era (16–18th century) in Europe. Beginning in the 18th and 19th centuries, the Industrial Revolution brought about mass production and mechanization, which revolutionized business practices and industries. In the twentieth century, management science and theories began to emerge, providing the framework for more structured business modeling. There was again a seismic shift in the late 20th century with the advent of the information age. Companies began to incorporate technology and data-driven approaches into their models based on internet and e-commerce, transforming the way businesses interacted with customers and delivered value. At the turn of the century, the information age transitioned quickly into what is now referred to as the digital transformation age, which further impacted most organizations' business models. Companies began to quickly adapt to the digital age through online platforms, data analytics and alternate revenue streams.

The Innovation Approach:
Overcoming the Limitations of Design Thinking and the Lean Startup, 215–236
Copyright © 2025 by David C. Roach
Published under exclusive licence by Emerald Publishing Limited
doi:10.1108/978-1-83797-799-420241015

The pace of change within the business environment continues to affect firms' ability to adapt in a timely manner. What used to evolve over a century, now transforms within a generation. Many believe that the pace of business model innovation (and the incumbent's sustainability) will once again be challenged by artificial intelligence (AI) and that this new era is already upon us. Business modeling is now more imperative than ever and those firms unwilling or unable to transition will undergo what Joseph Schumpeter so appropriately referred to as a process of creative destruction (Schumpeter, 1934).

Modern Incarnation

Business model "innovation" is a relatively modern concept, and its history is closely tied to the evolution of business practices and the dynamic economic landscapes as discussed above. This multidisciplinary field draws upon concepts from strategy, innovation management, entrepreneurship and economics.

The Boston Consulting Group refers to business model innovation as "the art of enhancing advantage and value creation by making simultaneous – and mutually supportive – changes both to an organization's value proposition to customers and to its underlying operating model" (*Business Model Innovation*, 2024). When referring to business model innovation, academics such as Henry Chesbrough merely state that "a better business model often will beat a better idea or technology" (Chesbrough, 2007, p. 12). He does, however, break down this belief into six parameters, including value proposition, target market, value chain, revenue mechanism(s), value network and competitive strategy. Regardless of the definition, most would agree that a business model is about value creation and capture.

Most of what has been written involves the discussion of "types" of business models. During the early industrial era, businesses experimented with various approaches to production, distribution and sales. For instance, the development of the assembly line by Henry Ford in the early 20th century revolutionized manufacturing and contributed to the creation of a new business model for mass production. The mid-20th century saw the rise of such innovations as franchising. Companies like McDonald's introduced franchise models, allowing individuals to operate their businesses using established brand names, processes and support systems. This approach extended the reach of businesses and became a significant innovation in the fast-food industry.

The advent of the digital age in the late 20th century ushered in a new era of business model innovation. Companies like Amazon, eBay and Google created entirely new business models based on e-commerce, online advertising and search engines. Companies such as Netflix and Spotify popularized subscription-based business models. This era also saw the rise of platform-based business models, like those of Facebook, Amazon – AWS and Apple, who revolutionized how businesses connect and interact with customers and partners. The early 21st century witnessed the emergence of the sharing economy, characterized by companies like Airbnb and Uber. These platforms introduced business models that focused on facilitating peer-to-peer transactions and the sharing of resources. All these business model innovations disrupted traditional industries and created entirely new marketplaces.

Other emerging models included sustainability and the circular economy in response to environmental challenges. These models emphasize reducing waste, reusing resources and promoting environmental responsibility. Open innovation also forms the basis of many modern business models, where companies collaborate with external partners, customers and even competitors to develop new products and services. What has become known as "open business models" are now widely accepted as a key component of business model innovation (Chesbrough, 2003).

Business model innovation continues to evolve rapidly, driven by technological advancements, changing consumer preferences and global challenges. Companies that can adapt and create innovative models often find a competitive edge in the ever-changing business landscape.

Business Model versus the Business Plan

Entrepreneurship and the Business Plan

Based on this evolution over the past three decades, the concept of business modeling began to creep into the pedagogy of entrepreneurship. Based on the early work of the late Jeff Timmons at Babson College and his drive to legitimize entrepreneurship as a field of management studies, entrepreneurship became respected as a rightful area of business strategy. Dr. Timmons was the first academic to highlight the word entrepreneurship in the title of his doctoral thesis and was subsequently recruited by Babson College in Wellesley, Massachusetts to develop what is now the world-renowned Babson Model of entrepreneurship education.

The Timmons model was both intuitive and simple to understand. It was based on a tripartite relationship between the "opportunity," "the team" and "resources." Where there is synergy and balance between these three constructs, the probability of successful outcomes increases. If there are disconnects or imbalances, then the probability of successful outcomes decreases. Many of the cases used at Babson focused on this relationship to show living examples of successful and unsuccessful executions of entrepreneurial strategy. Dr. Timmons, in his understated Texas style, would reinforce this model with many sayings. This led to many anecdotes such as "Always bet on an A-team with a B-opportunity versus a B-team with an A-opportunity," or my favorite, "Big hat...no cattle" when referring to B-grade entrepreneurs trying to promote their B-opportunity. The Timmons model also promoted the process of "opportunity recognition" as the basis for venture selection. He believed (as many still do) that not all ideas are opportunities and that opportunities have distinct characteristics. In his seminal textbook – *New Venture Creation* which survives to this day (Spinelli & Adams, 2016), he spends several of the early chapters devoted to the understanding of opportunities prior to the process of business planning. In his model, once opportunity characteristics are understood, gifted entrepreneurs can craft B-opportunities into A-opportunities from which they can develop and execute a business plan.

Based on this approach, the product of a successful entrepreneurship process should result in a business plan that is well thought out, balanced in its approach and properly costed. The classic sections of the business plan include industry, product, marketing, operations, team, risks and financials, all of which culminate in pro forma financial statements. This process is laborious but forces the entrepreneur to understand the relationships between all aspects of the venture and its marketplace while establishing an executable financial and management plan.

However, as the widespread reach of the internet began to take shape in the mid-1990s, entrepreneurial ventures needed to find a quicker way to conceive, develop and promote their new startups. As a result of this pressure to quickly execute, the rigor of the business planning process lost its luster and began to be replaced by vastly abridged versions of these plans. The business plan was reduced to a set of PowerPoint slides, each representing a key aspect of the business plan. This satisfied the gold rush mentality of the early days of the internet, where most investors considered speed the dominant opportunity characteristic. As you can imagine, thousands of these ventures ultimately failed and the entrepreneurial realm was in search of a balance between agility and rigor.

Shift to Business Modeling and the LS

After the dotcom bust in the early 2000s and because of the failings of the abridged business plan, business modeling took on a greater role in the new venture process. This philosophical difference even shifted terminology from "venture creation" to the construct of "startups." This terminology may seem unimportant; however, it had a profound impact on the approach to early-stage venture creation. The approach began to focus on a mixture of opportunity recognition and key drivers of the business. Investors became much more interested in the fundamentals of the business than five-year pro Forma projections. Speed was still of essence, but if the fundamentals of the business were favorable, then startups could quickly raise capital to prove out their model.

As this approach to early-stage ventures proliferated, along came the business model canvas as a visual tool to represent the key aspects of the business model considered essential for the success of the venture. This concept, popularized by Alexander Osterwalder and Yves Pigneur in their 2010 book *Business Model Generation*, quickly became a best seller. Although lacking in rigor relative to the business plan, it brought a more structured and visual approach to designing, discussing and analyzing business models. It became very popular with engineers, scientists and computer scientists, who were now able to gain an understanding of the various aspects of the business model and their interaction. Better yet, it now allowed them to converse with partners and investors on their terms by answering questions related to the business rather than their technology or idea.

The genius of the canvas was in its simplicity. It asked nascent entrepreneurs to suspend their myopic focus on the concept and expand their thinking to aspects of the business model. These included the value proposition, customer segments, channels, customer relationships, revenue streams, cost structure, key partnerships, resources and activities. All these activities reflected much of the Timmons approach to opportunity recognition; the first stage of business planning. The canvas, if used properly, allowed for a process of iteratively crafting a concept into an opportunity, reflecting another of Dr. Timmons many anecdotes of "transforming the caterpillar of an idea into a butterfly of an opportunity."

In very short order, a book entitled The Lean Startup (Ries, 2011) emerged in response to the quick and efficient requirements of the internet startup community in Silicon Valley. This became a "how to" companion to the business model canvas and expanded on requirements in fast-changing environments. It stressed concepts like customer discovery, hypotheses-driven inquiry and the use of MVP testing. As a result, these related approaches became inseparable. One complimented the other and the canvas became a method of chronicling changes to the business model based on feedback. Through these combined approaches, nascent entrepreneurs or teams could essentially craft or transform their concept from an idea to an opportunity. Once their opportunity was properly packaged, investors could decide whether to invest in the resources required to execute a full business plan.

Business Model versus Business Plan

There are significant differences between a business model and a business plan. A business model establishes the key drivers of the business but does not in itself form an execution plan. Both begin from the same point – namely, opportunity recognition and crafting. The business plan scope goes a step further and establishes how to resource the opportunity, over what time frame, by whom and how. It conforms to Jeff Timmons' initial model where the opportunity, resources and team must have synergy to align for success. Although the LS methodology is designed to lead to financing the venture, it really sees this as the culmination of the process, not the process itself. Business planning on the other hand, details the resource requirements of the business and how financing will be used to pursue the opportunity. As a result, the business planning process has a much stronger emphasis on both the revenue and cost models required to pursue the opportunity.

In summary, a business model is a fundamental concept that defines how a business creates and delivers value, while a business plan is a detailed document that covers all aspects of the business's operations and is often used for external funding and planning purposes. Both are essential in different stages of a venture's development and are complementary tools for strategic thinking and planning.

Heuristic Approach to Business Modeling

The innovation process is about *value creation*, while the business model is about *value capture*. The business model fundamentally relies on a properly managed innovation management process to deliver on the value creation aspect of the business model. Examining the business model canvas (see Fig. 22), we can see that value creation drives both the revenue model and cost model. I refer to this

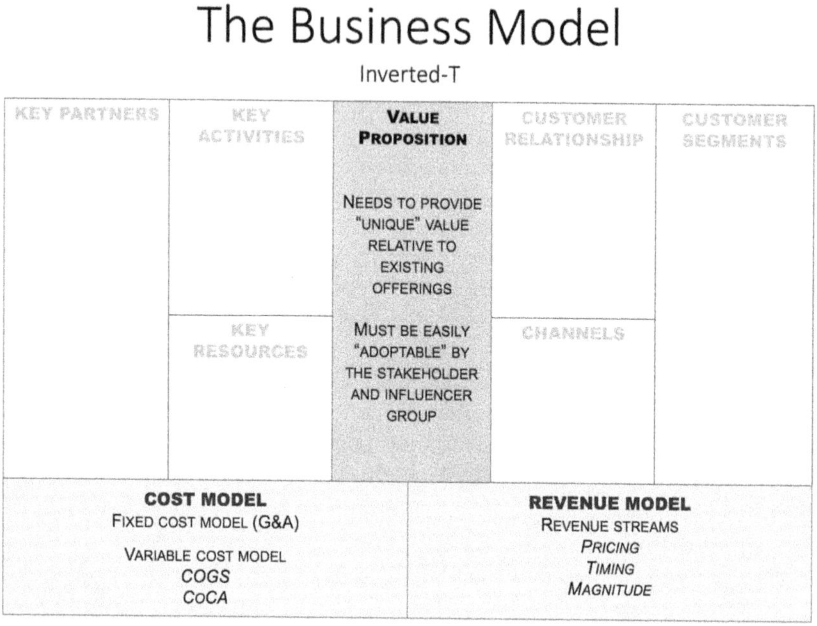

The Business Model

Inverted-T

KEY PARTNERS	KEY ACTIVITIES	VALUE PROPOSITION	CUSTOMER RELATIONSHIP	CUSTOMER SEGMENTS
		NEEDS TO PROVIDE "UNIQUE" VALUE RELATIVE TO EXISTING OFFERINGS		
	KEY RESOURCES	MUST BE EASILY "ADOPTABLE" BY THE STAKEHOLDER AND INFLUENCER GROUP	CHANNELS	

COST MODEL	REVENUE MODEL
FIXED COST MODEL (G&A)	REVENUE STREAMS
VARIABLE COST MODEL	*PRICING*
COGS	*TIMING*
CoCA	*MAGNITUDE*

Fig. 22.   Business Model Inverted-T. *Source*: Adapted from Osterwalder and Pigneur (2010).

as the business model canvas "backbone" or "inverted-T" (see shaded section of the diagram), which is the core of business modeling (Zacharakis et al., 2019). This value must be converted into a revenue and cost model to establish the viability of the business model but does not in itself determine financing requirements[1]. Below, I will examine the three essential "baseline" approaches to business modeling: the fixed cost model, the variable cost model and the revenue model.

Fixed Cost Model

I find it best to begin with the fixed cost model. For business modeling purposes, fixed costs are considered General and Administrative Expenses (G&A); this is standard terminology based on the income statement.

There are two ways to establish (or bookend) fixed costs. One is a grassroots *estimation*; the other is by using *comparables*.

---

[1]One persistent myth about business modeling is that it is related to financing. Financing is based on the capital requirements of the firm. Although it is impacted by the quality of the business model, it is determined by other aspects of the business such as cash conversion cycles, growth aspirations and inventory requirements to name a few. The business model reflects the viability of the business but does not establish how much capital is required to reach profitability or growth targets. This must come from the business plan.

Beginning with grassroots estimation, the following standard categories generally comprise G&A expenses (in no order).

General and Administrative Expenses (G&A)
    Salaries and Commissions
    R&D and other expenses
    Marketing, sales and promotion
    Operations and telecommunications
    Rent, insurance and bank charges
    Professional fees
    Amortization and Depreciation

Salaries and commissions: Nascent entrepreneurs assume that every startup begins with a brilliant idea formulated through a flash of inspiration and executed by a small group of individuals living only on Red Bull™ and pizza, while working in a garage. Under this persistent myth, the entire team will work for founding shares or stock options and take no other compensation until the venture gets their Series A investment. The probability of this happening is exceptionally low; however, this is not the point. From a business modeling perspective, not including reasonable fixed-cost salaries severely underestimates the viability of the long-term business model. This often results in pursuing a concept that was never viable in the first place. Thus, I always caution young entrepreneurs to (i) determine what critical skills are required in the venture and (ii) structure compensation at market rates. Then, if team members decide that they want to work for no pay in perpetuity, this becomes a *financing decision*, not a business modeling decision.

For long term viability of the business, as a rule of thumb, *critical skill sets* should be costed as if they are individual managers. These include (i) general management, (ii) senior technology officer, (iii) financial management, (iv) marketing, (v) sales and (vi) operations. Whether these individuals are on staff or contract is irrelevant for business modeling purposes. Over what period of time these skills enter the business will be reflected in financing requirements.

R&D and other expenses: All early-stage ventures require some initial R&D expenses. Looking at two ends of the spectrum, if one was starting a coffee shop, the research would involve looking at best practices, assessing location and determining a competitive menu. Development would include sourcing appropriate equipment, hiring interior designers and engaging a trustworthy contractor to build the space. At the other end of the spectrum would be medical devices where research would involve lengthy research activities, clinical trials and regulatory approvals. Development would involve setting up manufacturing, developing quality systems and customer support systems. Regardless of where the fledgling venture sits on this spectrum, the objective is to establish the viability of the long-term business model. As such, a good rule of thumb is to establish reasonable estimates for both "R" and "D" activities (including materials, testing and staff), then add a 25% contingency to compensate for "other" expenses. For early-stage companies, it assumes that research activities are on-going throughout the life of the venture.

Marketing, sales and promotion: These are ongoing fixed costs for any venture. For business modeling purposes, marketing and promotions costs should include "out of pocket" expenses above and beyond the compensation to the management team (i.e., salaries). Classic examples include advertising, tradeshows, client entertainment, travel expenses and development of marketing materials (e.g., website, brochures or promotional videos). These are normally considered recurring every year, although they tend to be higher in the early stages of market entry. A good rule of thumb is to establish reasonable estimates for the above (including materials, testing and staff), with an added 50% contingency to compensate for market entry costs. NOTE: This does not include *variable costs* associated with sales and marketing activities, including sales commissions, promotional discounts or pay-per-click advertisements, to name a few. This will be examined in more detail when accounting for variable costs in the next section.

Operations and telecommunications: These are month-to-month costs associated with operationalizing the venture. These range from such mundane things as software licenses, maintenance and miscellaneous administrative expenses to telecommunications charges such as mobile phones, computers and internet. Most nascent entrepreneurs leave this section blank, since they contend that they have all of this at their disposal either individually or obtained through various freeware sites on the internet. As discussed, to properly explicate a business model these costs must be included.

Rent, insurance and bank charges: These fixed expenses really speak for themselves. These are the basic costs of running any business, large or small, and this category is often a "catch-all" for fixed costs that don't fit nicely into other categories. Nascent entrepreneurs often ignore these costs, since they justify that in the early stages, everyone can work virtually, that they will use personal banking, and that other charges such as insurance are not required since they have nothing to insure. Again, this may be true, but not accounting for these long-term fixed costs in the business model underrepresents the long-term viability of the business. In the CASE EXAMPLE, I will show how to account for these.

Professional fees: These are charges that can easily impact the business model and include such things as accounting and bookkeeping, legal fees, year-end reporting, patent advice, general business consulting and so on. Nascent entrepreneurs tend to ignore these costs since they contend that they can do most of this themselves by doing their own bookkeeping, taxes and online patenting. The flaw in this logic is twofold; not only does this underestimate the business model but also creates a tsunami of problems when the venture eventually shows signs of traction.

Amortization and depreciation: These fees are an accounting method for the allocation of fixed costs over a longer period, in effect converting a fixed cost to a variable cost. For instance, classic costs such as purchasing equipment and, in some instances, cumulative patent and R&D costs can all be amortized over time. For business modeling purposes, they only need to be estimated, since amortization is a non-operational technique (i.e., does not materially impact the cost model). Thus, for the purposes of explicating a "fledgling" business model, a good rule of thumb is to estimate 3–5% of overall fixed costs. Once the business model is considered viable, the business planning process can take over and proper cost accounting principles can be applied. This will be required at some point to establish financing requirements.

Case Example – Golf putter (fixed costs)

Developing a grassroots estimation of fixed costs is the starting point for business modeling. As described in this chapter, fixed costs are costs that *don't change with an increase or decrease in the quantity of goods produced* by a firm. The business model objective is to establish a realistic fixed cost model (known as General and Administrative Expense – G&A) that matches the revenue and variable cost model. Together these establish the viability of the business model.

The golf putter example developed in Chapter 5 – Benchmarking will be used to determine reasonable costs associated with each fixed cost category.

INPUTS

All innovation cycle activities

PROCESS

The process begins with establishing reasonable annual fixed costs for each of these General *and Administrative Expense (G&A)* categories:

Salaries and commissions
R&D and other expenses
Marketing, sales and promotion
Operations and telecommunications
Rent, insurance and bank charges
Professional fees
Amortization and depreciation

To determine *Salaries and commissions*, an estimate must be established. In 2024, the average tech worker salary in Canada was $60,426 per year (*Tech Salary in Canada – Average Salary*, 2024), while US tech workers made 46% more than Canadian counterparts (*U.S. Tech Workers Make 46% More*, 2023). This results in a range of approximately $60,000–$88,000. Thus, a reasonable estimate would be $75,000/year. For long-term business model viability, we have established that there should be six individual managers (see *Salaries and commissions* previous discussion)[2]. This would result in an ongoing annual fixed cost of **$450,000/year**. There will be fluctuations

---

[2]This estimate often seems excessive to nascent entrepreneurs, since they contend that management responsibilities can be shared in the initial stages of the venture. Although I agree with this sentiment, I remind them that the objective of business modeling is to establish the long-term viability of the business NOT the short term scale up.

between individual salaries, but this average will suffice for business modeling purposes.

R&D and other expenses should cover out-of-pocket expenses such as design, prototyping, pre-production expenses, minimal viable product experimentation, etc. These types of expenses are often contracted to specialists, so they may involve more than just material costs. In the case of our golf putter example, there would be costs associated with design, prototyping, business model experimentation and manufacturing ramp-up. These will also require at least one non-management individual to operationalize. It would not be unusual for a simple product like a putter to go through several rounds of design and development until a final design is reached. Thus, for the purposes of business modeling, these costs could easily reach $40,000 in material and testing costs and another $40,000 in human resources. Adding a 25% contingency would result in an estimated annual cost of **$100,000/year**[3].

Marketing, sales and promotion are traditionally under-budgeted by nascent entrepreneurs. As the old saying goes, "sales focused, marketing driven." Marketing sets the strategy and framework, while sales execute the revenue plan. For the purposes of business modeling, marketing and promotional costs are non-salaried activities that are required to support the sales effort. These include, but are not limited, to advertising, tradeshow participation, client entertainment, travel expenses, development of marketing collateral (e.g., website, videos). Let's assume for the moment that the human resources costs for sales are covered in variable costs (see Cost of Sales (CoS), below). Typical costs for non-salary marketing and promotion activities can be estimated to be at least $1,500 per month. However, in the early stages there can be a significant amount of upfront costs. As a result, a 50% contingency should be applied for an estimated annual cost of **$36,000/year.**

Rent insurance and bank charges can be estimated as follows: Rent $3,000 per month; Insurance $500 per month; misc. $500 per month for a total of $4,000 per month or **$48,000/year.**

Operations and telecommunications: $2,000 per month or **$24,000/year.**

Professional fees: Accounting and Legal – $1,000 per month; business consulting (incl. patents) $3,000 or **$48,000/year.**

Amortization and depreciation: assume 3.5% of fixed costs expenses of approximately **$25,000/year.**

For a total G&A of **$731,000** per annum.

---

[3]For more complex projects this could easily increase 5 fold or greater. For example, even developing a simple App could easily require three programmers @$60,000/year.

OUTPUTS

The fixed cost breakdown thus looks like the following before revenue and variable costs are applied.

Table 5. Fixed Cost Model

PROFIT & LOSS STATEMENT	ESTIMATE	
General and Administrative Expenses		
Salaries & Commissions	$	450,000
R&D and other expenses	$	100,000
Marketing, sales & promotion	$	36,000
Operations and telecommunications	$	48,000
Rent, insurance and bank charges	$	24,000
Professional fees	$	48,000
Amortization and Depreciation	$	25,000
Total Fixed Expenses	$	731,000

These fixed costs can now be matched with a revenue model and variable cost model to complete the development of a fledgling business model.

Revenue Model

The revenue model begins with pricing, which must be relative to the competitive space. From this perspective, value creation impacts what price can be charged based on an assumption of "relative value." Whether pursuing a product or service, all pricing must be based on the customer's next best option(s). Thus, pricing is the key driver of the revenue model along with volume of transactions. In the *business planning* process, assumptions are made on both the size of the transaction (i.e., what I refer to as the *magnitude*) and the timing (i.e., over what *timeframe* it occurs). In business planning, these are normally projected monthly over a 24-month period to establish an aggregate revenue model. However, this is not necessary for *business modeling* since the objective is to determine a plausible and financially stable model. It highlights key drivers that form the basis for hypothesis development and MVP testing.

Unlike a business plan, the development of a business model can begin once competitive products or services are established through the benchmarking process as described in Chapter 5. In benchmarking, price is established as a byproduct of each competitor's value proposition based on their features and benefits. This process produces a *pricing range for the category*, establishing the top and bottom of the competitive space. Often nascent entrepreneurs pick the lower end of the pricing range (or below) in the misguided belief that their price must be lower than the competition to gain market share. We know from decades of research that this is effectively a straight line to business death for a startup. It also unknowingly projects to customers that the product or service is inferior to the incumbent's offering. This is where the business model and the innovation management process intersect. The objective of the innovation management process is to create a uniquely superior and differentiated product, while the business model establishes its viability. If the product is in fact superior and differentiated in the category, the objective should be to enter at the top of the category and compete based on superior value. As a matter of fact, if the innovation process has been successfully executed, in many cases, the venture should be able to support a premium price relative to the next best option.

Many factors can affect pricing strategy (Nagle et al., 2023), but from a business model perspective, the objective is to select a strategy as a "straw man" test.

Case Example – Golf putter (Revenue model)

As discussed, the initial pricing approach should come from a benchmarking exercise. Here, features and benefits are examined to establish the competitor's value proposition relative to price. In our benchmarking exercise we established that there is a wide price range based on each competitor's offering. Since our innovation objective is to produce a high value, differentiated product, we have chosen not to compete in the low end of the market, and thus chose products representative of top end of the category.

Using the golf putter benchmarking example developed in Chapter 5, a pricing range of the category can be established.

INPUTS

All innovation cycle activities
    Fixed cost model
    Benchmarking matrix (see below)

Table 6.   Pricing Model

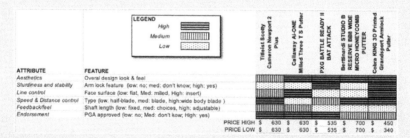

ATTRIBUTE	FEATURE	Titleist Scotty Cameron Newport 2 Plus	Callaway AI-ONE Milled Three T S Putter	PXG BATTLE READY II BAT ATTACK	Bettinardi STUDIO B RESERVE BB8 WIDE MICRO HONEYCOMB PUTTER	Cobra KING 3D Printed Grandsport Armlock Putter
Aesthetics	Overal design look & feel					
Sturdiness and stability	Arm lock feature (low: no; med: don't know; high: yes)					
Line control	Face surface (low: flat, Med: milled, High: insert)					
Speed & Distance control	Type (low: half-blade, med: blade, high:wide body blade)					
Feedback/feel	Shaft length (low: fixed, med: choices, high: adjustable)					
Endorsement	PGA approved (low: no; Med: don't kow; High: yes)					
	PRICE HIGH	$ 630	$ 630	$ 535	$ 700	$ 450
	PRICE LOW	$ 630	$ 630	$ 535	$ 700	$ 340

LEGEND: High / Medium / Low

NOTE: The above is a collapsed version of the benchmarking matrix developed in Chapter 5 and does not reflect all the features and benefits.

PROCESS

The prices range from a high of $700 to a low of $340 and take into consideration many factors including (but are not limited to) overall value proposition, brand effect, channel strategy, etc. From the background research conducted, the team should understand the overall category "value equation" and have determined where and how they intend to compete. From a business model perspective this is the only element that is within the control of the innovation team. If the team has in fact chosen to compete on value, then they can decide at which price point they want to compete. Opportunity recognition literature states that startups should enter the market at either market parity or with a small premium (ranging from 10% to 15%) (Spinelli & Adams, 2016). From a pricing theory perspective, there are many factors that can affect pricing policy; however, they are all based on *perceived value*. Since this is not a book on pricing strategy, I will refer readers to Nagle et al. (2023).

One aspect that must always be taken into consideration is the brand effect. Brand effect is a *perceived* value-added *attribute* of any product or service. Depending on the category, the brand effect can be large or small, however, in our case the brand effect in golf products can be considered quite large. How should a startup deal with this effect? Our benchmarking analysis can provide some clues. For instance, if we look at the most entrenched incumbent in the category – namely Titleist™, we can infer that they carry the strongest brand effect. If we look at an aggressive new entrant – namely PXG™, we can infer that barring brand effect, they both have relatively similar value propositions (see Chapter 5). The top-of-the-line PXG™ putter however is priced at roughly a $90 discount compared to the Titleist™ putter, or put another way, the latter is priced at about a 14% premium. However, remember PXG™ has now developed some brand recognition of its own, thus we may account for this by adjusting for the brand effect from 14% to say 20% (a subjective estimate). If we assume that our objective is to provide a uniquely better proposition, our strategy should be to extract a 10% "value" premium from the market based on our innovation approach. As a result, we could assume that the Titleist™ putter is our customer's next best option at a price of $630. We should than add our 10% premium ($630 + 10% = $693), minus the 20% brand effect ($693 – 20% = $554.40). Now, this price will *inevitably be wrong* (i.e., either too low or too high) but is a reasonable starting point to build a fledgling business model. To keep with pricing conventions, a good estimate would be a selling price of **$549.99**.

Now that target pricing is established, the next revenue model question to be answered is "how many." I refer to this as the *magnitude* of revenue that must be developed to support a viable business model. Like the fixed cost model, this should be approached on an annual basis. The question to be answered is "what magnitude of revenue is required to support our cost model"? Thus, from a heuristic business modeling perspective we will use our fixed cost model as a driver to establish our revenue model.

OUTPUTS

Target selling price of **$549.99**.

Prior to developing our variable cost model, some basic strategic decisions must be made, namely whether the venture plans to go directly to consumer (B2C), sell through traditional channels (B2B) or some form of mixed strategy. For the sake of this example, let's assume a B2C strategy.

Once a "strike price" for the innovation is established, the next step is to match the revenue and cost models to support the fledgling strategy. To accomplish this, I propose the use of heuristics (i.e., rules of thumb) based on business model averages. But first, the variable cost model must be estimated.

Variable Cost Model

Variable costs refer to a *type of cost that display variations proportionate with changes in the level of production (or revenue).* As production increases or decreases, so do the associated costs. Most often, there is also a relationship between production and revenue, where revenue generated per unit draws from the production process, with excess production moving temporarily to inventory. However, for the purposes of business modeling, we will *ignore inventory* for two reasons. First, for service firms or firms that act as brokers (i.e., hold no inventory), this is a moot point. Second, for firms that produce or hold goods, inventory does not affect the underlying business model, since it will take the form of a *financing activity* through working capital. Thus, for business modeling purposes *variable costs should be treated as directly proportional to revenue.*

There are three notable variable cost categories that impact the viability of the business model. These include Costs of Goods Sold (COGS), CoS or discounts and Channel margins.

COGS: This is the most classic variable cost. It normally assumes the cost to produce a unit of production, or, if acting as a distributor, the cost of obtaining and holding a unit of production ready for sale. Now, cost accountants will invariably say...wait a minute...cost accounting can be quite complex and involves many issues, from volume projections to how fixed costs are allocated (i.e., amortized). Again, I would wholeheartedly agree with my colleagues, but for the purposes of initial business modeling, this (i) has little impact on the business model, since fixed costs should already be allocated and (ii) it overcomplicates (for no gain) the process of developing an initial business model. Thus, for the purposes of business modeling, I recommend beginning with "comparables," then aligning actual costs with this target. For more detail, see the CASE EXAMPLE section below.

Case Example – Golf putter (Variable cost model)

To establish the variable cost model, COGS must first be established. This allows the team to then calculate what is known as "contribution margin." The term contribution margin essentially refers to the *amount of margin left over after COGS, which "contributes" to the fixed costs* of the enterprise. To put it more simply, it is the profit generated before General and Administrative expenses (G&A) (Gallo, 2017).

Not to be confused with "markup," contribution margin is calculated as Revenue (REV) – COGS. When converted to a *ratio* (i.e., (REV-COGS)/REV), it is a standard business metric used to establish business viability. For instance, most entrepreneurship textbooks use a 40% contribution margin as the cutoff for opportunities (Spinelli & Adams, 2016). We also know from entrepreneurship literature that in early stage ventures, *margin makes up for mistakes*, since there are many unknowns that can affect both revenue and COGS calculations. Thus, although the team should strive for higher contribution margins as the project develops, a good rule of thumb (i.e., heuristic) is to target a *40% contribution margin* for business modeling.

INPUTS

All innovation cycle activities
  Fixed cost model
  Pricing

PROCESS

Although there are two ways to estimate COGS, namely (i) grassroots estimation (i.e., bottom up) and (ii) heuristics (i.e, comparables), the recommended approach is to use heuristics to establish the *boundaries* of what would be acceptable. Later it can be confirmed via grassroots estimation. This becomes the genesis for hypothesis development and confirmation through MVP testing. Thus, for business modeling purposes our target COGS would then be calculated to be $329.50 ($549.99 X 1-40%).

Building on our fixed cost model, the following table reflects a fledgling business model with a COGS of 40% based on a breakeven scenario.

Table 7.   Variable Cost Model

PROFIT & LOSS STATEMENT	ESTIMATE Breakeven	ESTIMATED RATIOS Breakeven Percentages	NAICS AVERAGE Top quartile (25%)	VARIANCE Top quartile (25%)
Revenue increase (%)	0%	Percentage	Percentage	Percentage
Revenue	$ 1,827,500	100%	100%	0%
Minus: Cost of Goods Sold (COGS)	$ 1,096,500	60%	60%	0%
Income. Before fixed costs	$ 731,000	40%	40%	0%
General and Administrative Expenses				
Salaries & Commissions	$ 450,000	25%	16%	-9%
R&D and other expenses	$ 100,000	5%	6%	1%
Marketing, sales & promotion	$ 36,000	2%	5%	3%
Operations and telecommunications	$ 48,000	3%	2%	0%
Rent, insurance and bank charges	$ 24,000	1%	2%	1%
Professional fees	$ 48,000	3%	2%	-1%
Amortization and Depreciation	$ 25,000	1%	2%	0%
Total Fixed Expenses	$ 731,000	40%	34%	-6%
Total expenses (COGS + G&A)	$ 1,827,500	100%	95%	-5%
Net profit/loss	$ -	0%	5%	5%

This indicates that approximately $1.8M in revenue is required to break even on an annual basis. This is reflected in the adjoining estimated ratios (i.e., percentages). As can be noted, there is a variance with the North American Industry Codes (NAICS) averages, suggesting that adjustments should be made to this fledgling business model. For instance, NAICS[†] averages reflect a 5% *Net Profit* (i.e., profitability) and our *Salaries and Commissions* seem to be higher than the NAICS average.

A quick analysis suggests that either revenues need to increase, salaries reduced, or some combination of both. The knee jerk reaction is to try to cut expenses to match the revenue model, however I would *strongly advise that this is the wrong approach*. For heuristic business modeling, I recommend adjusting the revenue model to match industry profitability first. This is reflected in the following table.

Table 8.   Revised Variable Cost Model

PROFIT & LOSS STATEMENT	ESTIMATE	ESTIMATED RATIOS	NAICS AVERAGE	VARIANCE
	Breakeven	Breakeven Percentages	Top quartile (25%)	Top quartile (25%)
Revenue increase (%)	15%	Percentage	Percentage	Percentage
Revenue	$ 2,101,625	100%	100%	0%
Minus: Cost of Goods Sold (COGS)	$ 1,260,975	60%	60%	0%
Income. Before fixed costs	$ 840,650	40%	40%	0%
General and Administrative Expenses				
Salaries & Commissions	$ 450,000	21%	16%	-6%
R&D and other expenses	$ 100,000	5%	6%	1%
Marketing, sales & promotion	$ 36,000	2%	5%	3%
Operations and telecommunications	$ 48,000	2%	2%	0%
Rent, insurance and bank charges	$ 24,000	1%	2%	1%
Professional fees	$ 48,000	2%	2%	0%
Amortization and Depreciation	$ 25,000	1%	2%	0%
Total Fixed Expenses	$ 731,000	35%	34%	-1%
Total expenses (COGS + G&A)	$ 1,991,975	95%	95%	0%
Net profit/loss	$ 109,650	5%	5%	0%

As can be noted, a 15% increase in revenue aligns our fledgling business model with industry averages for profitability. It still shows a variance in our *Salaries and Commissions* category, although it has been reduced from –9% to –6%. Given the nature of early-stage companies, startup complications, and lack of process/infrastructure, I would argue that this builds in a slight contingency in the fixed cost model and should remain.

Thus, a target revenue model would be approximately $2.1M per annum.

OUTPUTS

This fledgling business model reflects a breakeven sales volume of 3819 units per year ($2.1M/$549.99)

† NAICS averages are derived from a blended average of NAICS 339 – Miscellaneous Manufacturing and NAICS 44-45 Retail trade based on Government of Canada Financial Performance Data.

The above example reflects a direct-to-consumer (B2C) model and assumes that there are no additional variable costs of selling the product. Nascent entrepreneurs often tell me that they intend to rely on their social network to raise awareness, along with a clever viral marketing campaign and the world will be a beat a path to their door. Rarely does this impress investors who want to know whether the business model is viable. To accomplish this, a realistic variable cost of selling must be established, which involves either channel partnerships or transactional costs of sales (also referred to as Cost of Customer Acquisition – CoCA). I suggest beginning with channel partnerships to set the boundaries of the model.

Channel margins: I am always amazed at the lack of understanding of channels in general and channel margins specifically. Before the advent of the internet, most products, whether consumer or business, required the use of channel partners. In any marketing textbook, there is always at least one chapter on channels. These include descriptions of the various forms of channel partnerships covering the spectrum from wholesalers, distributors, value added resellers, to sale agents. Channel partnerships through their networks provide deep access to markets that individual companies cannot easily access through direct sales. Each partner provides unique access to their customer base and as a result charge a margin for their services[4]. If you believe in a perfect economic market, channel partners' margins should reflect the value they provide...no less...no more. If they overprice their services, they would eventually be replaced by more nimble competitors. If they charged less, they would eventually be out of business. Thus, for the purposes of business modeling, channel margins offer a great benchmark from which to begin modeling, since they are proportional (i.e., a percentage) of sales. They set the boundaries for alternate approaches such as building a direct-to-consumer (B2C) strategy, internet-based sales , social media advertising or mixed methods.

Case Example – Golf putter (Variable channel – i.e., selling costs)

Let's assume the strategy is to hire a *sales agent* who then sells through to *retailers* (i.e., a two-level channel strategy).

INPUTS

All innovation cycle activities
  Fledgling business model (i.e., fixed cost model, COGS and revenue model)
  Breakeven units

---

[4]In this day and age, social media influencers have infiltrated this role but unlike traditional channel partners rarely work on a percentage of sales. They act more like "advertising" where they charge a fixed cost to deliver the company's message. As a result, for business model purposes they are considered a fixed cost, not a variable cost.

PROCESS

A quick investigation of Canadian contribution margins indicates that retail margins range from 26% to 61% between the bottom to top quartiles of businesses in this category†. Thus, we can assume that 40% contribution margin is a reasonable blended average for golf equipment retailers. As a startup with no brand visibility or track record, we would likely need to provide an incentive to both the retail outlet and agent. However, for the sake of calculations we can initially assume an average of 40%.

Agents also need to be "incented" to represent our product to their customer base (i.e., retailers). While the golf industry uses a lot of high-end golfers to promote their products directly to golf courses, these are not the agents who can negotiate channel partnerships directly with retailers. The agents capable of conducting these sales activities work on a percentage of sales. It is not unusual to pay between 15% and 20% on the *transfer price* to these sales professionals. Thus, for our purposes we should assume the higher end of this range at 20% contribution margin.

Revisiting our pricing model while accounting for channel arrangements, our revenue model would like something like this:

Table 9.   Revised Variable Cost Model

Retailer MSRP	$	549.99
Transfer price to retailer	$	329.99
Sales Agent margin	$	66.00
Selling price	$	263.99

Thus, when considering this channel strategy, our net revenue per unit would need to be $263.99 to compensate for the combined variable cost of our channel partners.

Reflecting on our fledgling business model, reducing our transfer price from $549.99 to $263.99 has significant implications. To maintain our model, we would need to increase our unit sales to 7,955 units (i.e., $2.1M/$263.99) and adjust our COGS to reflect this new volume. To maintain the viability of our fledgling model, our COGS should remain at $1,260,098. This new volume would reduce our COGS per unit from $220.00/unit to $158.39/unit ($1,260,098/7,955).

Our adjusted fledgling model (or working model) requires a selling (transfer) price of $263.99 with a COGS of $158.39. This leaves a contribution margin of $105.60 per unit to cover our fixed costs.

Our business model remains the same, however our business model *drivers* have changed.

OUTPUTS

From this simple exercise we can deduce the following:

- Any alternate selling strategy must not exceed $105.60 per unit ($263.99 – $158.39)

- The COGS must not exceed $158.39 per unit
- The business must be configured to sell approximately 8,000 units (rounded up) per year

Once a business model can account for sales through channel partnerships, this can then be used as a baseline for examining alternate approaches. These drivers can now be used for hypothesis development and testing.

† NAICS averages are derived from a blended average of NAICS 339 – Miscellaneous Manufacturing and NAICS 44-45 Retail trade based on Government of Canada Financial Performance Data.

Alternate methods include *CoS* which refers to a cost that varies or is proportional to the revenue derived per unit. Three pertinent examples are (i) sales commission, (ii) pay-per-click advertising and (iii) sales discounts. In these cases, costs vary with unit sales. Under a sales commission or other sorts of arrangements, a commission is paid to an outside party normally on percentage of sales. A modern example would be the transactional costs associated with selling through Amazon or eBay. There may be staged levels involved, for instance, increased percentages as volumes increase, but for the purposes of business modeling a steady state average will suffice. Pay-per-click advertising behaves similarly since it depends on some combination of impressions, click-through rates and conversion rates. In essence, the latter – conversion rate is the measure that impacts the business model since the metric used is *revenue generated per dollar spent* (a target metric for business model viability). Finally, sales discounts also act as a variable CoS since they are normally based on a percentage of the manufacturer's suggested retail price (MSRP). This is a classic strategy in industries such as medical devices, where hospital systems expect deep discounts based on volume contracts. As a result, depending on which sales strategy the venture choses, these costs may form a significant part of the business model.

Again, following the heuristic business modeling approach summarized in the CASE EXAMPLE, these alternate strategies do not initially need to be estimated at the grassroot level. The heuristic business model has estimated the *boundaries of the business model* and established *targets* from which to compare alternate approaches. These form the basis for hypothesis development and MVP testing. Rather than pursuing an ad hoc approach to viability testing, heuristic business modeling quickly establishes targets as the basis for testing, making hypothesis development and MVP testing much more *effective*.

Heuristic Business Modeling and Hypothesis Development

Now that a baseline business model has been established, the process of hypotheses development can begin.

One of my concerns with the LS methodology is that business model hypotheses development is generally ad hoc. It relies on the intuition of the founders or their team, who often (i) do not understand the basics of business modeling and (ii) have no real experience in business management. They also confound the *value creation* process with the *value capture* process. As a result, their hypotheses tend to be created in a vacuum, based on the next question that arises from their latest customer discovery exercise, MVP test or pivot. This is not a very *effective* mechanism for establishing the viability of the business model. As a result, hypotheses tend to be vague questions (i.e., not hypotheses at all) with even fuzzier tests. A classic example is asking customers how much they would be willing to pay for the product, the most difficult question to answer in marketing research. However, through simple heuristic business modeling the boundaries of hypotheses can be focused, significantly improving the effectiveness of the process.

Building on our example, we now have hard targets that must be confirmed or refuted through MVP testing.

Price. Our pricing policy is based on best estimates grounded on relative value. As discussed, pricing is a highly complex activity that is not easily determined through customer discovery. The best that can be garnered is (i) whether the value proposition resonates with the customer and (ii) whether they see increased value relative to their next best option. This becomes mainly a subjective exercise early in the innovation process, followed by more involved testing with progressively more complex techniques as the process unfolds. However, using our heuristic business model, a target price has been determined for testing. Initial hypotheses should involve establishing the relative value *perceived* by the customer based on the next best option. In our case, the Titleist™ putter is considered the customer's next best option. MVP testing should then involve probe and learn discussions based on the *relative merits of features* vis-à-vis this benchmark. Not only should the team probe for *perceived merits* but also focus on *perceived losses*, since the latter disproportionately impacts the customer's aggregate value equation. This not only increases the team's understanding of desirability but creates a link between desirability and viability, since it is now referenced to a price point.

COGS. Our COGS is based on industry-standard heuristics. It does, however, give us a target from which to measure. Initially, I recommend developing an MVP based on a grassroots COGS based on an "off the shelf" strategy. Using our golf putter example, can we buy (or cost) all components from suppliers, delivered to our location, even though we may require slight modifications to certain components. This will involve estimating minimum lot requirements, shipping, import duties, etc. This can easily be accomplished based on numerous online supply chain sites (e.g., Alibaba). There may be some components that are not available, but these same sites can be used to develop reasonable estimates for the costs of these components based on comparables. For instance, custom packaging can be estimated based on projected volume requirements. Additionally, a labor component should be added for assembly, testing, packaging and shipping. Once all of these have been estimated, a 40% factory overhead should be applied – an industry standard. This costing can then be compared to the COGS developed through the heuristic business modeling process. These costs will invariably differ, leading to subsequent hypothesis development and MVP testing. NOTE: Although the heuristic business model is based on a contribution margin of 40%, this MVP testing should strive to target a 50% contribution margin to account for startup inefficiencies.

Selling or channel costs. Alternate *selling approaches* such as (i) sales commission, (ii) pay-per-click advertising and (iii) sales discounts can now be hypothesized and tested. Focusing on direct-to-customer strategy (B2C) is overwhelmingly the choice of LS enthusiasts. They see it as easy to execute, inexpensive and profitable. They also naively believe that their social media strategy is the entire focus of their marketing spend which will generate unstoppable word-of-mouth (i.e., free) advertising. From our heuristic business model, we have a target customer acquisition cost (CoCA) of slightly over $105 per unit sold (see CASE EXAMPLE). Thus, hypotheses and MVP testing must determine if this is viable. A golf putter is a one-time purchase (i.e., no repeat purchase). As a result, the business model cannot rely on a customer lifetime value (LTV) model (i.e., multiple purchases over time). All activities require locating a "prospect" and driving them through a set of activities to an ultimate purchase. Each step can be the subject of hypothesis development and MVP testing. A viral video (or other awareness endeavor) is only the beginning of the customer acquisition cost process. Nascent entrepreneurs are often shocked at the average cost to acquire a customer on the internet. Also, they fail to estimate the human resource requirements to sustain such promotional activities (a 24/7 activity). To sustain such a campaign (at a minimum) requires the dedication of one full-time employee willing to manage the relentless back and forth associated with social marketing. There are also other significant costs that must be included such as pay-per-click advertising and social media influencers. Pay-per-click can be easily modeled, and conversion rates quantified. Social media influencers, on the other hand, are paid whether the prospect is converted to a paying customer or not. They effectively act as a fixed cost of advertising which must be accounted for in some fashion. Thus, costing of a full-time employee, along with pay-per-click advertising and influencers, must be weighed against the target CoCA developed through the heuristic business model.

Unit capacity. Nascent entrepreneurs often significantly underestimate the capacity of their organization. In our example, our heuristic business model requires producing and selling approximately 8,000 units per year. This requires supply chain logistics, quality control, assembly, packing, shipping and so forth. It also requires the ability to convert and process customers at the same rate. The infrastructure must be able to support *665 units per month* (8000/12) or *33 units per day* (based on 20 working days per month). At this rate, 4 units per hour must be processed in an average working day. This requires a significant amount of logistics, infrastructure and support personnel. With the target set by the business model, hypotheses and MVP tests can be developed to confirm or refute aspects of the business model.

Once a heuristic business model is established, there are many more hypotheses that can be developed, and MVP tests envisioned. Most will evolve from the *drivers* of the business model, many of which are highlighted in the business model canvas. These involve such drivers as key partners, resources, customer relationships and channel arrangements (Osterwalder & Pigneur, 2010)[5]. However, all will ultimately result in impacting the revenue and cost models of the business. Thus, beginning with a heuristic approach to business modeling forces the team to confront the realities of the business model, resulting in a more *effective* approach to hypotheses development and MVP testing.

Conclusion

Business modeling has many facets. Much that has been written about business modeling discusses aspects (or drivers) of the business model, rather than concentrating on the core of the business model, namely the revenue and cost models. The revenue model is driven by the pricing policy and the magnitude of revenue that is required to reach viability. Viability cannot be established before fixed and variable costs are determined. The cost model should begin by estimating fixed costs (or G&A expenses) to establish the magnitude of the fixed costs required to operationalize the business. Once a fledgling fixed cost model is developed, variable costs can be established based on standard business heuristics. These set the parameters for a key opportunity metrics such as industry contribution margins. These estimates need not be highly accurate since they can be adjusted to industry averages. Once a baseline business model is developed, the process of hypotheses development and MVP testing can begin in earnest. The business model then drives a focus of confirming of refuting key drivers of the business model through hypotheses development and MVP testing.

---

[5]A good guide to alternate forms of business models is Osterwalder & Pigneur's *Business Model Generation: A Handbook for Visionaries, Game Changers, and Challengers.* All of these can be modeled using the same heuristic approach outlined in this chapter.

Postface

As I reflect upon this body of work, I believe I've done justice to my objectives. My primary objective with this manuscript was to revisit the body of knowledge developed over the past several decades with respect to managing the innovation process. This allowed me to establish the lineage of what ultimately became two very popular approaches to innovation, namely, Design Thinking (DT) and the Lean Startup (LS). These systems did not develop in a vacuum, and much of their thinking reflects the knowledge that came before. My second objective was to outline an approach to managing the front end of innovation, which builds upon the best of these practices. Outlining this approach has, upon reflection, made me think more deeply about aspects of innovation management that I've successfully used throughout my career. The third objective was to establish the limitations of both DT and the LS, not so much in their approach, but in the way that I've observed their implementation. As with many of these systems, their approach is reasonably solid; however, as with most populist approaches, they have been deployed in a less-than-*effective* manner.

In the initial chapters, I argue for what I believe are the limitations of DT and the LS as they are currently practiced. Although I will not reiterate them all here, some of the key issues revolve around their ambiguous problem focus, their weak ability to extract latent needs, the rush to ideation or creativity and their ad hoc approach to economic viability. I then propose a complementary model that I strongly believe alleviates many of these concerns while remaining open to the strengths of both systems. This model is not meant to replace these otherwise beneficial approaches but to enhance their use in practice. One of my key recommendations is separating linear activities from those that must remain flexible, agile and iterative. These occur at the transition between natural linear *cycles of innovation* as these activities pass from one phase to another. These phases are based on *adoption, lead user* and *sustainability* themes, which *enhance and amplify* the value proposition of the innovation concepts. I believe that most practitioners will find this a more *effective* way to manage the innovation process.

There are also organizational system-level capabilities that cannot be separated from any effective approach. These include the appropriate balance of team capabilities, propensities and skills. They involve the ability to manage innovation projects and an aptitude to truly comprehend and grasp the business model. These supporting capabilities provide the bedrock for any innovation approach and must be embraced by senior management with all of their foibles and nuances. These core capabilities are essential for the effective management of the innovation process.

As I stated in the preface, I expect many of the discussions to be somewhat controversial. There are always those who will defend their approaches to the end.

For those critics, I only ask that they keep an open mind and perhaps find some aspects of interest. For organizations that have not realized the potential of these recent methods, perhaps this can provide a focal point to re-energize their innovation activities. For my academic colleagues, perhaps there are some avenues of inquiry that may be of interest to the Academy and beyond.

With this, I rest my case and will now leave this manuscript to be judged by the wider community.

Sincerely,

David C. Roach

References

3 M Lead User Research. (2012). https://www.google.ca/search?sca_esv=74c740cd3a771c52
&sca_upv=1&sxsrf=ADLYWILX4cU86Guo-L5g_TdzMj9DgSt6OQ:17151866795
95&q=3m±lead±user±research&tbm=vid&source=lnms&prmd=ivsnbmtz&sa=X
&ved=2ahUKEwjGtYWmwP6FAxVqAHkGHbhBACUQ0pQJegQIDhAB&biw=
1669&bih=828&dpr=1#fpstate=ive&vld=cid:a2036170,vid:jY6kGFLUBGc,st:0

Amyx, D., Jong, P., Lin, X., Chakraborty, & Wiener, G. (1994). *Influencers of purchase intentions for ecologically safe products: An exploratory study*. AMA Winter Educators'
Conference Proceedings, Chicago, IL.

Anderson, A. M., & Jurgens-Kowal, T. (2020). *Product development and management body
of knowledge* (2nd ed.). The Product Development and Management Association.

Antonelli, C. (2015). Innovation as a creative response. A reappraisal of the Schumpeterian
legacy. *History of Economic Ideas*, 2, 99–118. Accademia Editoriale. https://www.
jstor.org/stable/43924236

Aulet, B. (2013). *Disciplined entrepreneurship: 24 steps to a successful startup*. Wiley. https://
www.d-eship.com/

Bakker, C. A., Wever, R., Teoh, Ch., & De Clercq, S. (2010). Designing cradle-to-cradle
products: A reality check. *International Journal of Sustainable Engineering*, 3(1),
2–8. https://doi.org/10.1080/19397030903395166

Best-selling imported beer brands U.S. 2022. (2023). Statista. https://www.statista.com/
statistics/188728/top-imported-beer-brands-in-the-united-states/

Birkinshaw, J., Bouquet, C., & Barsoux, J.-L. (2011). The 5 myths of innovation. *MIT Sloan
Management Review*. https://sloanreview.mit.edu/article/the-5-myths-of-innovation/

Brainstorming. (2024). Wikipedia. https://en.wikipedia.org/

Brouwer, M. T. (2000). *Schumpeter and Keynes on investment and entrepreneurship*.
University of Amsterdam. http://www1.feb.uva.nl/pp/bin/1080fulltext.pdf

Business model innovation. (2024). BCG Global. https://www.bcg.com/capabilities/
innovation-strategy-delivery/business-model-innovation

Carlgren, L., Rauth, I., & Elmquist, M. (2016). Framing Design Thinking: The concept in
idea and enactment. *Creativity and Innovation Management*, 25(1), 38–57. https://
doi.org/10.1111/caim.12153

Chesbrough, H. W. (2003). *Open innovation: The new imperative for creating and profiting
from technology*. Harvard Business Press.

Chesbrough, H. W. (2007). Business model innovation: It's not just about technology anymore.
Strategy & Leadership, 35(6), 12–17. https://doi.org/10.1108/10878570710833714

Churchill, J., von Hippel, E., & Sonnack, M. (2009). *Lead user project handbook: A practical guide for lead user project teams*. https://www.wu.ac.at/en/entrep/forschung/
userinnovation/leaduser-1/

Cognition. (2024). Oxford Reference. https://doi.org/10.1093/oi/authority.20110803095622199

Cooper, R. G. (1986). *Winning at new products: Creating value through innovation*. Basic
Books.

Cooper, R. G., & Fürst, P. (2023). Agile development in manufacturing companies: Best
practices and pitfalls. *IEEE Engineering Management Review*, 51(4), 65–76. https://
doi.org/10.1109/EMR.2023.3304792

Daymond, J., & Knight, E. (2023). Design Thinking in business and management: Research
history, themes, and opportunities. In *Oxford research encyclopedia of business and
management*. https://doi.org/10.1093/acrefore/9780190224851.013.386

de Bono, E. (1977). *Lateral thinking: A textbook of creativity* (1st ed.). Penguin Books.

de Bono, E. (1985). *Six thinking hats* (1st ed.). Little, Brown. https://books.google.ca/books?id=0lNmQgAACAAJ

Design Thinking bootcamp bootleg. (2010). Stanford d.School. https://dschool.stanford.edu/resources/the-bootcamp-bootleg

Diekmann, A., & Preisendörfer, P. (2003). Green and greenback: The behavioral effects of environmental attitudes in low-cost and high-cost situations. *Rationality and Society, 15*(4), 441–472.

Dorst, K. (2011). The core of 'design thinking' and its application. *Design Studies, 32*(6), 521–532. https://doi.org/10.1016/j.destud.2011.07.006

Falsifiability. (2024). In *Wikipedia*. https://en.wikipedia.org/w/index.php?title=Falsifiability&oldid=1213895126

Gallo, A. (2017). Contribution margin: What it is, how to calculate it, and why you need it. *Harvard Business Review*. https://hbr.org/2017/10/contribution-margin-what-it-is-how-to-calculate-it-and-why-you-need-it

Gourville, J. (2005). *Note on innovation diffusion: Rogers' five factors*. Harvard Business School Publishing. https://hbsp.harvard.edu/product/505075-PDF-ENG

Griffin, A., & Hauser, J. R. (1993). The voice of the customer. *Marketing Science, 12*(1), 1–18.

Guinée, J. B., Heijungs, R., Huppes, G., Zamagni, A., Masoni, P., Buonamici, R., Ekvall, T., & Rydberg, T. (2011). Life cycle assessment: Past, present, and future. *Environmental Science & Technology, 45*(1), 90–96. https://doi.org/10.1021/es101316v

Heijungs, R., & Suh, S. (2002). *The computational structure of life cycle assessment*. Springer Science & Business Media.

Hopkins, M. S. (2010). How sustainability fuels design innovation. *MIT Sloan Management Review, 52*(1), 75–81.

IDEO Product Development. (2000). *IDEO Product Development 600143-PDF-ENG*. Harvard Business. https://hbsp.harvard.edu/product/600143-PDF-ENG

IDEO the deep dive. (1997). https://youtu.be/2Dtrkrz0yoU?si=y0L2r3dvVjH_sS6m

IDEOU Certificate Programs. (2024). IDEO U. https://www.ideou.com/collections/certificates

Innovation at 3M Corporation (A). (2002). *Innovation at 3M Corporation (A), 9-699-012*. Harvard Business School Publishing.

International, B. (2023). What is a cognitive map? B2B International. https://www.b2binternational.com/research/methods/faq/what-is-a-cognitive-map/

International Standards Association. (2006). *ISO 14040:2006*. ISO. https://www.iso.org/standard/37456.html

Johansson-Sköldberg, U., Woodilla, J., & Çetinkaya, M. (2013). Design Thinking: Past, present and possible futures. *Creativity and Innovation Management, 22*(2), 121–146. https://doi.org/10.1111/caim.12023

Kelly, T. (2006). The ten faces of innovation. *Rotman Management Magazine*, Spring/Summer, 4.

Kennedy, M. N. (2003). *Product development for the lean enterprise: Why Toyota's system is four times more productive and how you can implement it* (1st ed.). Oaklea Press.

Klöpffer, W. (2006). The role of SETAC in the development of LCA. *International Journal of Life Cycle Assessment, 11*(Suppl 1), 116–122. https://doi.org/10.1065/lca2006.04.019

Knight, F. H. (1921). *Risk, uncertainty and profit*. Hart, Schaffner & Marx.

Laroche, M., Bergeron, J., & Barbaro-Forleo, G. (2001). Targeting consumers who are willing to pay more for environmentally friendly products. *Journal of Consumer Marketing, 18*(6), 503–520. https://doi.org/10.1108/EUM0000000006155

Larson, E., & Gray, C. (2021). *Project management: The managerial process* (8th ed.). McGraw Hill. https://www.mheducation.com/highered/product/project-management-managerial-process-larson-gray/M9781260238860.html

Lee, D., & Boni, L. (2009). *Cradle-to-Cradle Design at Herman Miller*. Harvard Business School Publishing. 607003-PDF-ENG.

Leonard, D. A. (1995). *Wellsprings of knowledge: Building and sustaining the sources of innovation*. Harvard Business School Press. https://www.hbs.edu/faculty/Pages/item. aspx?num=72

Leonard, D. A., & Straus, S. (1997). Putting your company's whole brain to work. *Harvard Business Review, July–August*, 2–10.

Leonard, D., & Rayport, J. F. (1997). Spark innovation through empathic design. *Harvard Business Review, 75*, 102–115.

Levitt, T. (1981). Marketing intangible products and product intangibles. *Cornell Hotel and Restaurant Administration Quarterly, 22*(2), 37–44. https://doi. org/10.1177/001088048102200209

Levitt, T. (1984). Marketing myopia. *Journal of Library Administration, 4*(4), 59–80.

Lewrick, M., Link, P., & Leifer, L. (2020). *The Design Thinking toolbox: A guide to mastering the most popular and valuable innovation methods*. Wiley. Wiley.Com. https://www.wiley.com/en-us/The±Design±Thinking±Toolbox%3A±A±Guide±to±Mastering±the±Most±Popular±and±Valuable±Innovation±Methods-p-9781119629214

Liedtka, J. (2018). Why Design Thinking works. *Harvard Business Review, 96*(5), 72–79.

Mainieri, T., Barnett, E. G., Valdero, T. R., & Unipan, J. B. (1997). Green buying: The influence of environmental concern on consumer behavior. *The Journal of Social Psychology, 137*(2), 189–204. https://doi.org/10.1080/00224549709595430

McCarty, J. A., & Shrum, L. J. (2001). The influence of individualism, collectivism, and locus of control on environmental beliefs and behavior. *Journal of Public Policy & Marketing, 20*(1), 93–104. https://doi.org/10.1509/jppm.20.1.93.17291

McDonough, W., & Braungart, M. (2002). *Cradle to Cradle: Remaking the Way We Make Things*. North Point Press.

McKenzie-Mohr, D. (2000). New ways to promote proenvironmental behavior: Promoting sustainable behavior: An introduction to community-based social marketing. *Journal of Social Issues, 56*(3), 543–554.

McQuarrie, E. F. (1998). *Customer visits: Building a better market focus* (2nd ed.). SAGE Publications, Inc.

Moore, G. A. (2003). *Crossing the chasm* (3rd ed.). Perlego. https://www.perlego.com/book/589426/crossing-the-chasm-3rd-edition-pdf

Nagle, T., Müller, G., & Gruyaert, E. (2023). *The strategy and tactics of pricing: A guide to growing more profitably* (7th ed.). Routledge. https://www.routledge.com/The-Strategy-and-Tactics-of-Pricing-A-Guide-to-Growing-More-Profitably/Nagle-Muller-Gruyaert/p/book/9781032016825

Norman, D. A. (1988). *The design of everyday things* (pp. xi, 257). Basic Books.

Norman, D. A. (2004). *Emotional design* (1st ed.). Basic Books. https://www.nngroup.com/books/emotional-design/

Osborn, A. F. (1963). *Applied imagination: Principles and procedures of creative problem-solving* (3rd ed.). Scribner.

Osterwalder, A., & Pigneur, Y. (2010). *Business model generation: A handbook for visionaries, game changers, and challengers*. John Wiley & Sons.

Ovans, A. (2015). What is a business model? *Harvard Business Review*. https://hbr.org/2015/01/what-is-a-business-model

Plous, S. (1993). *The psychology of judgment and decision making* (pp. xvi, 302). Mcgraw-Hill Book Company.

PMBOK Guide. (2021). Retrieved May 6, 2024, from https://www.pmi.org/

Quality function deployment. (2024). In *Wikipedia*. https://en.wikipedia.org/w/index.php?title=Quality_function_deployment&oldid=1216422976

Reusable takeout options are popping up across Canada | CBC News. (2021). https://www.cbc.ca/news/science/what-on-earth-takeout-container-reusable-1.6016558

Ries, E. (2011). *The Lean Startup: How today's entrepreneurs use continuous innovation to create radically successful businesses* (1st international edition). Currency.

Roach, D. C. (2006). *Advanced tools and techniques across disparate industries* [PowerPoint]. Managing the innovation process, University of New Brunswick.

Roach, D. C. (2007). Experiencing entrepreneurship in the classroom. *Focus, 15*(2). https://cdn.dal.ca/content/dam/dalhousie/pdf/dept/clt/Focus/Vol15No2.pdf

Roach, D. C. (2012). *Product management as firm capability.* https://DalSpace.library.dal.ca//handle/10222/15720

Roach, D. C. (2020). Is it time to reassess the front-end innovation approach? *IEEE Journals & Magazine* | IEEE Xplore. *IEEE Engineering Management Review, 48*(1), 10–13. https://doi.org/10.1109/EMR.2020.2964741

Rogers, E. (2003). *Diffusion of innovations* (5th ed.). Free Press.

Rossi, M., Charon, S., Wing, G., & Ewell, J. (2006). Design for the next generation: Incorporating cradle-to-cradle design into Herman Miller products. *Journal of Industrial Ecology, 10*(4), 193–210. https://doi.org/10.1162/jiec.2006.10.4.193

Ryman, J. A., & Roach, D. C. (2024). Innovation, effectuation, and uncertainty. *Innovation, 26*(2), 328–348. https://doi.org/10.1080/14479338.2022.2117816

Sarasvathy, S. D. (2001). Causation and effectuation: Toward a theoretical shift from economic inevitability to entrepreneurial contingency. *The Academy of Management Review, 26*(2), 243–263. https://doi.org/10.2307/259121

Schumpeter, J. A. (1934). *The theory of economic development.* Harvard University Press. https://doi.org/10.4324/9781003146766

Seidel, V. P., & Fixson, S. K. (2013). Adopting Design Thinking in novice multidisciplinary teams: The application and limits of design methods and reflexive practices. *Journal of Product Innovation Management, 30*, 19–33.

Shane, S. A., & Eckhardt, J. T. (2003). Opportunities and entrepreneurship. *Journal of Management, 29*(3). https://journals.sagepub.com/doi/abs/10.1177/0149206303029 00304?casa_token=7Baq_tiIOZMAAAAA:Zk5cAlk50n8cpIVuuIdwyrJz5_qTzm-fR4rGEjJVRvCKfxfZKYKrSjdHwjZL2FK0S2sT0SBBL9beDUw

Skilton, P. F., & Dooley, K. J. (2010). The effects of repeat collaboration on creative abrasion. *The Academy of Management Review, 35*(1), 118–134.

Soman, D. (2014, Fall). The innovator's challenge: Understanding the psychology of adoption. *Rotman Management Magazine,* 5.

Spinelli, S., & Adams, R. (2016). *New venture creation: Entrepreneurship for the 21st century.* https://www.mheducation.com/highered/product/new-venture-creation-entrepreneurship-21st-century-spinelli-adams/M9780077862480.html

Stren, P. C. (2000). Toward a coherent theory of environmentally significant behaviour. *Journal of Social Issues, 56*(3), 407–424.

Team New Zealand (A). (1997). Harvard Business School. https://www.hbs.edu/faculty/Pages/item.aspx?num=22705

Tech salary in Canada—Average salary. (2024). Talent.Com. https://ca.talent.com/salary

Ulrich, K., & Eppinger, S. (2012). *Product design and development* (5th ed.). McGraw-Hill. https://www.mheducation.com/highered/product/product-design-development-ulrich-eppinger/M9781260043655.html

U.S. tech workers make 46% more. (2023, October 12). The Globe and Mail. https://www.theglobeandmail.com/business/technology/article-canadian-tech-workers-make-46-less-than-us-counterparts-tmu-study/

von Hippel, E. (1986). Lead users: A source of novel product concepts. *Management Science, 32*(7), 791–805. https://doi.org/10.1287/mnsc.32.7.791

von Hippel, E., Thomke, S., & Sonnack, M. (1999). Creating breakthroughs at 3M. *Harvard Business Review.* https://hbr.org/1999/09/creating-breakthroughs-at-3m

Wagner, S. A. (1997). Understanding Green Consumer Behaviour. *A Qualitative Cognitive Approach.* Routledge.

Webb, D., & Mohr, L. (1998). A typology of consumer responses to cause-related marketing: From skeptics to socially concerned. *Journal of Public Policy & Marketing,* *17*(2), 226.

What is Project Management, Approaches, and PMI. (2024). https://www.pmi.org/about/what-is-project-management

What is the Kano Model? (2023). American Society for Quality (ASQ). https://asq.org/quality-resources/kano-model

What's the BIG Idea? (2001). Harvard Business School Publishing. https://hbsp.harvard.edu/product/602105-PDF-ENG

Wheelwright, S., & Clark, K. (1992). *Revolutionizing product development* (1st ed.). Simon & Schuster. https://www.simonandschuster.com/books/Revolutionizing-Product-Development/Steven-C-Wheelwright/9781451676297

Zacharakis, A., Corbett, A. C., & Bygrave, W. D. (2019). *Entrepreneurship* (5th ed.). Wiley. https://www.wiley.com/en-ca/Entrepreneurship%2C±5th±Edition-p-9781119563099R150

Zaltman, G. (2003). *How customers think: Essential insights into the mind of the markets* (1st ed.). Harvard Business School Publishing. https://www.hbs.edu/faculty/Pages/item.aspx?num=11643

Suggested Readings

Aulet, B. (2013). *Disciplined entrepreneurship: 24 steps to a successful startup.* Wiley. https://www.d-eship.com/

Cooper, R. G., & Fürst, P. (2023). Agile development in manufacturing companies: Best practices and pitfalls. *IEEE Engineering Management Review, 51*(4), 65–76. https://doi.org/10.1109/EMR.2023.3304792

de Bono, E. (1977). *Lateral thinking: A textbook of creativity* (1st ed.). Penguin Books.

Design Thinking bootcamp bootleg. (2010). Stanford d.School. https://dschool.stanford.edu/resources/the-bootcamp-bootleg

Kelly, T. (2006). The ten faces of innovation. *Rotman Management Magazine, Spring/Summer,* 4.

Leonard, D. A. (1995). *Wellsprings of knowledge: Building and sustaining the sources of innovation.* Harvard Business School Press https://www.hbs.edu/faculty/Pages/item.aspx?num=72

Levitt, T. (1981). Marketing intangible products and product intangibles. *Cornell Hotel and Restaurant Administration Quarterly, 22*(2), 37–44. https://doi.org/10.1177/001088048102200209

Lewrick, M., Link, P., & Leifer, L. (2020). *The Design Thinking toolbox: A guide to mastering the most popular and valuable innovation methods | Wiley.* Wiley.Com. https://www.wiley.com/en-us/The±Design±Thinking±Toolbox%3A±A±Guide±to±Mastering±the±Most±Popular±and±Valuable±Innovation±Methods-p-9781119629214

McQuarrie, E. F. (1998). *Customer visits: Building a better market focus* (2nd ed.). SAGE.

Norman, D. A. (1988). *The design of everyday things* (pp. xi, 257). Basic Books.

Norman, D. A. (2004). *Emotional design* (1st ed.). https://www.nngroup.com/books/emotional-design/

Osterwalder, A., & Pigneur, Y. (2010). *Business model generation: A handbook for visionaries, game changers, and challengers.* John Wiley & Sons.

Ries, E. (2011). *The Lean Startup: How today's entrepreneurs use continuous innovation to create radically successful businesses* (1st International ed.). Currency.

Roach, D. C. (2020). Is it time to reassess the front-end innovation approach? *IEEE Journals & Magazine | IEEE Xplore. IEEE Engineering Management Review, 48*(1), 10–13. https://doi.org/10.1109/EMR.2020.2964741

Spinelli, S., & Adams, R. (2016). *New venture creation: Entrepreneurship for the 21st century.* https://www.mheducation.com/highered/product/new-venture-creation-entrepreneurship-21st-century-spinelli-adams/M9780077862480.html

Ulrich, K., & Eppinger, S. (2012). *Product design and development* (5th ed.). https://www.mheducation.com/highered/product/product-design-development-ulrich-eppinger/M9781260043655.html

von Hippel, E., Thomke, S., & Sonnack, M. (1999). Creating breakthroughs at 3M. *Harvard Business Review.* https://hbr.org/1999/09/creating-breakthroughs-at-3m

Zaltman, G. (2003). *How customers think: Essential insights into the mind of the markets* (1st ed.). Harvard Business School Publishing. https://www.hbs.edu/faculty/Pages/item.aspx?num=11643

Index

Academic researchers, 174
Adoption, 145–146
    adoption-focused primary research,
        145
    lens, 48
    mobilize, 140–146
    principles, 140
    of problem statement, 52
    theory in practice, 134–140, 181
Agile product innovation, 7–8
Agility, 15
Alpha dog (*see* "Alpha" syndrome)
"Alpha" syndrome, 89, 115
Analogies, 112
Analogs, 84
    markets, 151
Analytical–comprehensive quadrant,
        127
Artifacts as focal points, 99–100
Artificial intelligence (AI), 126, 216
Attributes, 15, 75, 151

Babson College approach, 33
Back end of innovation (BEI), 3,
        167, 204
Backward thinking processes, 111
Barrier busting technique, 180
Basadur Applied Innovation, 12
Basadur Creative Problem-Solving
        Profile, The, 192
Basadur Innovation methodology, 12
Basadur problem-solving index,
        192–193
Baseline business model, 233
Benchmark orientation matrix, 76,
        79–82, 84
Benchmarking, 73, 180
    analogs and complementors, 84
    benchmark orientation matrix,
        79–82

and best practices, 61
category features and benefits,
        75–76
consumers' relationship to
        products, 74–75
evaluation and analysis, 83–84
example, 80–83
product summary table, 76
summary table example, 77–79
systematic evaluation, 76–79
Benefits, 75
"Big business" management systems,
        6
Biological stream, 176
"Black and white" approach, 174
Body of Knowledge (BOK), 5, 194
Boston Consulting Group, The, 216
Brainstorm sessions, 109
Brainstorming, 17, 26, 108–110
Brand, 75
Brand effect, 227
Build–Measure–Learn Loop, 32
Business model, 32, 46, 62, 123,
        215–217, 219
    heuristic approach to, 219
    innovation and, 41, 43, 45–47, 217
    innovation invariably collides with,
        18–19
    shift to business modeling and LS,
        218–219
Business Model Canvas, 10, 29–30,
        34, 45
Business plan, 217–219, 225

Canvas, 32
Chief Technology Officer (CTO), 207
Circular economy, 217
Cognition, 101
Cognitive consumer research, 169
Cognitive dissonance, 170

Cognitive mapping, 101–104
Collaboration, 202–203
Collaboration opportunities, 61
Communication, 202–203
Company building, 30
Compatibility, 135, 139, 143
Competitor analysis, 59
Complementors, 84
Complexity, 135–136, 139, 143
Complimentary model of innovation
    management
  creativity lens, 41
  economics lens, 40–41
  entrepreneurial standpoint, 42–43
  innovation, 40, 43–45
  innovation and business model,
      45–47
  innovation approach, 47–50
  innovation helix, 53–54
  problem statement, 50–53
  strategic management perspective,
      41–42
Compound Annual Growth Rate
    (CAGR), 58, 87, 205
Comprehensive prototypes, 35
Computer-aided design system (CAD
    system), 158, 187
Concept development, 107
  brainstorming, 108–110
  concept selection, 118–119
  converging, 115–116
  lateral thinking and diverging,
      110–115
  qualitative approach, 117–118
  quantitative approach, 116–117
  with selected lead users, 154
  tools and techniques, 108
Concept evaluation, 121
  desirability, 125–126
  DT, 123–124
  evaluation approach, 124
  evaluation models, 122
  feasibility, 126
  LS, 123
  Stage Gate™ approach, 122
  viability, 125

Concept scoring system, 117
Concept selection, 118–119, 121
Conceptualizers, 192
Conducting interview, 95–97
Conjoint analysis, 90
Construct mapping, 91
Consumers, 170
  behavior, 169
  behavior analysis, 59
  relationship to products, 74–75
Continuous learning, 27
Conventional functional model of
    development, 187
Convergence process, 27
Converging, 115–116
Cost-benefit analysis, 125
Costs, 201
Costs of Goods Sold (COGS), 228,
    234
Cradle to Cradle (C2C), 175–176
  approach, 167, 181
  methodology, 177, 179
"Cradle-to-grave" linear model, 175
Creative destruction, 40
Creative process, 26
Creative reaction, 40
Creative team abrasion, 14
Creativity, 16, 36
Critics, 95
Cross-functional teams, 14, 189
Customer creation, 30
Customer development, 30
Customer discovery, 30
Customer empathy, 27
Customer journey mapping, 100–101
Customer listening, 33, 36, 88
Customer segmentation, 62
Customer validation, 30
Customer-centric approach, 43
Customer–product inquiry, 70

Data analytics, 61
Data validation, 59
Decision-making unit (DMU), 27, 36,
    44, 69, 96, 108
Decision-making process, 18, 20

Deep Google search, 153
Dependent activities, 201
Design for disassembly (D4D), 176
Design for Environment (DfE), 168
Design for Sustainability (D4S), 168
Design process, 181
Design Thinking (DT), 3, 9, 20,
      23–26, 42, 45, 51, 58, 88,
      107, 121–124, 134, 157,
      161, 188–189, 203, 237
  enthusiasts, 110
  implications, 35–38
  innovation system gap analysis, 37
  methodology, 16
  modern incarnation of, 24
  perspective, 61–62
  proponents, 96
  recommendations, 38
  strengths of system, 26–27
  as system, 23
  weaknesses in practice, 27–29
Desirability, 124–126
Development process, 8, 194
Digital transformation age, 215
Direct-to-consumer model (B2C
    model), 231
Discovery phase of problem
    statement, 52
Discussion guide, 93–94
Disk operating system (DOS), 159
Disruptive innovation, 44
Diverging, 110–115
Do it yourself (DIY)
  combination, 44
  community, 152
  solutions, 73
Do-it yourselfers (DYIers), 164
Dominant ideas, 111

Eco-behavior, 169
Eco-design, 168
Eco-development, 168–169, 171, 174,
    182
Eco-innovators, 174
Economic uncertainty, 20
Economic viability, 38

Effectiveness, 20
Efficiency, 20
Elusive green consumer, 169–171
Engineering-anchored innovation
    domain, 24
Entrepreneurial innovation, 43
Entrepreneurial perspective
    innovation, 43
Entrepreneurial setting, 160
Entrepreneurs, 43
Entrepreneurship perspective, 60
Entry point, 112
Environment Agency, 172
Environmental, social and governance
    (ESG), 167
Environmental Resources
    Management Limited
    (ERM Limited), 172
Environmentalists approach, 171
Environmentally meaningful
    consumer behavior, 169
ETEE™, 181–182
Ex post facto process, 172
External communication, 13–14

Feasibility, 121, 124, 126
Features, 75
Field trials, 90
Fixed cost model, 220–225
Fledgling business model, 223
Fledgling concept, 47–49, 52, 134
Fledgling model, 125
Focus, 155
Focus groups, 89
Focused prototypes, 35
Focused–analytical quadrant, 127
Focused–physical quadrant, 127
Forward-thinking processes, 111
Fractionization, 111
Front end of innovation (FEI), 3, 13,
    40, 58–59, 74, 108, 153,
    167, 189, 202, 208, 214
  management, 204–205
  process, 155
  projects, 196
  tool, 88

General and Administrative (G&A Expenses), 220, 223, 229
Generators, 192
Google Glass, 138–140
Graphical user interfaces (GUIs), 127, 136
Green consumers, 169
Greenhouse gas emissions (GHG emissions), 174

Halo effect, 170
Handheld GPS, 102–104
Helix, 53
Heuristic approach to business modeling, 219
Heuristic business model (ing), 35, 235
  approach, 233
  business model, 215–216
  business model *vs.* business plan, 217, 219
  fixed cost model, 220–225
  heuristic approach to business modeling, 219
  heuristic business modeling and hypothesis development, 233–236
  modern incarnation, 216–217
  revenue model, 225–228
  shift to business modeling and LS, 218–219
  variable cost model, 228–233
Heuristics, 170, 228
Hierarchy, 126
Highly user-centric, 26
House of Quality, 11
Hypotheses, 129
  development, 233–236
  hypotheses-driven criteria, 124

Ideation process, 25–26, 36, 47, 119
IDEO Deep Dive video, 67–68, 107, 113
IDEO ten faces of innovation, 191–192
IDEO video, 117
Implementers, 192

Incremental innovation projects, 7
Independent activity, 201
Inductive process, 50
Industrial design approach, 87
Industrial Revolution, 215
Industry and technology assessment, 61
Industry trends and forecasting, 59
Innovation, 39–45, 60, 133
  agile product innovation, 7–8
  approach, 47–51, 167–168, 179–180
  Basadur applied innovation, 12
  boundaries, 17–20
  and business model, 45–47
  check-in, check-out, 18
  common themes and approaches, 13
  creativity enhanced, not driven, 16
  cross-functional and multidisciplinary, 14
  design thinking, 9
  diffusion, 134
  economic viability, 237
  helix, 53–54
  IDEO ten faces of, 191–192
  information driven, agile and effective, 14–15
  innovation invariably collides with business model, 18–19
  innovation systems, tools and techniques, 10
  internal and external communication, 13–14
  invariably collides with business model, 18–19
  IPD, 6
  lead user research, 10–11
  lean product development and innovation, 6–7
  lean startup, 9–10
  market innovation, 40, 42
  methods, 6
  MIT model, 8–9
  PDMA, 4–5
  philosophy, 8
  problem focused not solution focused, 16

process, 70, 219
process innovation, 40, 61
project management component,
    19–20
QFD, 11–12
relative value, 17
requirements and attributes, 15–16
Stage Gate™ System, 5–6
systems, 8, 193
theory, 40
tools or techniques, 4
TRIZ, 12–13
uncertainty management, 20
Innovation management, 3, 174
    approach, 15, 18, 133
    perspective, 5
    process, 141
    systems, 14
Integrated product development
    (IPD), 6
Intellectual property (IP), 60
Internal communication, 13–14
Interviews, 88, 91

KANO model, 63–65, 70
Key opinion leaders (KOLs), 76
Key performance indicators (KPIs), 31
Knowledge, 200–202

Latent needs, 36
Lateral thinking, 109–115
Lead user research (LUR), 10–11, 74,
    149, 153–157, 163–165
    downside of, 157–160
Lead users, 149–150
    analog, 162–163
    attributes, 158–160
    downside of LUR, 157–160
    LUR, 153–157
    in market, 156–157
    misconceptions, 152–153
    phase of problem statement, 53
    use, 160–163
Leadership, 196, 203
Lean product development and
    innovation, 6–7

Lean Startup (LS), 3, 6, 9–10, 20,
    28, 30–32, 45, 58, 83, 88,
    121–122, 134, 157, 188,
    203, 237
    canvas, 19
    decision making unit, 108
    economic viability, 237
    gap analysis, 36
    implications, 35–38
    innovation system gap analysis, 37
    latent needs, 36
    linearity, 38
    methodology, 29, 108, 215
    minimum viable product, 63
    organizational innovation, 40
    perspective, 62–63
    prototyping, 91, 95
    recommendations, 38
    shift to, 218–219
    strengths of system, 32–33
    weaknesses of system, 33–35
Lean system, 6
Life cycle analysis (LCA), 167, 171–172
    studies, 180
Life Cycle Impact Assessment (LCIA),
    171
Linear activities, 54
Linearity, 28, 38
"Lock-in" effect, 173

Management support, 196–197
Manufacturer's suggested retail price
    (MSRP), 233
Market
    analysis, 59
    innovation, 40
    lead user in, 156–157
    research perspective, 59–60, 153
    trends and opportunities, 60
    uncertainty, 20
Marketing research approach, 87
Mathematical equation, 15, 116
memsorb™, 141–144
Metaphor elicitation technique, 90–91
Metaphor elucidation technique,
    99–100

Mind mapping, 26
Minimum viable product testing
        (MVP testing), 9, 31, 38,
        63, 123, 127–130, 215
Mirra™ Chair, 177–179
Mission statement, 51
Modern incarnation of DT, 24,
        216–217
Moment of inertia (MOI), 78
Monstrous hybrids, 176
Multidisciplinary teams, 14, 189
Myers-Briggs Type Indicator (MBTI),
        190–191

Nappies, 172–173
Nascent entrepreneurs, 235
Novelty, 43
Novice innovation teams, 16

Observability, 136, 139, 143
Observational research, 89
Off ramp, 38
Open business models, 217
Open-ended transaction, 211
Opportunity recognition, 42
Optimizers, 192
Organizational innovation, 40
Osterwalder's approach, 30
Outdoor professionals, 156

Personality assessment tools, 190
Physical–comprehensive quadrant,
        127
Pivoting, 33
Plastics, 176
PM software, 208–209
Polyvinyl chloride (PVC), 178
Portfolio management, 5
Pragmatic business modeling
        approach, 19
Pricing policy, 234
Primary market research, 88
Primary research, 84, 180 (*see also*
        Secondary research)
    approach to, 87–88
    artifacts as focal points, 99–100

cognitive mapping, 101–104
conducting interview, 95–97
customer journey mapping,
        100–101
developing, executing and
        analyzing interviews, 91–93
discussion guide, 93–94
interpreting results, 100
observation within interviews, 97–99
primary research best practices, 91
types of, 88–91
Primary Target Audience (PTA), 96
"Probe and learn" interview
        techniques, 93
Problem focus, 36
Problem statement, 47, 50–53
Process innovation, 40
Processes, 36
Procrastination, 210
Product Development Management
        Association (PDMA),
        4–5, 194
    BOK, 5
Products, 133
    consumers' relationship to, 74–75
    design and development, 8–9
    innovation, 40
    product-related adoption
        principles, 141
    statement, 209
Profiling tools and techniques, 190,
        193–194
    Basadur problem-solving index,
        192–193
    IDEO ten faces of innovation,
        191–192
    Myers-Briggs, 191
Progressive organizations, 190
Project execution, 58
Project management (PM), 50,
        199–200
    collaboration and communication,
        202–203
    component, 19–20
    education. 19
    FEI management, 204–205

knowledge, 200–202
leadership, 203
managing uncertainty and risk,
    203–204
skills, 202
tools and techniques, 204
Project Management Institute (PMI),
    199–200
Project Management Professional
    (PMP), 199, 208
Project selection process, 57–59
Project structure, 194
Project-related issues, 209
    self-management, 210–214
Prototyping, 26, 38
    approach, 128–130
    and MVP, 127–130

Qualitative approach, 117–118
Quality Function Deployment
    (QFD), 11–12, 63, 73
Quantitative approach, 116–117
Questionnaires, 88

"Re-ideation" process, 145
Reduce, Reuse and recycle approach
    (3R approach), 175
Regulatory compliance, 60
Relative advantage, 134, 137
Relative value, 225, 234
Research and development (R&D), 3
Return on investment (ROI), 18, 116
Revenue model, 225–228
Reversal, 112
Rhode Island School of Design
    (RISD), 188
Risk assessment, 60
Risk management, 203–204
Risk-taking, 43
Rough-rapid-ready prototypes
    (triple-R prototypes), 35
Rudimentary approach, 109

Scope, 200
    changes, 209
    creep, 209

Seasonal affective disorder (SAD), 118
Secondary data, 59
Secondary research (*see also* Primary
    research)
    entrepreneurship perspective, 60
    guiding models, 63
    IDEO Deep Dive, 67–68
    importance, 57–58
    informing next steps, 69–70
    KANO model, 63–65
    market research perspective, 59–60
    perspectives of, 58
    process, 61
    secondary research in action, 66–68
    secondary research information
        important for innovation
        management, 63
    technology management
        perspective, 60–63
    user-centered model, 65–66
Segmentation, 59
Self-management, 210–214
Silicon Valley approach, 34
Simplex system, 12
Small-to medium sized enterprises
    (SMEs), 18, 160
Software industry, 8
Solution, 44
Solution-based approach, 174
Solution-centric position, 34
Sprints, 7
Stage Gate™ System, 5–6, 121–122,
    124
Stanford School, The, 25
Startup community, 19
Steering, 31
Sterilization, 14
Strategic management
    business perspective innovation, 41
    perspective, 41–42
Stream separation, 176
Strengths, Weaknesses, Opportunities,
    Threats analysis (SWOT
    analysis), 59
Success, 45
Surveys, 88

Sustainability, 49, 167, 217
    C2C, 175–176
    eco-behavior, 169
    eco-development, 168
    eco-development and consumer
        behavior, 169
    eco-development and innovation
        management, 174
    eco-development and LCA, 171
    elusive green consumer, 169–171
    ETEE™, 181–182
    innovation approach, 179–180
    LCA, 171–172
    limitations of LCA, 172–
    material problem, 174–175
    other aspects of, 180
    other aspects of sustainability, 180
    of problem statement, 53
    work, 176–179
Swift market analysis, 62
Systematic approach, 26, 28
Systematic evaluation, 76–79
Systems, 4
Systems thinking, 4

Team approach, 188–189
Team empowerment, 14
Team resource management, 206–208
Team selection approaches, 189–190
Technical feasibility, 18, 122
Technical uncertainty, 20
Technological landscape, 62
Technology management
        perspective, 60
    DT perspective, 61–62
    LS perspective, 62–63
Terminology, 7
The MIT model–Product Design
        and Development, 8–9
Thrashing, 206, 210
3M Corporation, 10, 157–158
Time, 201

Timmons model, 217
Total addressable market (TAM), 133
Total available market (TAM), 58
Total Quality Management (TQM),
        73
Traditional market research, 10, 150
Trialability, 136, 139, 143
TRIZ, 12–13

Ubiquitous IDEO Deep Dive video,
        108
Uncertainty, 205
    management, 20, 43, 203–204
    PM software, 208–209
    team resource management,
        206–208
Unilinear approach, 28
Unique selling propositions (USP),
        76, 99
Unit capacity, 235
Up-cyclability, 176
User-centered design (UCD), 65,
        97–98
User-centered model, 65–66, 97
User-driven development (UDD), 65

Validated learning, 32
Value capture process, 46, 219, 234
Value creation, 46, 219, 234
Value proposition, 124, 127
Value Proposition Canvas, 30
Value relatively, 36
Variable costs, 222, 228
    model, 228–233
Viability, 121, 124–125
Voice of the customer (VoC), 6, 36, 65,
        83, 88, 91
Volatile, uncertain, complex or
        ambiguous conditions
        (VUCA conditions), 203

Young entrepreneurs, 34